BOB KLEBERG AND THE KING RANCH

BOB KLEBERG

AND THE

KING RANCH

A WORLDWIDE SEA OF GRASS

by John Cypher

UNIVERSITY OF TEXAS PRESS  AUSTIN

LIBRARY OF CONGRESS CATALOGING-IN-PUBLICATION DATA

Cypher, John.
    Bob Kleberg and the King Ranch : a worldwide sea of grass / by John Cypher. — 1st ed.
        p.   cm.
    Includes index.
    ISBN 0-292-71171-9 (cl.)   ISBN 0-292-71187-5 (pbk.)
    1. Kleberg, Robert Justus, 1896–1974.   2. Ranchers—Texas—Biography.   3. King Ranch (Tex.)—History.   4. King Ranch, Inc.—History.   I. Title.
SF194.2.K58C96   1995
338.7'636213'092—dc20
    [B]   94-22454

CONTENTS

FOREWORD   vii

ONE   The Beginning, Century II   1

TWO   Embellishing a Legacy   11

THREE   Let's Go to a Roundup   25

FOUR   Simple Styles, Simple Habits   35

FIVE   On Entering Another World   53

SIX   Going International: The First Step   74

SEVEN   Inventing a Beef Factory—Venezuela   84

EIGHT   Meanwhile, Back at the Ranch   111

NINE   Brazil, a Multifaceted Adventure   121

TEN   Argentine Problems, People Problems   141

ELEVEN   Versailles via Flushing Meadows   153

TWELVE   Another World, Down Under   165

THIRTEEN   From the New Cattle World to the Old   187

FOURTEEN   Decision Making, the Contorted Process   201

FIFTEEN   The Trials of the Two Kings   209

SIXTEEN   We Say Good-bye   221

AFTERWORD   229

INDEX   231

Photographs follow page 52

I AM A LIFELONG rancher and I plan to tell a rancher's tale, avoiding, if I can, the garrulousness associated with my kind. It is about my employer, King Ranch, and the brains and heart at its focus, Bob Kleberg, how he guided it into a period in its 140-year history that made it unique to American agricultural enterprise. Mine is the oftentimes fruitful, sometimes tragic, story of that era, why and how the ranch grew from a typical South Texas range cattle operation, albeit quite a large one, to a global agribusiness conglomerate managed by this cattleman genius. He organized ranching ventures in nine countries, along an earth-circling cattle trail from Australia to Africa to Latin America, over a span of fifteen years, expanding and consolidating them in his remaining five.

Then he mounted for his ride to Valhalla, leaving to his extended family his worldwide legacy to do with as they willed. Piecemeal, over the next decade and a half, they sold off the bulk of it. From Texas to Texas in less than forty years—an empire that ended as suddenly and as breathtakingly as a stampede. The world's few international agricultural enterprises tend to permanence. His must have been unique for its brevity.

My forty years with King Ranch—December 1948 to precisely December 1988—spanned this unparalleled epoch. Much of my career I was the assistant to Bob Kleberg, the chief executive, architect, and overlord of his 15-million-acre domain. So my story will be about the ways he went about his work and how I and others provided him sets of hands to accomplish it.

The focus will largely be on the period in Mr. Kleberg's life that brought me into his orbit, from the early 1950s to 1974. To provide this view of the pace he set for himself, I must jump across time zones and continental boundaries in not seeming but actual disarray; that was the way life was during those tumultuous and fascinating decades.

In a day we shifted through all five gears: from hours upon boring hours waiting on telephone connections (the international fax was down the road a bit), to the exhilaration of being boosted into the substratosphere in the posh comfort of a Grumann G-2 jet (surely one of the nobler technological utensils)—or bouncing in the back of a Toyota four-wheeler over an unfenced semiarid plain, or under the canopy of a steaming rain forest, or holed up in a palm-thatched lean-to to let a sudden downpour pass, or doing our laundry in camp water dirtier than our shirts.

But it was worth the toss, as our Australian mates say. For in these seemingly haphazard circumstances, Bob Kleberg eventually reached a moment and a place where he got out of the Toyota, walked out a way, folded his arms across his chest, and—eyeing mainly untended land that he had walked over, dug into, smelled, assessed—projected on the screen in his mind a picture of fat cattle grazing tall grass. By just watching the back of his head under the faded Stetson, we too witnessed a transformation—raw land into beef. Then those of us around him pitched in to turn his visions into creations of splendid proportions, the King Ranch chain of foreign operations.

At the end of most of the chapters, I have included a diversion, an intentional one. Bob Kleberg bore the burden and reaped the benefits of the King Ranch's near-legendary name, symbolic of our country's unique western culture. It became almost a cliché that visiting the ranch was the best glimpse one could get of American ranching life; it wasn't—many attributes of King Ranch business were not typical of the livestock norm. In the early 1950s, Bob tried to explain this to Miss Edna Ferber when he denied her request to come and settle down at the headquarters to do, in her words, a book on a "typical Texas ranch." Her interpretations of the word "typical," as she detailed them in her best-selling novel *Giant*, Bob and Helen were forced to live with for over a decade.

More recently in the public mind, the TV series *Dallas* became the stereotype of the family-owned Texas spread. Some of our visitors have appeared downright disappointed that they didn't step into an evil empire where Kleberg pursued Kleberg with invective, stiletto, and gun.

The upshot of these commonly held erroneous beliefs was that they brought us a steady stream of visitors—there were few days when from

one to several hundred did not pass through the front gate. Bob was generous in the extreme with his time with them, accommodating his schedule
to them at every opportunity. Strangely, most of his management people
did not follow his example; they were more likely to shy away, making
excuses that their business of the day was too pressing to interrupt even
when the visitor might be on the ranch to study their particular field of
work. So it most often fell to me to break into whatever I was doing to
look after them, and as it turned out, I, along with the boss, benefited from
these worldwide contacts. The friends I made are my lifetime's richest
reward.

Their backgrounds were as varied as their numbers: presidents and
princes, reigning monarchs and deposed ones, ministers, business leaders,
artists, entertainers, learned doctors, students, ne'er-do-wells sent off on
world tours to get them out of the family hair, lots and lots of attractive
ladies. I have chosen a few among them to represent this important facet
of King Ranch life. Rather than being typical of the flow, these are some of
the ones who interested me.

They often appeared on very short, sometimes no, notice, and that's
the way I'll introduce them here—as interruptions in the flow of events in
Bob's and the ranch's routine.

So together let's explore American ranching, the finest our world has
ever seen, as it unfolded in an immeasurably exciting way under the hand
of the man who was, for over half a century, at its pinnacle.

JOHN CYPHER

BOB KLEBERG AND THE KING RANCH

CHAPTER ONE

THE BEGINNING, CENTURY II

I HAD HAD ABOUT ALL I could take—my hide, thin at the outset, had been peeled away in layers, my nerve ends exposed; I was a cadaverous zombie for lack of sleep. From the time this trip had begun two weeks ago, relations between my boss, Bob Kleberg, and me had jutted up and down the graph like the daily stock market averages, changing every fifteen minutes, markedly declining. Too many people with too many agendas were bidding for the old boy's attention, while he by turns was distracted by his three older grandchildren, an assortment of pretty girlfriends, and an assortment of bottles.

Lifting off from Kingsville on a spring day in 1974, Bob had aboard his jet his Brazilian partner, Dr. Augusto Antunes, and the doctor's assistant, Ambassador Barbosa da Silva and his wife, King Ranch do Brasil president Francis Herbert, and his granddaughter Helen Alexander. Landing in Houston, we exchanged the Barbosa da Silvas for a ravishing Mexican friend named Sandra Riverole—next leg, to Manhattan. By the time we had unpacked, a cadre of glittering types had ascended to the King Ranch suite on the thirty-seventh floor of the Pierre Hotel, drinks aplenty, a move to the

21 Club—heavy food, heavy conversation, to bed at 1:30, one of the earlier nights.

The ensuing days varied little in context and substance, a great deal in time and place. In New York, grandfather said good-bye to the others, escorted aboard Helen, and two more grandchildren, John and Emory Alexander, and the five of us headed out over the Atlantic bound for Madrid. Waiting at the Ritz was George Moore, the recently retired chairman of the board of First National City Bank. George still is to the top echelon of entrepreneurship as the Zambezi in monsoon is to Victoria Falls: in his enthusiasm he cascades over the precipice, obscuring the fundamentals in a rising mist of words. His proposal at the time was for his friend Bob to go into business with Iran (Iran, my God!—but George was a great friend and adviser of the Shah), either by selling the Iranians part of Bob's holdings in Argentina or by buying a property there and managing it for them. Bob: "No."

"No? Well, then, try this one. Iran buys a property in Kenya and King Ranch comes in to run it for them." Bob loved Kenya. "I like that one. Let's have a drink"—and a drink—and a drink.

From Madrid we headed for King Ranch, España, on the frontier west of Seville. Bob's Spanish friends found us, Mercedes and helicopter loads of men with their wives or girlfriends in tow. They were ready for a day's sight-seeing and partying, maybe two; then they returned to their tight-knit business and social worlds and were replaced by the next batch of partygoers. A pleasant interlude for them, an endurance contest for us. Bob fell ill of a stomach complaint—sadly, we did not give it the attention it eventually merited. After all, his innards had every reason to complain at the fluids he had been pouring into them. We were wrong in not watching him more closely; his ever-darkening mood was a warning I didn't heed.

His bickering and complaints intensified, some directed at me, with reason. I was helping him to bed most nights and returning to his guests for another two or three hours of conviviality. I had lost my edge; things were slipping by me.

The next leg took us to Rabat, where Bob had an appointment with King Hassan. It was bound to be confrontational—Morocco had not kept its part of an agreement with King Ranch to furnish an allotted amount of land to their joint ranching venture. In the past, Bob's meetings with His Majesty had been cordial, but he could not be looking forward to this one. Michael Hughes, the president and general manager of both the Spanish and the Moroccan operations, had located a piece of land up on the Mediterranean coast that he thought the government might acquire, a possibility for relieving the pressure somewhat. When we walked over it, Bob didn't like it—which added little to his frame of mind.

My end-of-the-line crisis came two days before the audience. Coming away from a three-hour lunch, Bob, Mike, and I were driving through a reforestation project on the outskirts of the capital. Bob, in front with the driver, had been silent, withdrawn, in a vapor; Mike and I were chatting in the back seat. Rousing himself, Bob said, "I think I'll send John home. We don't need him anymore." Then he turned and faced both of us, his eyes blank, vacant. Mike was nonplussed—I was flabbergasted. We had been together the whole day and he didn't realize I was in the car!

So to hell with him, this lousy trip, this kind of life. My mentor, the only one I had ever had aside from my father, had turned on me. Back at the hotel I made reservations, packed, and the next morning went in to tell him I was on my way. He was silent for an embarrassing minute, two, then, "I don't want you to leave." That's all.

I stayed another day, the last one for all of us. Following his afternoon meeting with the king, Bob was taking his grandchildren on a safari to eastern and southern Africa. At the hotel entrance, I watched the car door close on him and the prime minister and whistled for my driver. I could have waited over another day to take the plane from Rabat to Paris, but there was one from Casablanca in just three hours and I wanted to be on it, away from these miserable surroundings.

Three days in Paris and the rational world reclaimed me. Out over a sparkling North Atlantic, watching occasional icebergs drift past the window and make dazzling white triangles in a calm sea, I was a bit more at ease with myself, a bit more rational. What in the world could have happened to change the old boy's attitude toward not only me but every facet of his surroundings? That the change was irreversible I had little doubt. He was seventy-eight, in the grip, the mind-set, of about his only fear: old age. Yet this had come on so puzzlingly sudden; there were missing bits in the scenario.

During the next several weeks I received not a direct word from him. What course would be best for me and my growing family to take on his return? (Culminating nearly half a century of bachelorhood, I had married Patricia Riba y Rincon Gallardo of Mexico City and entered another exciting world, a distinctly different culture. We had a son and were expecting our second child in just a few months.) Was I to let two weeks color a relationship of twenty-six years, even though they were the latest, most decisive two weeks? In my mind, a scale weighed that minuscule period of time against two decades and more of watching a genius put together unparalleled accomplishments. Those accomplishments, the paths leading to them, for me began like this . . .

ON A BALMY FALL evening in October 1953, 150 guests, the top ranchers in Texas and around the world, together with an elite group of animal and range scientists, overflowed the dining room and the large central patio in the main house on King Ranch. It was a black tie occasion, the closing night of a conference rather cumbersomely titled "Breeding Beef Cattle in Unfavorable Environments." The gathering was commemorating the centenary of the King Ranch's founding, and the previous four days had been taken up with reading eighteen scientific papers, each on some aspect of producing beef in tropical and subtropical climates, presented by seventeen of the most eminent agricultural researchers of our generation. The papers were interspersed with field trips—to roundups, to inspect the pastures and the herds and the bands of horses, and to see the wildlife. The nights were for partying.

Now the symposium was closing with an address by the president and general manager of the ranch, Robert Justus Kleberg, Jr. His speech that night was long; it was read, delivered in a monotone, in marked contrast to the opening remarks made four days earlier by his brother, Richard M. Kleberg, the chairman of the board, whose ability on his feet was legendary. Bob had anguished over putting into words the ideas that had taken a lifetime to mature in his mind. Rereading them, I find that he said the things that I later learned he most deeply felt, regardless of the delivery. They have as much import for our world of the 1990s, restructuring itself from its forty-year division into Communist/Free World camps, as they had for his divided, divisive world of the 1950s.

> Today our civilization is advancing . . . in the direction of an increased world population. Food, always important to the progress of civilization, has taken on a new significance, a new dimension. Not only is food important to human progress, but today food is important in and to human affairs. Food has become an effective instrument of diplomacy. More than ever before food has become a weapon of peace.
>
> . . . We believe that the future expansion of large-scale beef production will be in the wet and dry tropics and the semidesert areas of the world. That is where the largest undeveloped regions lie.
>
> We must operate within our sphere to contribute the most possible to the common-good effort that is man's struggle for freedom— for freedom from hunger, for freedom from oppression.

My association with him, from that evening until the end of his life, reaffirmed for me over and over that he was speaking from his intellect and from his heart. He truly sought, in his past accomplishments and in his plans ahead, to do his part to nurture his fellow humans, pretentious as it sounds.

THE CONFERENCE CLOSED; everyone rose from the tables. Bob was standing in the dining room doorway sharing a much-needed glass of champagne with Holland McCombs, a former editor in the Time-Life-Fortune group who had helped him with his speech, when I happened by on an errand. I had knocked my brains out over the past several weeks, helping to put this thing together and acting as nonstop gofer while it was under way. Bob knew this and he caught me: "Stop whatever you're doing and have a drink with us."

I raised my glass to congratulate him on the things he had said. He didn't thank me; his assessment: "I got through it."

I have since wondered if that night he realized that at fifty-seven, with a full lifetime's accomplishments behind him, he was embarking on enterprises that in themselves would have been a full life's accomplishment.

TO ASSESS HIS remaining twenty-one years, let's examine briefly the elements that made this particular Kleberg the man who could, with the faith and confidence he expressed in his speech, with élan and with dispatch, create a string of jewellike ranches to girdle the world's temperate and tropical waist.

The son of King Ranch manager Robert J. Kleberg, Sr., and grandson of the founder, Captain Richard King, Robert, Jr., was born just before the century ended, on March 29, 1896, born, as it turned out, to transform the Captain's legacy. Having adjusted to his calling (he told me that in college he had wanted to study electrical engineering), he first had to pass through the character-forming seasoning that eventually prodded his own household into placing the mantle of authority on him.

Alice, Captain King's youngest daughter, had married Robert, Sr., and borne him two sons and three daughters, all living in the mansion of the matriarchal owner of the ranch, the widowed, revered grandmother, Henrietta M. King. From an office in her home, armed with his mother-in-law's power of attorney, Robert, Sr., managed her considerable holdings. Bob was the younger brother of a more-favored child, Richard M. Kleberg; he grew up overshadowed by his older sibling. Childhood photos, brown and faded, tell part of the story; they picture young Dick as handsome as a 1920s movie idol, sitting his horse ramrod straight, his chin high. Bob had a relaxed slouch in the saddle—his head low, his hat propped on his ears—that did nothing for his image. Hardly any of those early pictures show him smiling.

Dick knew everyone; he had a ready, cheerful word for his myriad Latin and Anglo friends. Completely bilingual, he cultivated a lyrical form of speech in both Spanish and English that made him the most sought-after orator in our part of the country—"orator" being a term still used in Mr. Richard's best years. This talented man—it seemed that everything he put his mind to came easy for him—never fully explored those talents; he wore them like a bush jacket, casual and easy. Trained in the law, in 1931 he was elected to Congress from our district and made his contribution to ranching from a Washington base. While constrained by his opposition to Franklin Roosevelt and some of the president's New Deal programs, Mr. Richard was able to make contributions where his expertise counted. A notable one was his sponsorship of the Duck Stamp Act; this pioneering legislation in the fields of ecology and wildlife management is still providing funds to support the preservation of waterfowl habitats. With years of perseverance, he was able to convince the Department of Agriculture to recognize the Santa Gertrudis breed as the first to be developed in the U.S., an achievement that had brother Bob's eternal gratitude.

BY CONTRAST, BOB was not at all versed in words or at ease with strangers. To compensate, he had a will as hard and durable as a forged horseshoe—and the incentive, the intensity, the brains, the ability to focus his concentration, and the overpowering energy to excel by unremitting hard work.

Mrs. King's ranch foreman was a bachelor named Sam Ragland, respected in our region for his knowledge of livestock and of men. As a part of Bob's early training, his father sent his young son over to the bachelor quarters near the main home to live in a room next to Sam. It could have been an astute move on the part of the elder Kleberg; even as an unseasoned youth Bob did not see eye to eye with his father on many things. They did not share a philosophic view of the ranch's management and direction under the South Texas conditions of the early 1900s; shifting quarters must have reduced those tensions. So days in camp and nights in the bachelor digs, Sam tutored his young charge in the basic things, in turning grass into beef. From Sam, Bob mastered the fundamentals.

Mr. Kleberg chose the University of Wisconsin for his son to attend on completing high school in nearby Corpus Christi; it was one of the leading agriculture institutions in the country. Bob was enrolled for two years, a good time in his life. But by 1916 the war clouds were roiling over the U.S., and his father ordered Bob home, got him an agricultural exemption from the draft, and put him to work. This was a mistake that darkened the rest of young Bob's life. The Klebergs were of German origin, so the local loud-mouths branded Bob and his brother draft dodgers with enemy sympathies, an undeserved smear that lasted long after the war was over. It was a tragedy that need not have happened; Bob very likely would have enjoyed the military experience—he would have made one hell of a cavalryman. Only once did he speak to me of this; even after five decades, his temper and his anguish flared at an act that was not of his doing. The local harass-ment tended for many years to isolate Bob on the ranch, away from the people in the village of Kingsville that his grandmother and father had founded. It was possibly the reason he had but few local friends.

IN 1900, MRS. KING brought Caesar Kleberg, a nephew of Robert, Sr., to South Texas to work for her. It was cousin Caesar who was to most pro-foundly influence young Bob's life. Though Caesar was the older, the two became lifelong, binding companions. Caesar was another bachelor and another outgoing Kleberg—his friends were legion, embracing every spec-trum of American life. He and Bob shared the same interests: cattle, horses, wild game, and improving the land. Bob's contributions to each of these placed him above his peers in ranching; Caesar, the mentor with the remarkably level head, guided him along the way. Caesar managed the south half of the ranch, and Bob was the general manager from the head-quarters on the north end. Their homes were forty miles apart. When a problem of any proportion arose, Bob did not let the distance interfere; he set out to talk it over with Caesar.

Many years after Caesar died, I glimpsed the depth of this Bob/Caesar bond, at Aqueduct racetrack on a summer afternoon in 1970. During this particular season, racing was dominated by an outstanding colt named Buckpasser. (The second-best horse was Buffle, owned by King Ranch.) Buckpasser was winning everything, as he did the feature event this par-ticular afternoon. Shortly after the race, an agent came by Bob's box to try to interest him in buying a breeding share in Buckpasser's syndicate when the stallion retired to stud (a share representing the right to breed one mare a year to the syndicated horse). The agent didn't get the time of day, just a short reply and a dismissal.

That night Bob had invited a group of eight or nine to dinner at the 21 Club, his perennial watering hole in Manhattan. Over drinks, I asked him why he wasn't interested in getting a breeding to a proven champion like Buckpasser. He got mad at me, telling me I knew so little about race-horses that he couldn't explain it on my level. "Not only that, Buckpasser's not syndicated!"

This took me aback; I asked if he didn't remember being approached about purchasing a share that afternoon.

"John, how long have you known me?"

"Well, I suppose nearly all my life."

"Then you should goddam well know I never listen to anybody!" and he turned to his pretty dinner companion.

But I couldn't let this tiny portal into his character close on me. So at my peril I nudged back into the conversation.

"But at some time in your life you must have listened to someone."

He turned quiet and thoughtful for a moment, then said, "Yes, I listened to Caesar."

LET ME INTERJECT HERE a clarification. I will be using two forms of address for Bob Kleberg: "Bob" and "Mr. Bob." When I refer to him, "Bob" will suffice. It's a short, compact name that will easily identify the principal. But when I relate conversations I had with him, he will be "Mr. Bob." On the ranch, especially among his employees and those a generation younger than he, he was "Mr. Bob," a uniquely southern-southwestern form of address, evolved over time to render respect for one's elders. In our region, it is never misconstrued as subservience. To Spanish speakers, here and in Latin America, he was "Don Roberto." By my father I was taught to use "Mr." Even though his friends and employees in the East and overseas, many younger than I, called him "Bob," I never varied from the "Mr. Bob" I had become accustomed to in my youth.

REGARDING HIS ATTACHMENT for Caesar, I sensed an ambivalence in Bob's perceptions of his family. On the one hand, he made it the focus of his thought and work; his dedication was to leaving the ranch in perpetuity to his relatives and their descendants. He looked on his family as the sole heirs and future managers of their inheritance; it was so much a part of his being that he often repeated, "I have no business except King Ranch business."

On the other hand, he was of two minds in his assessment of his individual kinfolk, not extending to any of them his complete trust and confidence. The only two about whom he was unreserved were Caesar and his cousin Richard King of Corpus Christi, of whom he said publicly, "The best man I have ever known." Had it not been for problems Richard King had within his immediate family that precluded his putting his inheritance into King Ranch when it was chartered in 1934, he would have been at Bob's side in management.

Two times, Bob gave me an insight into his assessment of his relatives' abilities. On one occasion he said, "In this family, it's the women who make the difference." The other was at a roundup at Norias. We were reined in side by side, watching Adán Muñoz and Ed Durham cut year-lings. He told me, "After me, there are three people who can select and improve our cattle and horses: Adán [his chauffeur and constant compan-ion], Helenita [his daughter], and Bobby [Shelton, his nephew]." Consider-ing that these animals were at the center of his life, it was an accolade beyond measure.

BOB'S LIFELONG MATE equaled Sam and Caesar in molding his char-acter. Moving at the pace he usually did when he made up his mind, in 1926 Bob courted, proposed to, and married Helen Campbell in just seven-teen days. Helen was the daughter of longtime congressman Phillip Pitt Campbell of Kansas. The product of a Washington upbringing, upper-level-educated, widely traveled, Miss Helen made a place more than normally wide in her husband's and in the ranch's development.

In 1927, their daughter and only child, Helen King, was born. Though Helen passed much of her adolescence away from the ranch in school, she was a product of her parents' upbringing, loving everything about the rough-and-tumble and the intricacies of ranch life. Nor did she grow up an isolated only child; Bob and Helen raised in their household two of Helenita's cousins, B. Johnson and Bobby Shelton, the sons of Bob's young-est sister, Sarah, who was locally the most popular of the Klebergs. Three years after the birth of her elder son, Belton D. Johnson, Sarah had lost her first husband. She later married Dr. Joseph H. Shelton, and they in turn begot B.'s younger brother, Robert R. Shelton. In 1942 Sarah was tragically killed in an auto accident, and B. and Bobby were taken in by their aunt and uncle, who raised them, oversaw their education, and in every way treated them as the brothers of their daughter. All three were duly edu-cated in the cow camp, and all three have stayed close to the ranching enterprise.

My early 1950s impression of Helen was of the ivory cool, eminently proper, straight-backed, auburn-haired, throaty-voiced mistress of the ranch, a perfectionist in dress and decorum who saw to it that those of us around her behaved the same way, husband excepted. As I began to develop habits that suited her standards, she occasionally smiled on me, a smile as radiant as her half-smile was deadly.

Miss Helen was especially a confidante and mentor of the young brides who married into her husband's family. Possibly she sought to spare them the jolting adjustments she had had to make to conform to the insular life the remote South Texas ranch demanded. Her encouragement and confidence were things to cherish, and they created in her circle as loyal and devoted a group of relatives and friends as I have ever known. But not all her in-laws succumbed to her intricate personality and her tastes. Her eastern connections, her education, and her European travels gave her an outlook that set her apart from the more provincial of Bob's relatives. For instance, she had a bias for English titles and emulated their ways, which were not the ways of her kinspeople and friends. But she toughed it out— she had that kind of fiber in her—and eventually became the *dueña* of a good-sized piece of Texas. For me, if I have but a few attributes of a gentleman, I am indebted to the lessons I received from her, sometimes at the symbolic back of her hand.

THE WIFE OF A RANCHER plays a larger role in her husband's professional life than is the norm in other occupations. The couple's relative isolation throws them together. If she is outdoor-inclined, and usually she is, since she made that choice along with her choice of suitor, she accompanies him to the cow camp and to the working pens to help on horseback, to keep records, or to keep tabs on the little ones.

Helen not only assumed this place in her husband's life on the ranch, but by years of gentle persuasion and guidance, exercising uncommon judgment on when to move in and when to back off, she broadened his horizon to encompass the world. Bob was innately provincial, a not-surprising characteristic in a young man raised on a huge spread with an open coast on one side and an unpopulated semitropical plain on the other three. She changed him, gave him an international outlook. It is my opinion that, but for Helen, Bob would not have ventured to any extent outside of Texas, though I expect that by the end of his life he would have expanded his local holdings to include a vastly larger piece of our state.

CHAPTER TWO

EMBELLISHING A LEGACY

BY 1953, BOB KLEBERG had headed the corporation for about thirty years. His succession had not been precise. His father—the manager under his mother-in-law, the venerable Henrietta M. King—had been debilitated by a series of strokes, and Bob, a youthful twenty-seven, had gradually taken the reins. His trials crowded one upon the other. Mrs. King passed away in 1925, stipulating a ten-year trust period in her will before her estate was settled. Bob, a trustee, had that time to find the money to pay her inheritance tax. He found the cash not on the ranch but under it, by negotiating a mineral lease.

With a loan secured by the lease in the bank to settle with the government, Bob and brother Dick plunged into the legal morass of forming a corporation among themselves and their sisters, readjusting the ranch boundaries, and settling with Mrs. King's other heirs—a drawn-out legal donnybrook that was not fully adjudicated until 1950. But during this thirty-five-year tenure, from his taking up his youthful duties on the ranch in 1916, Bob had by no means channeled his energies solely into seeing that the King Ranch survived as a viable business enterprise. His restless mind saw opportunities to improve or transform its every facet, and he set out to upgrade his inheritance.

While he worked toward making King Ranch a modern, efficient beef factory, Bob had strong feelings about spending money on improvements, feelings both for and against. He made his considerable cash outlays adhering to another of his axioms, repeating it over and over: "One of the easiest things in the world to do is overcapitalize a property. Once you've done that, there is no way on God's earth it can pay itself out."

But his self-imposed rule gave him the leeway to bring his home ranch up to a level of efficiency found on very few ranches around the world. For instance, he developed an unparalleled road system: six hundred miles of asphalt-topped pavement connecting each of the headquarters and the twenty-six sets of corrals, and passing through nearly every one of the pastures. In his early working days, in the rainy season the heavy soils would become a bog and in a drought the sand would be loose and impassable. Bob created a transportation system whereby men and livestock could move every day of the year. The roads made life easier for the men; they no longer had to live outdoors in camps for weeks on end, away from their families and from the amenities in the nearby communities; they could now get home every night.

The fences, the gates, the watering places, the sets of pens he had built were all the best, the most durable—sometimes overbuilt—to cut repair costs and maintenance time.

THIS UPGRADING PROGRAM could have been completed by nearly any competent, energetic ranch manager; within his profession, Bob set himself apart from his contemporaries—indeed from his fellow livestockmen throughout history—with three developments that were to change the industry dramatically and permanently. Though many of the things to which he dedicated his life have already disappeared, these achievements have passed into the worldwide domain and will be his enduring memorial. These three are developing the Santa Gertrudis breed of beef cattle, creating one of the four foundation families of the American Quarter Horse, and, in soils where they were deficient, identifying the trace elements necessary to animal diet and reproduction.

BY 1900, THE TEXAS LONGHORN, the durable, contrary critter that had given birth to the U.S. beef business, had virtually disappeared. It had been replaced on the King Ranch, and nearly all other ranches, with the improved beef breeds from Great Britain: the Hereford, the Shorthorn, and the Aberdeen Angus. While the British cattle were great meat producers in temperate zones like their cool, green homeland, in the semidesert Southwest and the steamy swamplands of the Southeast they suffered a variety of maladies. Ticks found a free lunch in the campground under their matted hair, flies carrying the screwworm larvae laid eggs in their open wounds. The poor Hereford, the most popular of the three, had a white face that lacked pigment in the skin around its eyelids. The lids sunburned, formed tumors, and eventually cancered, causing the animal to lose the eye. Felled by this disorder, about half the Hereford cows on King Ranch went to slaughter before they reached the end of their productive lives. Something had to be done.

Shortly after 1900, Bob's father had purchased two Brahma bulls, the white, humped, sacred cattle from tropical India, to crossbreed with a few of his British cows. The results were portentous; the calves were short-haired, hearty, fast-growing, and indifferent to the summer heat. Using these Indian and British breeds as building blocks, Bob was able to create a small, close-bred family. He then identified within the family one superior bull that combined the attributes he needed: excellent beef characteristics and climatic adaptability. The bull's name was Monkey. Over thirty-five years, Bob built on this bloodline, the immediate family of Monkey.

The high standards for selection he had set for his animals—year after year culling the majority of the herd that did not meet the ideal he had fixed on the screen behind his eye—resulted over time in his creating an extended gene pool. Dr. J. K. Northway, the ranch's longtime chief veterinarian, told me that he was at times completely exhausted from standing from sunup to sundown on the side of a cattle chute, keeping records while Bob inspected over a thousand heifers. Bob deemed it a most profitable day when he was able to select six of the thousand to go into his experimental herd. Using the only tool he had available, his remarkable eyes, plus talent, study, immense concentration and energy, and patience, he garnered the prize.

Through judicious inbreeding, the animals in the pool he created—all of them uniform in type and carrying the genes of the foundation bull, Monkey—had the climatic attributes of the Brahma and the beef qualities of the British Shorthorn. Most important of all, by transmitting Monkey's homozygous genes to future generations, these crossbreds were able to reproduce their own kind.

Thus a new breed was born to the bovine world and named the Santa Gertrudis, the name of the Spanish land grant upon which the headquarters of the ranch sits. After years of effort in Washington, in 1940 Dick

Kleberg was able to convince the U.S. Department of Agriculture to rec-ognize the Santa Gertrudis as the first breed of cattle developed in the Western Hemisphere. Until the early 1950s, Bob multiplied their numbers and improved their type on his home range.

PARALLEL WITH DEVELOPING his new breed of cattle, Bob was doing the same sort of experiment with the ranch horses. Horses were indispens-able to getting the cattle work done, and to accomplish it he wanted himself and his men mounted on animals of superior stamina, speed, cow sense, a gentle nature. He often told me that there was nothing more worthless than a poor horse and hardly anything more valuable than a fine one. He meant it—the following episode shows how forcefully he meant it.

After World War I, the horse market dried up; the army was no longer buying remounts for the cavalry and artillery. With sales at a standstill on the ranch, the horses multiplied until they were overrunning the pastures; Bob could not dispose of them at any price. The local railroad, which Mrs. King and Bob's father were instrumental in building, ran from Houston to the U.S.-Mexican border at Brownsville, with a spur line paralleling the Rio Grande River to the northwest. Bob ordered a train of cattle cars loaded with several hundred of these useless horses. During the night, he had his train shuttled onto the spur and stopped in a remote stretch of brush adja-cent to the riverbank. His cowhands slid back the doors, jumped the horses onto the embankment, and herded them into the river, where they swam into Mexico. Bob had reduced his inventory while putting the poor peas-ants on the other side in reach of a useful asset.

His approach to creating the superior type of horse he visualized was the same as with the cattle. He identified one outstanding stallion that had the qualities he sought, then multiplied his genes in a close-knit family. This stallion, never properly named, just called the Old Sorrel, Bob persuaded Caesar to purchase as a foal from a neighboring rancher, George Clegg. He grew into a magnificent animal, ideally matching the picture behind Bob's eye. Riding him at the roundups, Bob made an outstanding cutting horse of him. The animal's intelligence and ability made him a versatile performer, as Bob proved on one occasion.

Pursuing her English leanings, in the later 1920s Helen had con-structed—in a pasture near the headquarters—a jumping course to train her Thoroughbreds over the fences. One evening Bob made some com-ments about her affinity for her rangy mounts, saying that his horses could learn to jump just as well. She bridled at this; Thoroughbreds had been trained as jumpers and hunters for centuries. It was a bright, moonlit night. Bob had Old Sorrel brought out to the course and led him around it. Then he mounted, bareback with no bit in the horse's mouth, and took him over the jumps in perfect order.

Helen was astounded. "How did you know he could do that?"

"Easy—he's spent his whole life jumping cactus bushes in the pasture."

The world of reproduction is aggravating or fascinating, depending on your success at manipulating it. Bob found that with his horses he could not duplicate the breeding plan he had used with his cattle. When they were as closely bred as were his Santa Gertrudis, the offspring were disappointing. He backed off and bred relatives no nearer than uncle/niece, constantly innovating, breaking new ground in a remote, still mysterious realm. His results proved manifold: he created an animal that suited the King Ranch cowhand while at the same time developing a foundation family within a new breed, the American Quarter Horse. Mainly as a result of its versatility, the Quarter Horse has become the most popular, most numerous breed of horse in the world today.

MR. KLEBERG'S THIRD major contribution to his profession is more difficult for the layperson to appreciate than these first two. A magnificent stallion or bull, standing before you to be judged and admired, is a tangible contributor to humanity's well-being. Not so a near-invisible addition to the animal's diet that makes it a stronger, more efficient producer.

Over half the land on the King Ranch in South Texas is heavy sand, geologically not long up from the floor of the receding Gulf of Mexico. During seasons of adequate rainfall, cattle can support themselves on it; in fact they are about the only domestic animals, with perhaps the exception of sheep and goats, that can make the rolling sand dunes, shin oak, and mesquite produce even a minimum profit for the rancher. But when the pastures went through a drought, as they periodically do, the animals grew thin to the point of emaciation. Breeding cows were especially affected. They developed an arthritic condition that forced them into a slow, labored walk, a malady called the creeps. Creepy cows had no calves, so the calving percentages (the annual ratio of calves on the ground to cows exposed to bulls) dropped to unprofitably low levels, below 50 percent. The U.S. animal scientists of the day had no solution to the problem.

In 1929, Bob was engaged in importing from the Union of South Africa a small herd of cattle called Africanders; they are a tropical climate-adapted breed that he thought might contribute something to his evolving development program. He was told that in the dry areas of that country steers were periodically fed a spoonful of a phosphorus-bearing chemical to make them fatten more readily. He reasoned that if they put on weight faster, it must be because they were in better health. Possibly his cows did not have available to them in their natural pasture the phosphorus that they needed. He was able to interest the U.S. Bureau of Animal Industry in assigning one of their range scientists, Lowell Tash, to analyze the native grasses in the sandy country. Tash found them phosphorus-deficient.

In a second phase of the research, phosphorus was added to the animal diet to make up the deficiency. The same method of supplementing was used that had been described in South Africa: the cows were herded into a chute, their heads were pulled back by grasping them by the nose, and a large spoonful of the compound was ladled down their throats, followed by a beer bottle full of water.

The usual checks and controls were set up to ascertain if phosphorus was, in fact, the element they lacked; but this good scientific procedure, while appropriate, was not entirely necessary. When the cows learned what they could expect, they rushed into the chute with their saliva glands flowing, threw back their heads, and opened their mouths wide for their portion. They knew what they needed.

The experiment paid a huge dividend when methods were worked out to supplement phosphorus in the animal diet by either putting it in the drinking water or feeding it in a dry lick. As a consequence of getting a proper level of phosphorus into the cows, calf production in dry years jumped over 30 percent, from unprofitable to profitable levels.

What ranks this work beside Bob's pioneering in animal breeding is the fact that almost all of the arid land in the tropical, semitropical belt around the world is phosphorus-deficient. The discovery opened millions upon millions of acres to money-making beef production. Following upon his ground-breaking work, decades of research in agriculture centers around the world have gone into evaluating every component in the bovine diet. I have always felt that, second to founding the Santa Gertrudis breed, this mineral work was Bob's most significant achievement.

THESE ARE BUT THREE highlights in a life motivated by the pursuit of scientific discovery that could be put to practical use. Bob delved into every facet of turning grass into beef and made a contribution to nearly all of them. When I said something like this to him, he told me, pointedly, that he didn't undertake his experiments out of an altruistic motive, such as improving the human diet, or even to help the industry—he committed himself to them to improve beef turn off on the King Ranch.

But I never entirely believed him.

A FOURTH MAJOR ACCOMPLISHMENT during Bob's early career must be included with these three, though it was not a part of his research in animal husbandry but was a matter of exercising his business acumen. It was the negotiation that put the jingle in his pocket, making possible everything that he afterward undertook. He pursued and kept alive, through low-key contacts, the extended negotiations that eventually led Humble Oil and Refining, later Exxon, to develop the ranch's mineral resources.

Humble had first leased King Ranch property in 1919; several shallow wildcat wells were drilled—dry holes. The lease was allowed to expire in 1926. But the Humble chief geologist, perhaps the world's foremost geologist, Wallace E. Pratt, was convinced that the formations under this vast coastal prairie had potential for oil production. During the remainder of the 1920s and into the 1930s, he and Bob teamed up to keep that possibility alive before the president of Humble, Will Farish, who did not look kindly on further ranch exploration. In Pratt's view, Bob exercised patience, good judgment, and a flexibility with the intractable Farish that he seldom showed in dealings on his own turf.

By 1934, the Depression had settled over South Texas and the cattle industry, a particularly heavy pall just at a time when Bob needed an exorbitant amount of cash. Mrs. King's ten-year trust period was terminating and her death duties, plus interest, had saddled her heirs with a debt of over $3 million. Bob let Pratt know that his interest in leasing was particularly pressing and Pratt, a vice president and director of Humble, took on the board. Putting his reputation and his future on the table in a high-stakes game, he convinced them to make the company's largest single investment in lease holdings in its history: the entire acreage of the King Ranch. Humble agreed to pay an annual rental of $127,824 for a twenty-year agreement, and at the same time Bob negotiated with them a loan of $3.5 million, with the rental to be applied as installments on the loan.

In Pratt's view, the lease as it was finally written was one of the most unusual in the annals of oil and gas. According to *King Ranch and Exxon, an Historic Relationship* (a small publication privately printed by Exxon), Pratt recalled, "Kleberg's chief concern was with his cattle. Under the lease's terms, Exxon wasn't even obliged to drill."

Payday was six years away. On August 23, 1939, the first well came in; less than a month later Adolf Hitler invaded Poland, France and England declared war, and the world developed an insatiable thirst for petroleum products. During the next twenty years, Humble and successor Exxon drilled over 2,700 wells; over 830 have been active producers. This largess in royalty payments made it possible for Bob Kleberg not just to improve the King Ranch, whence the bounty came, but to make his cattle and horses, his grasses and his ranching practices, a part of the world domain, without incurring debt to the corporation.

AN ADDITIONAL KLEBERG undertaking has its place here. One of his ancillary programs, an important one, was developing practices to manage the ranch's varied native and exotic wildlife. These practices, systematized and published, in recent years have become a boon to the ranchers in South Texas. From the perspective of their overall income, taking advantage of King Ranch wildlife management experience has been comparable to the ranchers being able to increase their beef output by introducing the Santa Gertrudis into their herds. Nearly all of the ranchland in our part of the state is under lease to individuals or corporations, who pay a goodly stipend for the privilege of hunting during the season. Ranchers are able to maintain a balanced wildlife population by following the management practices developed under Bob's supervision.

Wildlife management was of particular interest to Caesar, and he instilled it in his cousin Bob. Because of the little value put on game in the 1920s and 1930s, and the consequently lax game law enforcement, the large animals and birds in our part of the country had virtually disappeared. As early as 1912, Caesar set shooting rules to conserve the little game that was left. They are still followed today: Deer and turkey are shot only with a rifle, to be hit in the head or neck. Quail are not fired upon at the covey rise. Deer-hunting season is ended when rutting reaches its peak. Game is not shot around watering places or under the stress of drought. Also at Caesar's suggestion, in 1946 Bob created a wildlife management division on the ranch and hired a manager located by Caesar, Valgene Lehmann.

By following Caesar's rules and introducing good management practices, implemented by Val Lehmann, the ranch realized dividends almost immediately. Midcentury found the pastures teeming with whitetail deer, turkey, javelinas, mourning and whitewing doves, geese and ducks, and the premier sporting bird of the Southwest, the bobwhite quail. Controlling predators, four- and two-footed, and improving the range and water habitat for all of the species were largely responsible for this dramatic turnaround.

Bob had invested a lot of time, energy, and money in turning the ranch into a showplace for wildlife management, and he and his family reaped the benefit by having around them one of the best shooting realms in the world. In perpetuity, bachelor Caesar continued to play his part. He left the bulk of his estate to a foundation to promote wildlife management world-wide. The ranch has become a habitat laboratory where specialists do their fieldwork, underwritten by grants from Caesar's legacy.

Caesar was also responsible for establishing an exotic species of ante-lope on the coastal plain. In the early 1930s, he acquired from the San Diego Zoo a few nilgai antelope, a large ungulate native to India and Paki-stan. South Texas rangeland is similar in most ways to their native habitat, but it still took over twenty years for their numbers to begin to increase substantially. Now the nilgai have multiplied sufficiently to be commer-cially harvestable, by the hunter and by the ranch. Their lean, venisonlike meat is in demand in a number of quality restaurants in the Midwest and the East.

In the 1940s, either there must have been an imbalance of males to females or they had a problem finding each other. The cowboys reported that while gathering cattle, they would occasionally hear brush crackling behind them and turn to find a charging nilgai bull, six hundred pounds of raging sex drive, bearing down with the obvious intent of breeding their mare, rider aboard. Nothing ever came of these quixotic attempted matings except hotly contested horse/nilgai races, the cowboy digging in his spurs to get the hell outta there.

BOB AND HELEN EVOLVED a sporting routine to do justice to the game population. The physical requirements for their quail shoots were as elabo-rate as the etiquette was rigid. Bob kept a large kennel at the Norias head-quarters, overseen by an old friend and retainer named Sam Chessire, an-other bachelor and a retired Texas Ranger. Sam lived out his life breeding the dogs and working with them. He also kept things lively around the headquarters and in the camp—sometimes perhaps a little too lively.

At one of my early roundups, in 1952, I drove Sam out on the cattle ground to watch the cutting; he was by then past the age when he rode very much. When the work was finished, I slowly navigated the open hunt-ing car, no doors, no roof, through a motte of sacahuiste grass—a tough, prickly bunch of close-packed spears about the size and shape of a half-barrel.

Bob clung to one of the fashions of the 1920s—he loved practical jokes. Sometimes they got painfully raucous. Quietly, he rode up on Sam's side, unlimbered his rope, and threw a loop over Sam's head, intending to pull him out on his butt. But a front wheel climbed over a tuft of grass, tilting us, and the rope slid off Sam's hat. With a speed that demonstrated a lifetime spent handling weapons, Sam whipped a .410 double-barreled shot-gun from the fender holster, spun, pointed it at Bob's head, and pulled both triggers. Down the car went, tilted by another lifesaving sacahuiste, the barrel bobbled, and the blast went off just under the horse's jaw. The animal showed more intelligence and cool than we humans—he kept to his gait without missing a step. The rest of the way in, Bob rode along razzing Sam over his terrible shooting—he couldn't even scare a horse. Unmentioned was Sam's original intent—Bob was still connected with his head, his joke having misfired in a resounding way.

In his extensive kennels, Bob bred English pointers and golden retrievers, each breed having its specialty. Sam reared them like his children and turned them over to the trainer, Joe Sandifer, who handled the pointers in the field. Adán, the day's master-at-arms, took care of the equipment, saw that the shotguns were assembled and in the proper holsters in the hunting cars, that special shell bags were filled with ammunition, that liquor, rain gear, warm clothes, all of the dozens of other things the hosts and guests might need, were in their proper places. Bob and Ed Durham conferred to select the pastures to be shot over, and Ed arranged for the food, either a chuck wagon meal or a picnic.

On a typical outing, the caravan rolled away from headquarters at a leisurely hour; quail shooting is not necessarily an up-before-dawn sport. The dog handler and his assistants were waiting at a prearranged meeting place and dropped down the dogs from their portable kennels at covers they had scouted days before. Sandifer moved forward with one or two dogs out front, whistling, shouting, and signaling them to check all the likely clumps and bushes. The boss and his guests followed in open four-wheel-drive hunting cars, their windshields laid on their hoods, two and three gun holsters built into their fenders.

When a dog went on point, the shooters trooped out in a predetermined order, two or three guns to a dog. Following behind the shooters, the retrievers were restrained by their handlers' leashes until they were released to sniff out and bring in the dead and wounded birds. Here, with your shotgun at the ready and the birds breaking cover under your feet, rules came into play that had taken years to codify: choosing your bird on the rise, swinging left or right, following over your shoulder, getting in front of the line, or behind, on and on and on. Somewhat like English common law, the rules had evolved over two lifetimes on King Ranch and you learned them one by one as you miserably broke them. Explanations were not forthcoming to anyone lower in rank than a duke—just Miss Helen's inevitable admonishment, falling with the weight of a guillotine blade: "It isn't done."

Most of these rules imposed safety measures as well as proper shooting etiquette, and considering the number of rounds that were fired in a season, the accident record was remarkably low. Nevertheless, in the excitement of a rising flutter someone occasionally blundered and fired in the wrong direction. This sort of conduct had a lasting effect on the boss.

Bob was standing at the wheel of his hunting car, watching the action out front. The dogs flushed a single that in low flight turned back toward him. He saw one of the shooters swing, following the bird, and threw his hand over his face, but his fingers were spread and a pellet went between them, hitting him in the left eye. It stung for a while, but the pain eased and he thought no lasting damage had been done.

In the living room at Norias that evening after dinner, his Venezuelan friend, Diana Marturet, perched on his knee and saw that the eye was inflamed. Looking closer, she told him something was lodged in it—and something was—the spent pellet. The next morning in Kingsville he had it removed, but the wound set up a pressure in the eyeball akin to a glaucoma condition; it troubled him the rest of his life.

SHARING IMPORTANCE WITH his contribution to scientific game management was Bob's use of hunting as a tool to develop a rapport with the men and women who were to help and guide him in the international arena. With his friend Tom Armstrong at his side, he first found hunting a means of bonding with the board of directors of Humble Oil and its parent, Standard Oil of New Jersey. In the hunting camps, he was able to build a relation with them that was almost unique for a leasor to a major oil company. It was helpful down the road, when he was able to negotiate a better price for King Ranch gas. Later, in a broadening circle, he invited his friends down from the Northeast and from foreign countries where he had interests. The game population being what it was on Norias in a normal year, a shooting invitation was honored; they were rarely declined in his most influential circle.

Viewing the Norias shoots from the perspective of the 1990s, one can envision them as a holdover from the age of the colonial Spanish grandee, exercising his right of domain in the New World in the ancient ritual of pursuing game. It was a patrician pastime that too soon was destined to fade and be gone: the King Ranch quail shoot.

The rigid hunting schedule that Bob kept even had a profound effect on my family life. I traveled with him almost constantly in the early 1970s, but he unfailingly spent the month of January at home entertaining his friends. Patricia and I have three children, spaced exactly two years apart, born within thirty days of each other—in September/October.

Helen and Bob invited all of their hunting guests to Norias and, during the rest of the year, also took most of them to this protected sanctuary to the south, rather than entertaining them in their home on Santa Gertrudis. Over the years, Norias virtually became a private fief for Bob and Helen. The other stockholders, the extended family, had access to the other three divisions of the ranch but felt constrained to have an invitation to visit Norias. Since it was the most diverse, most scenic, of the four parts of the ranch, this created a minor hang-up, a smoldering, unspoken resentment that lingered throughout their lifetimes.

On the other hand, Bob and Helen made very few demands on the main home at the headquarters, Santa Gertrudis. Though Miss Helen oversaw the running of the large building and the staff, she and Bob mainly left it to the use of their relatives and to the constant flow of ranch visitors. When they married, they chose to move into the bachelor quarters where Bob had grown up, rather than live in the mansion with their family and in-laws. They had planned to build a house of their own, but they never did, just adding to the modest frame dwelling as their family and their needs grew.

THE MAIN HOME, named for the Spanish land grant upon which it sat, Santa Gertrudis, was the premier ranch attraction for most people. Visitors, men and women, who had no interest in the beef business sought nonetheless to be guests there. From the ranch's founding in 1853, it was probably the fourth house to stand on the same site. Captain King's first structure was an adobe jacal, commanding a knoll overlooking a small flowing creek, a creek that was the only source of water between the Nueces and Rio Grande rivers, separated by 158 arid miles. This part of Texas, the Gulf of Mexico coastal plain, is flat; some of the largest expanses of level land in the world are here. So the Captain set up camp on the only elevation on his original ranch, a 200-foot-high pimple on an otherwise straight horizon.

When he married Henrietta Chamberlain, he built for her a small frame cottage to replace the jacal. As their family and their fortune grew, the Kings remodeled and enlarged until they had created yet another home, a Victorian-style, T-shape two-story atrocity that housed their extended family and their many guests. On a night in 1912, it was set afire by a demented arsonist and burned to the ground, taking with it nearly all the family possessions.

The widow King asked her son-in-law to build for her a new home, a fireproof one where men could walk in their boots. The senior Klebergs had just recently visited on a ranch in Mexico and had stayed in a typical

Spanish Colonial hacienda predating the independence, of the style that is preserved today on the sixteenth- and seventeenth-century ranches. The architecture suited South Texas, so Mr. Kleberg had plans drawn along these lines. Since 1915, this great square monument has dominated our landscape. The outside, with its white walls and red tile roofs, its Italianate carved friezes, arched columns and windows, is a wedding cake feast to the eye, a light-and-shadow delight. Inside: solid, comfortable, plain. The antique Mexican and Spanish furnishings that would find a congenial setting here are few, the artwork Texas early 1900s. All of the things that would have meant something to the King-Kleberg family had been lost in the fire. But for Klebergs and hands alike, it is a shrine.

COUNTING MR. KLEBERG'S passing years, we find him now in his midfifties. His habits, business and personal, were formed. His mind-set was formed too; for the rest of his life, few if any of his fundamental and secondary beliefs and positions materially changed.

He had developed a simple, paternal management style and a way of life that mandated his total involvement. Upon organizing the corporation in 1934, the stockholders put their shares in a trust administered by the two Kleberg brothers. Richard, Sr., was elected chairman of the board and Bob president and general manager. This arrangement lasted twenty years. In 1954, Bob's brother and sister and the other Kleberg family heirs altered the management structure to include a board of directors.

Bob was reelected president and chief executive officer, but for the first time in his managerial life he had a group with veto power looking over his shoulder. It did not suit his mind-set—he preferred the more dictatorial approach. During our travels, I sometimes had to remind him that a board meeting had been scheduled back in Kingsville. He would inevitably rework our itinerary and we would set off for the next country down the road. His lifelong habits persisted—in his realm, few decisions, certainly not any major decisions, were made without his review and consent.

THE PRICKLY DESERT FLOWER

While we entertained scores of visitors who extended their stays beyond propriety, a few I would have welcomed for as long as we could keep them. One of them was Georgia O'Keeffe. Miss O'Keeffe visited us on a cloudy spring day in 1955; about as gloomy as the weather were her dress and manner when she was introduced around. She had been judging an amateur art exhibition in Corpus Christi and had been accompanied to the ranch by as many simpering elderly ladies as could cram into a large sedan. I gathered she had had enough of the art and the artists.

The juices in me were running strong at the opportunity to get acquainted with a photographic legend: the wife and model of Alfred Stieglitz, the most famous of our lens pioneers. By the 1950s, O'Keeffe had, from her New Mexico base, surpassed her mentor to become the foremost American woman artist of her time.

She wore her signature flat-brimmed black hat over a scarf tied around her head. These formed a somber frame for a serious, gray-complected face that reminded me of a New Mexico topography map—lots of parallel ridges and valleys. The rest of the outfit matched: man's white shirt, black bolero jacket, tight-fitting gray trousers, as slim and straight as a reed.

Unfortunately, I got off on the wrong boot when I asked where her home was and then told her I was acquainted with Albuquerque. She bristled, "Not Albuquerque—Abiquiu!" But the set of her jaw softened somewhat during our ride through the pastures. She tuned out the chatter from the backseats, picking out the cacti and wildflowers that were native to her own beloved desert. Her smoky gray eyes roamed like a hungry raptor's; she missed nothing, not even the mice that skittered under the bunchgrass clumps. We bumped across the potholes and grass turfs and compared our semiarid climate with hers and found a little common ground.

Back at the main house I sat the ladies down in the library for coffee. O'Keeffe roamed, squinting into the dark, metal-grilled bookcases. She came on a set of Mrs. King's volumes I had never seen: Matthew Brady's collection of Civil War photographs. We pulled them out and in her enthusiasm her expression changed, smiling over pictures long familiar to her. I had the feeling that she warmed to King Ranch; any outfit valuing photographic work like this must be in the hands of worthwhile people.

As we were loading up to drive to the gate, Miss O'Keeffe glanced across the driveway toward the old garage. The stalls were closed by tall double doors made of cypress; they had been painted many years before but had peeled and weathered in lines of soft, silky gray. Quietly she remarked, "How lovely." Without thinking, I told her the building was scheduled to be repainted. One of the ladies leaped to what she must have thought was an O'Keeffe-defended artistic barricade: "Oh, no! You mustn't let them do that!"

But O'Keeffe came back with the longer view, a timeless put-down. "Never mind—they'll weather again."

CHAPTER THREE

LET'S GO TO A ROUNDUP

WHILE, AS WITH MOST of us, people exerted the strongest influence on Bob's life, there were other forces at play. Dominant among these was his work, and by far the most commanding was the cattle work. Taking his life as a whole, from his infancy to within three weeks of his death, Bob spent more time at the roundup than at any other pursuit, perhaps even a majority of his waking hours. It was here on the roundup grounds, day after day riding among four-hundred-odd head of his cattle, assessing every one of them, that he formed and refined the picture imprinted on his mind's eye of the perfect animal. In his profession, it set him apart. The image apparently wasn't just a photograph of the bovine exterior, its hair and horn. Of a metaphysical quality, it bored in to assess the muscle, the bone structure, the innermost organs. X-ray eyes? Not quite—more a divine gift born of intense concentration. For it permitted him to judge the worth of a bull or cow in any condition, fat or thin, young or mature. It gave him a decisive tool; with it he accomplished something that had not been done anywhere in the world in the last two hundred years: he created a cattle breed.

THE FOCUS OF BOB'S premier achievement was the roundup grounds; it was his research laboratory. Before we join him on one of his typical roundup days, let's look briefly at the setting, the physical layout of the ranch.

The South Texas property is spread along the Gulf of Mexico coast, from the outskirts of the city of Corpus Christi to near the delta of the Rio Grande on the Mexican border. That's a stretch of some eighty miles, but the land is not contiguous. It totals over 825,000 acres, divided into four sections that form on the map a rough square. The two northern divisions are Santa Gertrudis, 203,468 acres, where the headquarters is located, and to the east the Laureles, 255,026 acres, the division with the most varied soils, from the best to the worst. The Norias division, 237,348 acres, on the coast about forty miles south of Laureles, is in sandy, oak-motted land that was once a part of a Spanish land grant with the lyrical name San Juan de Carricitos. Encino, 131,017 acres, west of Norias and also sandy, anchors the southwest corner of the square.

We ranch hands have all of our lives heard it said, "The King Ranch— the largest ranch in the world!" It isn't nor ever has been, not by half. Since the world's largest landowners are chary of making public the number of acres they own or control around the world (it's almost like asking financiers the size of their bank accounts), the largest of them is known but to a few. Probably one of the English cattle companies, perhaps Vestys, operates on the most acres worldwide.

In the United States, while the King Ranch is the largest privately owned ranch, there is at least one—maybe more—public company that controls more land. The Kern County Cattle Company in California can likely lay claim to the title. From the 1930s onward, the King Ranch has been the largest ranch in Texas and by numbers of its breeding herd, the largest beef producer in the state.

From Captain King's day to the end of Bob's tenure, nearly all the cattle work was done in the open pasture in roundups; the exception was the top purebred herd that was sorted and culled in corrals. The drudging, boring, sweating-or-freezing part of the work got under way in the week prior to roundup day. The cattle—dry cows, cows with calves at their sides, bulls—had to be gathered into a fenced holding lot around a water tank. Since it took about 450 cows to make a day's work, in the sandy land the animals could quite possibly be spread over 8,000 to 10,000 acres. The fifteen to twenty cowhands who made up the *corrida* (the group of cowboys that work together) on Norias spent the week before roundup day riding past the dunes, through the mesquite and oak thickets, or across the prickly pear flats from sunup to nightfall, scouting out and bringing in the herd.

It was mandatory that the pasture get a clean work, which meant leaving not an animal behind. This entailed riding over a lot of ground; the largest pasture on Norias was 60,000 acres. Of course there were more than 450 cows in a pasture that size, but the bovine social structure made it possible to gather in only a portion of it. Cows form groups—usually around a dominant matron cow or an old bull—and these groups stay together, separated from the others. They water at the same place every day. Since water on King Ranch was drawn from wells by windmills spaced approximately three miles apart, catching all the cows watering at a particular mill amounted to a clean work.

Having been through a few roundups, older cows found all kinds of ways to hide themselves and their calves until the line of the *corrida* passed; they lay down in every thicket or depression they thought might serve as a screen. The men had to be able to outthink those pasture-wise mamas on their own ground. It was a contest, man against cow, that was played out in each of the pastures on the ranch every six months, year in and year out.

During his youth, Bob Kleberg spent his school holidays living in the cow camps with the men. The roads on Norias were sandy ruts in those days—it was possible to move from headquarters to pasture only by horseback or wagon. So he lived out in the open, sleeping on a cot under the stars. From a lifetime of riding over the pastures gathering cattle, he was able to tell *Fortune*'s Charles Murphy in 1968 that he had seen every foot of the ranch from horseback. "Unfortunately, I will be the last of my family to ever say that—things have changed—the younger ones won't spend a lifetime in the saddle—they won't need to."

AN HOUR BEFORE DAWN on roundup day, the camp truck loaded supplies at the headquarters commissary and made the rounds through the colony, picking up the men. With the advent of the hardtop road system on the ranch following World War II, the men were able to return home every night rather than having to camp out for weeks at a time. They still camped at distant work sites, but it was not a routine—more a bachelor lark away from home for a few days.

On reaching the roundup ground, everyone fell to. The cook stirred up the coals and got a large coffeepot brewing; everyone downed a quick, scalding cup, along with a slice of camp bread. Then the men scattered to organize the day's work. At first light, the horse wrangler called to the remuda (the assembly of geldings and working mares) that had been turned out overnight onto the 200-acre trap where the roundup would be held. He cracked a long braided whip above their backs, and the riflelike report told them their day was beginning.

Like the cattle herds, the remuda was bossed by a dominant animal, an older mare wearing a bell that allowed the other horses to keep tabs on her. She led them into a fenced water lot—an enclosure containing a drinking trough thirty feet in diameter that was kept filled from a nearby windmill. There the men had gathered, unlimbering their lariats. The ensuing promenade, with the sun's backlight a low arc just touching the horses' withers and manes, was as graceful as a ballet. The men, their ropes hanging in coils at their sides, gathered in the center of the lot while the horses, schooled to their roles, swung in a counterclockwise circle around them, moving at a slow trot that raised a powdery film, catching and diffusing the sun's rays. The lariats fanned out in slow, easy loops that just fell over the horses' heads. The horses, in turn, stopped and waited when they felt the weight upon them. Even if the ropes did not circle their heads but just lay on their necks, they knew their riders had chosen them.

All of the horses were sorrel (chestnut, light brown)—the color of the King Ranch family of horses. Each rider had four to eight mounts in the remuda. Between man and animal there existed an intimate relationship that enabled the rider to single out one of his mounts in this uniform chorus line. Then the horses were led to the saddling rack, usually just a long, skinned oak pole hanging between two trees.

The first task was to gather the cattle together, from under the trees and brush where they had scattered during the night, onto the roundup ground. Then there was usually time for a second breakfast, a heartier one than the camp bread and coffee that had been downed before the horses came in. When the boss and the foreman drove up, the work got under way.

The foreman on Norias during my years was Ed Durham. A broad-shouldered man of medium height, he had a large, most impressive head and a tyrannosaur jaw. His formidable appearance disguised a gentle nature that was evident in his slow, soft drawl. During the four decades I worked with him, he became aroused only a very few times—when he did, the earth shook and the men scattered. Ed's father, a former Texas Ranger, had been foreman before him, as had his older brother. The family was distantly related to the Klebergs, and Ed revered Bob; everything Bob said was Ed's credo (except politics); his orders were Ed's mandate.

The first part of the morning's work was the most important and was undertaken by Bob with Ed riding at his side. When cows pass a year without having a calf, or go permanently barren, they are transformed from an asset to a liability, a useless burner of grass that must be taken out of the herd and delivered to market. Among the producing cows, age catches up with them even though they are regular calvers. Especially in the sandy soil, their teeth grind down, and their organs slow to a point where they are not weaning a heavy, hearty calf. So they too must go. These cows had to be found among the 450 that were moving in a walking circle around the riders, and a decision had to be made on each of them.

If the decision was to cull, another ballet—a far more intricate one—began. First, Bob or Ed slowly nudged the cow toward the outside of the circle. She soon sensed she was being put upon and did a two-step of her own, attempting to duck around the horse and melt back into the herd. But the horse, fleeter and experienced to her ways, cut her off and forced her further out. She made a looping circle—he swung on his hindquarters and was a head and neck ahead of her. She saw her chances fade and turned upwind, sniffing the scent of another small herd in the distance. Two outriders picked her up and pointed her toward a small group of lead steers about a hundred yards away, gentle old animals schooled in the ways of calming feisty cows. Back in the herd, the next cow was already on the way.

By midmorning the culling was done and the pace quickened. The producing cows with calves at their sides had by now been rebred, and the calves—six to eight months old—were ready to wean. The same cutting technique that had been used on the barren cows was employed to take these youngsters out of the herd. But some of them—weighing five to seven hundred pounds and as fast and tricky as greased pigs—were even more of a challenge to the horses than the barren cows had been. They ducked and slithered and reversed their field with photoflash speed, anything to get back to mother's side and mother's milk. But the horse and rider rarely lost the contest—when they did they were serenaded by the hoots of the men holding the herd around them.

At first this work went fast; there were lots of heavy calves scattered through the herd. But as the morning wore on, it took longer to find those few remaining that were cleverer than the others and had managed to elude the riders. If it was a summer day, the heat and the wind began to rise around 9:30 or 10:00, and the dust that heretofore had been climbing straight up began blowing in thickening clouds over the men spaced in a circle around the back, or downwind, side of the herd. These were usually the younger ones who had not yet graduated to the higher school of horsemanship displayed by the outriders up front. Or they were the old men whose mended bones, swollen knees, and hernias had retired them from the more active lineup. Pulling their battered straws down tight, they tied bandanas over their faces, turned up their jacket collars, and hunkered down in the saddle to collect as little of the fine sand as possible. Occasionally they got some welcome action when a goosey cow broke and took to the brush; a looping dash brought her in again.

No matter how late the hour, the lunch call did not come until the weaning was finished and the barren cows, along with the weaned and bawling calves, followed the lead steers and outriders to a nearby corral, a mile or two away. Then everyone unsaddled and made for the water barrels to wash up. The long wooden tables set under the spreading oaks were piled with an almost unvarying camp menu: overnight bread called *pan noche* (unleavened, baked in large, flat cakes) and several kinds of beef—steak, ribs, and the cow camp pièce de résistance, saddle strings. Saddle strings were long, thin strips of grilled meat, pulled from between the ribs of the young animal that had been killed and dressed early that morning. No question, fresh beef every day. There were beans that had been simmering in five-gallon iron pots for a day or two; refried beans mashed and fried in a skillet; rice with peppers, tomatoes, and onions; cold, over-sweet tea in the summer and coffee in the winter. Hearty fare suited to men who took a lot of exercise—and the exercise was upcoming in the afternoon.

The conversation was good. It usually began with the cattle and the pasture conditions around the camp, moved on to current prices, the condition of the economy, and likely to politics, especially if there were state or national elections on the horizon. We Texans take our state politics more than ordinarily serious, and around the table at election time we were usually personally acquainted with the candidates. So the discussion was lively, obscene if all male, and personal. As you might expect, Bob was staunchly conservative. Though he claimed no party affiliation, I have no idea when he might have last voted for a Democratic candidate for president. Most of the locals were lifelong die-hard Democrats; decades of argument across the rough-hewn tables did not make a single party conversion one way or the other.

Next, inevitably, came a short siesta; everyone looked for a spot in the shade, cushioned if possible. The boss read the mail that I often brought out from the office. If any of it needed a speedy answer, he gave it to me and I hiked off to the nearest telephone; a lot of work besides cattle was done in the camps.

Preparations for the afternoon were under way. The men who ate early had wood fires built; the branding irons in the coals had reached a soft red glow. Serums had been taken off the ice and large, multiple-dose syringes were filled. The ranch psychiatrist, an older man deft with a knife, was stropping his blade. His mission was to take the male calves' minds off everything but eating.

When everyone was ready, two or three ropers rode into the herd. Among 450 cows, there were usually about 250 young calves, four to eight weeks old, that needed branding, inoculating, and castrating. The morning's weaners had had their turn in the last roundup; the ropers caught the babies and the horses pulled them—bawling and dancing in an arc at the end of their tethers—toward the branding fires. About half the *corrida*, the younger men again, were waiting on foot in the open space between the herd and the fires, their ropes at the ready. They ran behind the calves, throwing their loops on the ground, where they rolled like a hoop under the calf's belly. As the calf ran forward, he was caught by his two hind legs at the heels. A man nearby dropped his lariat and grabbed the calf by an ear and by the loose skin between his flank and his hind leg, throwing him to the ground and landing on top of him. With short strings, his feet were looped together.

When enough of the struggling youngsters were down, bawling and throwing up plumes of sand from their nostrils, the brander began his rounds, marking them in the middle of the left side rather than on the hip, as is the practice on most ranches. By branding on the animal's flank, the calf is able to turn its head and lick the wound, keeping it clean until it heals. Next came the knife wielder, in two swift strokes removing the male testicles. The injector followed, giving them one or two shots depending on their sex. It was all over in about forty-five seconds; the calf was untied to bolt back into the herd.

Here was a good demonstration of the difference between human and bovine physiology. The calves weighed from 150 to 250 pounds, about the same as a man. If we men received these same procedures in less than a minute, there would be no getting up. We would lie there, go into shock, and die—or wish we could. The calf jumped like a cricket as soon as he was released, scampered for the herd, and was contentedly nursing his mother as soon as he could find her.

A well-run *corrida* could brand ninety calves an hour, about three and a half hours' work in this herd. The first two hours, the air was thick with dust and smoke, a mixture of the aroma of the wood in the branding fires and the pungent, acrid stench of hair sizzling under the iron. Ears, as well as noses, were set upon: the bawling calves, their lowing mothers calling to them, the shouts among the men, the creaking saddle leather, combined in an off-key calliope. In the final hour, the calves coming out gradually slowed to a trickle; then the boss raised his arm, signaling there were no more to be found.

With everyone near exhaustion, the horseplay began. Usually there were several cows and bulls in the herd that needed attention: a cut or scrape, a damaged hoof. Sometimes an animal's horn was not firmly attached to the skull by the usual cartilage growth; as it grew it drooped down beside the cheek and rubbed a sore spot. They were towed onto the branding ground, heeled from horseback, stretched between two mounted men, and thrown by a mighty heave on the tail—they were too large to be manhandled by the men on the ground. When treatment was done, a rope was threaded around their middle and one of the more adventurous youngsters climbed aboard. The cow or bull, mad and frightened, lurched to its feet and ran—twisting, pitching, and bucking—back into the herd. The trick was to stay aboard as long as you could and still dismount—on your feet if possible—before the animal took you into the midst of sixteen hundred grinding hooves. Every ride was accompanied by a critique— unfailingly negative and profane.

Finally the herd was turned out to find its way to water and the horses were unsaddled, whinnying and galloping to their buddies that had not worked during the afternoon. The boss usually had iced beer to offer around. Hanging a boot heel on the running board of the open hunting cars, Bob and Ed discussed plans for the next roundup while the rest of us watched the sun—it too looking a bit bronzed and tired from its full day of punishing us—slip behind a mesquite thicket on the horizon.

WE HAD JUST PASSED a cattle-handling day that had come down to us out of the dust plumes of aeons past. Our practices were adapted from the Mexican *estancieros,* who in turn brought theirs over, along with their cattle, from southern Spain in the fifteenth century. The Spanish had learned from the Moors during their nearly eight-hundred-year occupation, and the invading Moors had transported their age-old horsemanship and cattle-handling methods from the Middle East by way of North Africa. Our tack—the saddles, bridles, chaps, and spurs—though adapted to our conditions and slightly modified, retain the forms and functions that have been handed down through these centuries. A roundup must be one of the oldest techniques for handling commercial commodities still in practice in today's technological world.

THE POTBELLIED PIXIE

On two hours' advance notice on a morning in 1955, Ludwig Bemelmans— the author, satirist, premier epicure—dropped in for a short visit. He was accompanied by his wife and a friend, a Mr. Day, a travel escort whose duties soon became evident.

Mr. Bemelmans was a man assembled from connecting and concentric circles. His perfectly round head framed a round face, set with bulging eyes and a little round mouth. His midriff was the largest of his spheres, bouncing and swaying on his stubby round thighs. He grabbed you—in his shapeless tweeds, with his never-ending patter, his chubby hands sculpting the air, he was a joy to the eye and ear, buttressing his reputation as one of our country's most diverting celebrities. His charm sprang in part from his jumping from subject to subject in midsentence, from place to place in midstride. He needed outriders to rein in his propensity to perpetual chaos.

On a driving trip from their home in New York City to Hollywood, the party was detouring through South Texas; Bemelmans had not before visited our part of the country. I expected that he did not have an interest in cattle that went further than an inventory of the various cuts of their loins, so I spent most of our time together showing him the young racehorses in training. He knew no more about them, but he found them masterpieces of fluid grace and energy. Taking the shank from one of the handlers so that he could get eyeball to eyeball with a colt to which he took a liking, he moved in to rub the animal's jaw. Bemelmans had a rim of wild, upstanding white hair that made a circle just above his ears; otherwise he was bald. The spikes tickled the colt's nose, so he took a bite. Not pulling but chomping, he ingested a mouthful and went after another, Bemelmans obligingly turning his head so that the horse could work his way around. His quiet, self-effacing little wife couldn't contain herself: "You look bad enough. Get your head out of that horse's mouth!"

Paying no attention at all, Bemelmans happily babbled as the colt nibbled.

A hasty lunch had been ordered at the main house and I approached the table with misgivings. Knowing of Bemelman's worldwide renown as an epicure and a sometimes humorously crucifying food critic, I envisioned our being hoisted on a roasting pike in one of his published articles. But the cooks had sensibly stayed with South Texas fare and it made a hit: much lip smacking, lots of exclamations.

When we rose from the table, he headed for the kitchen to thank the staff and to pry into some of the recipes.

During the course of the meal, he recounted his latest venture. He had recently returned from Paris, where he had opened a bistro, on the Right Bank I think, facing the river. Bad luck had dogged it—just as the decorating was completed, the Seine flooded to near its high point in recorded history. He got up on a chair and held his hand above his head to mark the waterline on his walls. In the weeks following the disaster, he was able to get the building cleaned out, but he could not get his plumbing fixtures installed. Impatient to try out his new kitchen, he made a deal with a friend who had an apartment nearby: he would provide a generous series of dinners to his friend in exchange for the use of his bathroom. On opening night, Bemelmans hired a fleet of taxis to sit at the front door. When his patrons felt the call they were whisked into a cab and driven to the apartment, where they climbed two flights of stairs and completed their mission, then were returned to the cafe. He was inordinately proud of his crazy solution to a seemingly insurmountable problem.

As much as we would have liked to extend his stay, it seemed that in only a moment he was off again, a little German leprechaun enchanting us for a few hours, leaving us behind to return to our everyday rounds.

CHAPTER FOUR

SIMPLE STYLES, SIMPLE HABITS

THOUGH BOB KLEBERG was for over fifty years nominally the chief executive officer of the King Ranch, he never developed a structured command tier within the organization. His system was elementary: he was in almost daily contact with a small group of people each of whom oversaw one of his divisions—cattle, horses, range management, machinery, bookkeeping, and so on. They reported directly to him and made none but the routine decisions without consulting him. This had its pluses and minuses. Since he was readily accessible and usually settled the matter on the spot, no one was in the dark about a course of action; the work moved ahead.

Past his middle fifties, he was physically fit to shoulder this unremitting load. In his youth he had been a slight, hollow-chested kid with a round, rather gaunt face and penetrating blue eyes, his most salient feature, shaded by a sloping forehead and a prominent brow. That brow, it seemed to me, equipped him for his profession—in our windy climate, even when he was riding at full gallop, I never even once saw his hat blow off. Manhood had filled him out, of course; his higher-than-average liquid intake gave him a fair-sized abdomen. He compensated for this by hold-ing himself erect, his head tilted slightly back. Those meeting him for the first time came away with the impression he was a large man—he wasn't, about five feet ten inches. But his presence created a larger-than-life illusion.

The minus in his system was that from the middle 1950s onward he traveled a great deal. When he was away from the ranch, except for the work done by rote, things came to a standstill. This wasn't as serious as it might seem; unlike other manufacturing businesses, the production line moved at a measured pace, controlled by the seasons and the breeding cycles. In the main, he planned his trips so that he would be on the ground in Texas during the busy times of the year.

His decision-making habits were a reflection of Bob's times. In com-municating, his generation fell between the widespread use of the tele-graph system and the current era of the fax; he and his contemporaries did their business on the telephone. A verbal agreement was usually binding on both parties, leaving a scant written record of the decision-making pro-cess. Daily Bob spent hours holding the receiver to his ear, keeping in touch with his far-flung interests.

His firm belief in finding the right man for the right place was another facet of Bob's management style; when the fellow had settled in and proved himself, Bob generally expected him to remain there the rest of his work-ing life. This was a part of his larger philosophy, to find the best possible solution to a problem and then stay with it, unless there was overwhelm-ing justification for change. It was also in keeping with his own experience. His father's illness had propelled him into the chief executive's saddle in his late twenties, and there he remained the rest of his life; he saw no reason why others could not be as contented with their lot as was he.

The same sort of thinking applied to remuneration. Wages were low on King Ranch, but workers were provided the necessities—their homes, utilities, basic food items (meat, milk, dry staples, canned goods)—and the men were furnished their work clothes and tack. Education was free in first-class schools; christenings, Christmas gifts, and funerals were pro-vided. While the monthly pay was minimal, during good years Christmas bonuses were generous, sometimes nearly equaling the annual wage. Em-ployees needing extra cash received an advance against wages just by ask-ing. While this prerogative was sometimes abused by papa's temptation to dip into next month's income and wander off to the local cantina, the fringe benefits always assured that his family had the necessary provisions.

The system found its roots in the sixteenth- and seventeenth-cen-tury Mexican hacienda, which provided birth-to-death security for all its people, the hard workers and the worthless. In most ways it suited South Texas, to the middle of the twentieth century. But as the ranch began its expansion, educated people with a more assertive outlook were needed. In the main, they were not willing to be fitted into a slot, there to remain for a career. While Bob always strove for quality—in his properties, livestock, improvements, and his personnel—he never reconciled himself to this perfectly normal human attribute in those around him. Too often his comers either left him or took on outside business interests that diverted them from applying their total energies to the ranch.

Bob's lifestyle also shaped his thinking about the things he felt others needed. For a man born to wealth, his tastes were simple; he did not surround himself with the material goods that were the norm in his income bracket. His homes were modest, with small staffs that knew his needs and habits and were meticulous in providing for them. His cars were middle-priced, and he drove them about twice as long as the average owner. But where quality counted, he went for the best, his clothes tailored by Edward Nelson and his shirts by A. Sulka, his shotguns a pair of custom Purdeys. Simplicity was the key to his taste; his lifestyle was far less lavish than that of his own family living around him.

Another anomaly set him apart: he lived in a cocoon, insulated from the preoccupation that daily nags all of us, our cost of living. His utilities were paid by the ranch; his food was ordered by his cooks and paid for by the accounting department; his transportation and entertainment were ranch-related expenses. The only bills he saw were for a few big-ticket items invoiced directly to him. This left him with little concept of the amount of money required each month just to cover ordinary living expenses. To Bob, inflation was a megaforce foisted upon our society by the evils of the left-wing welfare conspiracy, not an insidious little peril that day after day gnawed at the monthly paycheck.

While Bob was seemingly parsimonious with his people, his loyalty to them was unsurpassed. Since almost the entire labor force was made up of people born on the ranch, he had grown up with nearly everyone on his payroll. Some of the longest-tenured families had arrived with Captain King and had worked their way through seven generations. Their job security was probably the highest of any employees in the state. Bob did not believe in dismissal and exercised it, in extremis, only a handful of times.

Once we were driving in from the racetrack and I was telling him about a man under me with whom I was having problems. His advice: "Any damn fool can fire a man—it takes a lot of sense to get him to do what you want him to do."

On the ranch, loyalty was a two-way street; the employees, called

Kineños (King Ranch people) felt an abiding kinship with the owners. A local story goes this way: A woman visitor approached an old man who was puttering around near the headquarters. She opened a conversation by asking him if he worked there; he acknowledged that he did. "Then you work for my friend Bob Kleberg!"

"No, señora, I work for King Ranch. Mr. Kleberg, he work for King Ranch too."

THE KING RANCH was in a part of the state that was developing, that had need for expanding every facet of its economic and cultural life; during his tenure, it made the charitable demands on Bob considerable. He responded, intelligently and generously. However, his decisions on which petitions to grant and which to deny were generally paternalistic and sometimes capricious. In sync with his standards and inclinations, if he deemed a project good for the local citizenry, he supported it—if not, one thumb down, usually just that quickly. This was in step with his generation; in his formative years, our tax structure had not yet decreed that organizing corporate foundations and leaving these things in the hands of faceless boards was the best route to go. But to the locals a yes was just, a no unreasonable. This, added to the discretion surrounding most King Ranch gifts, resulted over the years in the stockholders' not getting due credit for their part in moving South Texas forward.

Open-handed when giving away money, Bob was chary in the extreme over giving away land—he followed the advice that Robert E. Lee gave Captain King when Lee was a colonel stationed on the Rio Grande. Lee is quoted by Tom Lea as telling his friend King, "Buy land and never sell." Over the years, the admonishment matured into a credo for the King-Kleberg family (although quite loosely interpreted of late), and Bob was especially its adherent. He usually countered a request for a few acres of ranchland for some civic purpose by offering to buy its equivalent elsewhere. On the few occasions when he did consent to a piece of pasture being put to public use, it was always with the reservation that the land revert to the ranch when it ceased to fill its designated function.

AT FORTY-FOUR, BOB took the first step toward arranging his succession. Only very late in his life did he even consider the possibility of having someone outside his family succeed him; his lifelong mind-set was that this family corporation would always be managed by a stockholder family member. The logical choice for the next chief executive was on the payroll: his older brother's son, Richard M. Kleberg, Jr.

In 1940, Dick graduated from the University of Texas and went to work as his uncle's assistant. He married Mary Lewis Scott, daughter of prominent Austin physician Dr. Z. T. Scott and sister of movie actor Zachary Scott. Mary Lewis has been the outgoing member of Dick's family; she probably has more friends in South Texas than any of the Klebergs.

Little by little, Bob turned over to Dick the management of the north half of the ranch, the two divisions that pastured the purebred cattle and most of the Quarter Horse breeding band. But just as Dick was taking over direction of the prize herds, he had a long run of bad luck. In the early 1950s, the country went into the worst drought in its history, a decade of scant rainfall. It's almost impossible to manage breed improvement in a drought; all available resources in men and money are expended either in moving cattle to the little grass that survives or in buying and distributing feed where no grass exists. Shifting animals around contravenes good breed improvement practices.

The load took a toll on Dick, a sensitive, somewhat introverted man who wanted most in life to be an exemplary father to his four children. He did not have the early drive, manifested by his uncle, to take the bit in his teeth and run with it. Bob kept his hand in to see that the animals he had created were managed in ways that suited him; he sometimes brusquely countermanded Dick, reversing his orders. A man with a tougher hide might have been able to shrug it off; Dick could not. By the early 1960s, his health began to fail. The decline was a gradual one, painful to watch. Throwing off bouts in bed and in the hospital, he stayed on the job until the end; it came in 1979. Though he never said so, Bob indicated he knew he had mishandled making Dick his successor, as he had hoped that he would be. Once, when I reported to him that Dick was back in the hospital, he said softly, "I've lost the race."

IN IDENTIFYING PEOPLE to take into his confidence, to perform as an extension of his mind and hands, Bob was equally modest. In the later part of his life, he sorted out a cadre of three upon whom he depended. The first of these was Leroy G. Denman, Jr., his attorney and his financial and business confidant. In length of service, Leroy had by far the most experience at Bob's side of anyone in the corporation. His grandfather had at times acted for Mrs. King, and his father was counsel for the ranch from 1924 until his death in 1950. Mr. Denman, Sr., was a cultured, formidable gentleman who shaped his son to succeed him, not only in his King Ranch position, but also as one of San Antonio's leading counselors and bankers. The indoctrination began when Leroy was of a tender age. One of Leroy's intimates once told me that Leroy never had a childhood; his father treated him throughout his life as a junior partner.

In Bob's group, Leroy was *primus par primus;* his knowledge, his experience, and most of all his sound judgment set a standard. Of memory he is formidable; Leroy has never forgotten anything. But to take advantage of his acumen, one had to put the question; in our long association I cannot recall Leroy volunteering an opinion before he was asked. I expect that a number of my contemporaries on the ranch shared my mind-set: when faced with making a decision to a problem that was a close call, I often asked myself, "What would Leroy advise?"

When, late in his life, Bob began to think about a person outside his family to succeed him, Leroy was his first choice. So it is in every way fitting that at this writing Leroy is rounding out a half-century King Ranch career by serving as chairman of the board.

The second man in this group of insiders was Michael J. P. Malone. Jack was a many-faceted man who combined competence with charm and wit. He entered Bob's life as the right-hand man to George and Riondo Braga, principals in a private New York sugar-trading firm. The Bragas formed a partnership with King Ranch in Cuba, and Jack was the liaison between them. His contacts in Washington and New York, and in many of the world's foreign capitals, were invaluable to a company that was at the outset Texas provincial. He was the U.S. arm in organizing the Venezuelan operation and a director of Big B Ranch, the King Ranch partnership in Florida.

Jack was on the telephone with the boss every day, and he was a rich lode of news, reports, and Irish-type gossip. When Fidel Castro overran Cuba, in Washington and Havana Jack was as effective as anyone in the country in attempting to protect American business interests. As communist unrest spread to some of the other countries where the ranch operated, Jack kept everyone up-to-date on the local situations, and on the risks of traveling in some of these Latin hotbeds to a man with as high a profile as Robert Kleberg. His contacts in the State Department and the CIA were invaluable.

The third in the trio was me. Leroy and Jack were night and day available to Bob on the telephone, and Leroy made a practice of spending at least one day a week in Kingsville. But after he lost Miss Helen, Bob needed someone with the mandate he gave me—to be at his side, not just to smooth the path through the working day by taking an order and carrying it through or by finding one of his managers somewhere out in the far-flung pastures. He needed a sounding board, a target to score his ideas, to get a feel for how they bounced back. When he had thought them through, it was important to him to put his plans into words; for him a plan crystallized that way. So he needed someone around—to exercise the judgment to be there when needed and disappear when he wasn't. It was time-consuming. I once went seven months without a day off, which is not too unusual in agriculture. And it didn't seem that way; in the boss's company was a good place to be—generally.

This is not to say that Bob leaned exclusively on us, not by half. Each of his administrators and partners in Texas, in the other states, and overseas was vital to him; in their domains he sought their advice and usually followed it. But he looked upon us differently, as extensions of his hands. Late one evening in New York, over a nightcap, he told me, "I depend on three people to help me accomplish the things I want to accomplish in the rest of my life: Leroy, Jack, and you. You will do what I ask you to do."

THE BOSS WAS NOT overdemanding—his orders were, for the most part, simple and direct—but he did occasionally short-circuit his own people. He was adverse to putting off a decision or an action; if it needed doing, do it now. So he had the habit of turning to the person at his elbow and giving an order, thus often putting the unknowing instructee onto someone else's turf.

If anyone in Bob's circle, employee or associate, failed at the task she or he was put to, the cardinal sin was to try to alibi your way out. His most often-used expression was "No excuses"; I heard it one or more times a day, an axiom he applied to himself as well as to others. He tolerated failure, but he would not stand for shirking responsibility.

Oddly, with his racehorses Bob made an exception. He and Max—and whoever else was around—rehashed every race where a King Ranch entry had run and lost. Bob took refuge in his "ifs": "If the horse had moved on the inside . . . if the jockey had held him in at the quarter . . . if he hadn't been bumped in the stretch. . . ." By the end of the critique, the horse had won the race.

TWO OTHERS SPENT THEIR working lives in his inner circle, his secretary, Lee Gillett, and his multiple duties man, Adán Muñoz. Lee had little secretarial training when she joined King Ranch after World War II, so she developed by conforming to his work habits. Her virtue was her dedication to her boss—responding to his calls nights and weekends, arranging his schedules, taking dictation over the phone for hours at a time, paying his bills, keeping his servants in line, buying presents for his six grandchildren. The reply to any questions about the mundane details in his life was, "Ask Mrs. Gillett."

Adán, born in an outcamp on the ranch, was a versatile phenomenon: outstanding all-around cowboy, horse trainer, chauffeur, mechanic, valet, bartender, gate opener, gun bearer, dog handler, chaperon—dispatcher of any number of other duties that he carried out with tact and finesse. He too was on call twenty-four hours a day, seven days a week; from before dawn to the quiet hours before the next dawn, he never seemed to tire or to get out of sorts. His thoroughness spoke for his dedication; the boss was never without food, a full liquor hamper, ice, the proper shotgun, rifle, and pistol, ammunition, warm jackets, foul-weather gear, provisions for every contingency. English butlers are renowned for their fidelity to their highborn masters. It's doubtful that any of them provided service the equal of homegrown Adán's.

Sometimes Bob's faith in Adán's versatility passed all understanding, as in this instance.

Princess Lala Niza, sister of his Majesty King Hassan of Morocco, was visiting at Norias, along with her coterie of ladies-in-waiting, as exotic a group of Moorish lovelies as one would wish to be surrounded by, and one emaciated little Arab manservant in a burnoose. Shortly after dinner, the princess rose, bid her host Bob good night, and retired, her company trailing out behind her. Sometime later, I was walking along the porch and passed the open door to their rooms. The girls were piled on the beds and the little Arab was on the floor before them, with gestures spinning a tale that held them spellbound. He was the princess's storyteller.

Back in the living room, I told Bob what was going on.

"Quick! Go find Adán and tell him to get down there and listen. He can tell them to us." Translated from Arabic, of course.

Sometimes there weren't enough hours in the day, even for Adán. We were out on a ride through the pastures one day, Adán in the backseat with his hand on the door handle, ready to run for the next gate. The boss was castigating him. His favorite roping horse was getting old and Adán didn't have a replacement trained for him. It was the only time I remember Adán getting back at him, then only gently: "Mr. Bob, if I didn't spend so much time sitting back here opening gates, I could spend more time sitting on your horses."

OUTWARDLY BOB'S RELATIONS with people with whom he came in contact at all levels were open, void of initial distrust. Until acquaintances showed themselves otherwise, Bob tended to accept them full face. But one word or action that even hinted at dishonesty was enough to turn him off with the finality of a knife stroke. For Bob honesty came first—even more than braininess in his associates, he valued honesty. The information he received from those around him he used as building blocks upon which he formed his judgments and planned his actions; if he made a decision based on a lie, he felt a party to it. He accepted the things he was told as the truth, that is, the truth as the person who told it to him saw it. He could forgive misinformation but not a lie. He did not accept lying as a human weakness—it was an unforgivable sin.

This facet of Bob's makeup came out in a curious way. He was a great storyteller, often illustrating a point with an incident drawn from his experience. Sometimes these stories had no endings. Unlike most of us who tend to wrap up our tales by embellishing the finale, he stopped when the chain of events played out, with no enhancement—no gloss. Often our real life encounters are like that; when Bob's were, he left the recounting hanging in the silent, expectant air. Puzzled as his listeners might have been, they got their tales from him unadorned.

During our many nightlong conversations, I don't recall Bob mentioning God or the hereafter. He was interested in the social work undertaken by religious organizations, particularly the Catholic mission in Latin America. Late in life, he tuned even them out, over his mistrust of their liberation theology. But he never showed an interest in church doctrine. If anything, he had a naturalistic, mystic kinship with the living things around him, but how well he defined this I never ascertained. The formal religion to which his parents were so devoted he put behind him. To my mind, the thing he most worshiped was truth in all its forms.

On a personal, human level, Bob had the attributes of most men, except more so. By the time he had become a public figure, after World War II, he had what must have appeared to those who came into contact with him a calm, even sometimes stony, facade. Inside, he ran the emotional gamut. His temper, for instance—he had one. It was understandable in a man raised the way he was. Even as a child everyone in his surroundings—with the exception perhaps of his immediate family—deferred to him. To the adults on the ranch and his playmates alike, he was the chief's son, the *hijo del patrón*. So on those few occasions when he got involved in unpleasant events beyond his control, unreasonableness surfaced. His outbursts were slow to develop, mercurial when they did, and providentially brief. Unduly provoked, he could explode with rage, almost to the point of losing restraint, but then he almost immediately exercised sufficient control to get himself in hand. Fortunately, this rarely happened to him; few of even his lifelong friends were aware that he harbored this trait.

At the opposite end of the emotional scale, a sad or a joyous happening could move him to sentimental tears. In the evenings when he had a crowd of young people about him, he often encouraged them to sing. Bob couldn't carry a tune—when he joined in for a few notes, he threw everyone off-key. Mostly he listened quietly, and when he did a tear sometimes trickled beside his nose. It seemed a contradiction to me that his favorite tune was "On the Street Where You Live," from *My Fair Lady*. With the possible exception of his two years at the University of Wisconsin, in his whole life his home was never on a street, and the image of him swinging from a lamppost or pining out his heart on a fair lady's doorstep defeated my imagination.

IN CONDUCTING our routine, mundane business, those of us around Bob developed our handling techniques—"handling" used here in its mildest, most comfortable form. Mine evolved from making the same mistake over and over. When I had a matter to raise with him that needed a decision, I marshaled my facts, intending to recite them beginning to end. But I hardly ever made it. When he thought he had grasped the substance, he would interrupt, begin thinking out loud, and make a decision before he had the whole story, at least in my view. If I interjected, "Yes, but . . . ," he would cut me off at the pause and go on to something else.

Then I learned how dependent he was on his eyes; anything he was handed he read through. So I switched to writing out my delivery rather than talking, silently handing him a sheet when I sat down. He would invariably read it without comment, then begin to talk.

I also tried to keep to a pattern; if possible I got everything attended to before lunch. Bob had a lifelong habit of eating a hearty breakfast—really hearty: orange juice, cereal, oatmeal, eggs, bacon, toast, several cups of coffee. I am a light, early eater; it made my stomach queasy watching him down one course after the other. But it held him until a late lunch; sometimes it was his only meal of the day. If he was at home alone (we conducted nearly all our business on his porch rather than in his downtown office), there was no problem; at midday he ate lightly, took a nap, and was ready for a worthwhile afternoon. But if there were friends about, inevitably he offered drinks around and began a conversation, while lunch—overlooked by him but not by his famished guests—stole silently and coldly away.

THE HABIT WAS a deep-rooted force in Bob's life—he was a heavy drinker. A strong bias against alcohol had been impressed upon him early in life. Captain King was addicted to the jug, despite every influence his

Presbyterian-raised wife, Henrietta, could exert on him. She conveyed her deep religious beliefs to her daughter Alice, Bob's mother; father Robert, Sr., shared with the ladies an intolerance toward imbibing of any kind. In Bob's childhood household, only cousin Caesar lifted an occasional glass, always in moderation. It was in Bob's makeup to be attracted by the unknown, the forbidden; in his teens, his years away at Wisconsin, he developed his lifelong affinity for the bottle.

Except for those occasions when he would for weeks forgo a drink, Bob hit it hard all of his adult life, a malady that seems to especially affect ranchers. Was he an alcoholic? Can alcoholism be precisely defined? Not by me; but as it affected Bob's ability to perform, my answer is no. To Bob alcohol was an escape, as it is for so many. But escape can take many forms: by, year by year, shutting yourself off in an inaccessible place where no one can get at you—or by, for a few hours, relaxing in a hideout close by. The second was Bob's refuge. Because he was not trained in the ability to delegate, the pressures built every day; a dozen or more decisions affecting the ranch and his extended family's welfare were demanded of him. He usually complied instantly, seeming effortlessly. But his unruffled facade masked the disquiet it left in him. Each day the pressures built so that when he had had enough, at noon or midnight, he picked up a glass and retreated for a time into his hideout, where the petitioners and the demanding relatives could not get at him. The booze was the latchkey to that private domain.

He often asked for a Glenlivet and soda, a single-malt scotch whiskey he favored. In his time, only 150 barrels a year were imported into the U.S.; he saw that Sherry Lehman in New York provided him a generous share. Or he chose a bourbon old-fashioned, mixed with another single-malt that his friend, former college roommate, and King Ranch, Kentucky, manager, Howard Rouse, located for him in the small distilleries around Lexington. These choices signaled that everyone could count on a good night's sleep; he would have two and go in to dinner. If he ordered a vodka martini, things could get hairy, but maybe not. If it was a martini, gin with a lemon twist, he was checking out for the rest of the day and the night—usually a long, long night.

Normally he was on this general, after-work schedule for imbibing, but there were exceptions, oftentimes when he was traveling with his friend Major Armstrong. Together they had a morning ritual cup called a *leche colorado* (red milk). It was a mixture of bourbon, milk, and a generous spoonful of honey. The Major, discriminating in all his tastes, favored a brand made by the bees in Greece. Neither considered a round or two of that to be drinking at all; it was "a nutritious breakfast substitute." To me it tasted bad enough to be one of those diet formulas, but they found it a felicitous start for the day.

While Bob never saw reason to waste money, personally or professionally, in one arena he was lavish: his wines and liquors were the best. Early in his imbibing career, he woke from a night with the boys to find his left arm paralyzed. In his words, "It scared the hell out of me"—he thought he had had a stroke. His sister Sarah was married to the family physician, Dr. Joe Shelton, and the doctor relieved him of his anxiety. Joe told him that he was allergic to fusel oil, a component of cheap booze. From then on, Joe cautioned Bob, he had to adhere to an inflexible rule: never drink anything but the highest-quality spirits.

Bob graciously acquiesced: "Joe, you're going to be my doctor for the rest of my life."

Bob certainly followed his brother-in-law's instructions in his choice of wines; his selections were limited, but limited to top quality. One of his longtime eastern acquaintances was Douglas Dillon, chairman of the board, Dillon Reed and Company, ambassador to France. According to the story Bob told me, Mr. Dillon invested in the stock market in Europe and one morning received from his agent a terse telegram reading "Buy Haut Brion." Thinking he was investing in a French publicly traded company, he replied affirmatively, to later learn he had bought one of the finest small vineyards in the world. Mr. Dillon introduced his friend Bob to his new acquisition; forever after it was Bob's red.

Keeping him supplied from the minuscule Haut Brion output was a challenge. In 1972 at a lunch Bob hosted at the Ritz in Paris, he sipped a vintage and told the sommelier, "This is a great year. Send three cases out to my plane." The steward leaned over and whispered in his ear, "Mr. Kleberg, if I searched all of Paris, I might find ten bottles."

But on another occasion, in New York, his wine-selecting discernment became befuddled. The eye he had injured in his shooting accident was troubling him, so one morning I accompanied him to the doctor, who dilated his eyes to make an examination. By the time we returned to the Pierre, he was feeling terrible and could see very little. At midafternoon we went into the grill for lunch; the room was deserted except for us and the staff. Bob kept a small supply of wine in the hotel cellar and ordered one of his Haut Brions. While the sommelier decanted it, he told Bob that his inventory was low and he needed to replenish it. "Mr. Kleberg, I have acquired a case that I'm confident will suit you."

"All right, let's try a bottle."

"I suggest that you might host a small dinner party, say four or five, and try it then."

"Bring the bottle."

Gently, away from the others: "Mr. Kleberg, it's a Medoc '29, ninety-six dollars a bottle." (The 1967 price.)

"BRING the bottle."

A ritual commenced. The decanting operation required the services of five men: one to uncork, one to hold the bottle, one to candle the sediment, one to hold a toothpick across the mouth, and one to hold the pitcher. Two glasses were set before each of us, test samples were poured. I sipped, to the fixed stares and concentration of the grandstand crowd across the table. Bob gulped—he needed some relief for that aching eye. Finishing off his Haut Brion, he beat the sommelier to the pitcher to replenish his glass. But he couldn't see—after two or three passes over the goblets, he poured the Haut Brion into the pitcher of Medoc. To a man, the crew exploded—eyes bulged, cheeks puffed out, bellies distended. But there was no sound—it was like watching a detonation in a silent movie.

Meanwhile Bob, oblivious to the emotional disarray around him, finally got some of the blend into his glass and passed his judgment. "I don't think I want the case; it tastes about like the one I already have."

Thereafter we went through a leisurely meal, Bob switching to martinis while I knocked back a pitcher of what must have been one of the more exotic blends in the history of the vintners' trade.

SOMEWHAT RELATED TO HIS addiction to spirits, Bob had a small maneuver he went through each time he entered one of his dwellings, domestic or foreign; it was possibly another manifestation of his motives for drinking as he did. From the doorway he studied his surroundings, particularly the seating arrangement. Then he chose a place—forevermore it became his station. In his home, it was an easy chair at the ell in his porch, near the end of a coffee table; in the Pierre apartment, an overstuffed lounger in the northeast corner of the living room; on the plane, the aft end of the couch, port side. It was the same on the foreign ranches. Even if he had not been in a place in months, he unerringly took the seat he had last occupied. In hotel rooms the habit persisted; he picked a chair and used it during his entire stay.

Everyone in his entourage had the sense not to get in ahead of the boss and take the throne. On the few occasions when an uninformed stranger landed in his place, not an objection was uttered—but it was a short assembly.

Bulls do this. They choose a place in the pasture to rest and repeatedly return to it; it's called a *querencia*, a stopping-off or resting place, a place where they feel secure. Bob had a number of *querencias*. They seemed to fortify the drink he often took when he occupied them. Perhaps one of humankind's most secure executives in his position, he nevertheless was drawn to his retreats, where he could work out his problems in his time, on his terms, with the rest of us at least at arm's length.

As I PUT DOWN here my thoughts on this aspect of Bob's life, I can't recall an instance when he was not ready for work the following morning, or at the latest by noon. I heard that there had been times in his life that were exceptions, but I didn't see them. Did his drinking habit affect his total output—would he have had an even more formidable lifetime record had he not lost part of so many days and nights in the company of John Barleycorn? Who is to say? There is evidence that the booze cut his output materially. On the days when, for one reason or another, he would forgo that first libation, his powers of concentration—his ability to focus on a problem or a project for hours without end—were impressive in the extreme. But would his particular constitution have allowed him to live, day after day without respite, at that unremitting pace? It's doubtful—the small disconnect-your-brain hideaway was seemingly vital.

It's possible that Bob's habit gave a continuity to the King Ranch's hundred-year history. I never heard him say it—I don't know if he even thought it—but he was extending into his generation a tradition established by the grandfather he never knew, Captain Richard King, to whom he owed everything in his life. The Captain was a devotee of Old Rosebud, the Glenlivet of the Rio Grande. Fortuitously, the Captain and Bob stayed faithful to their responsibilities through troubled, perilous times, and they did it in a way that suited them, by regularly taking their respective jugs into a quiet room nearby.

THE DECADE OF THE 1960s could have been a most satisfying one for Bob, a decade when he reaped the dividends of his life's accomplishments. It could have been, except that not far into it he suffered his life's most devastating tragedy: he lost Helen. Helen had periodic spells of illness, usually involving her lungs. Eventually she lost a portion of them in surgery, but she completely recovered. She and Bob were exceptionally close; she accompanied him on his travels when she was able and was as trusted an adviser on the intricacies of acquiring foreign properties as she had been during the course of his achieving his earlier goals. But life in the South

Texas dust and heat gradually took its toll on her, as it has on all of us; her illnesses became more prolonged. A swift, massive brain tumor unexpectedly struck her down—in New York City on June 12, 1963, age sixty-one. The throaty, calm voice was gone; the intelligence and dependability Bob needed were no longer there. A lasting void yawned before him.

In the year following Helen's death, he kept his custom-fitted leather case at his side, a traveling bar, and he frequented it more often than usual. His nephew B. Johnson called the squat, forbidding box the Norton bombsight, so accurately did Uncle Bob zero in on it. He partly filled the abyss by attracting young people around him, especially delighting in the company of beautiful young women. Largely diverting, they were not confidantes. They came, they went, they married, they were replaced by other pretty faces.

Daughter Helen was sensitive to her father's loneliness and isolation in his little cottage beside Santa Gertrudis Creek, and she spent as much time with him as her own family of six children and her other responsibilities permitted. Recognizing that he needed companionship, she gently made him aware that she had no objection to his remarrying—she even encouraged it. But she told me his reply was inevitably "I can't find anyone like your mother."

SETBACKS LIKE HIS might have provoked other men to relent, to be content with past accomplishments—by now Bob had put together unparalleled feats on his family's 825,000 acres. But they were to prove the foundation and the prologue to the things that lay ahead. Now he raised his sight above the top wire on the border fences and gazed out on the larger ranching world.

THE RACCOON SAFARI

The King Ranch, encompassing as it does a vast expanse of diverse soils, climates, and faunas, is an inviting laboratory in many areas of nature study. Thus it attracted scientists from over the world, and one of these was the most interesting and diverse scientist Bob ever hosted. Bob's son-in-law, Dr. Deaver Alexander, had done a year's residence at Guy's Hospital in London and while there he and Helen, Bob's daughter, had met an animal physiologist, Dr. Rufus F. S. Creed, of the Royal Veterinary College. Dr. Creed was a world authority on the physiology of wild animals.

The Alexanders arranged for the doctor to spend several weeks at Norias pursuing one of his current research projects. He had discovered that the raccoon is unique among vertebrates in that there is an exchange of blood between the mother and the developing fetus, the blood cells passing through the walls of the placenta. The sandy coast country at Norias, with its dense oak mottes and shallow lakes teeming with minnows, small fish, and lizards, was raccoon heaven. The population was as high as could be found in the U.S.

It turned out that in addition to his professional stature, Dr. Creed was a stimulating, interesting companion. He had been captured on the beach at Dunkirk at the beginning of World War II, had escaped from German prisoner-of-war camps three times, and had been recaptured three times, once in sight of the Swiss border. When he finally returned home, he reckoned that the rest of his time on earth was God-given—had his life taken its normal turn, he should have been dead for several years. So he determined to spend the rest of it doing only exactly those things that interested him. Raccoon collecting was one of them.

In his search for the process by which the blood exchange took place, Rufus needed a number of specimens of the uterus/fetus, in progressive stages of development, for examination under the electron microscope. Following the early spring breeding season, the female raccoon has a five-week gestation period; Rufus's goal was to obtain specimens during each week of pregnancy. One of our ancillary findings was that the female raccoon is loath to surrender any of her reproductive parts during any week of the year.

While Bob took a lively interest in the science involved in the project, he was not much interested in raccoon collecting. So he put Rufus in my charge as guide and equipment procurer. We in turn enlisted the aid of the local state trapper, stationed on Norias primarily to hold down the coyote population. Since the raccoon is nocturnal, we switched timetables, sleeping during the morning and early afternoon and setting off on our safaris after dark.

Each evening our party, along with one to four volunteers who came along for the fun of the chase, sat down to a large dinner. We learned that the little gray beasts did not move around much until 11:00 or so, giving us time for an after-dinner pep talk and strategy session, buttressed by trips to the bar. By the time we got the trapper's pack of coon hounds in their crates and the cars loaded with nets and cages, we were in a happy, positive mood over the fine hunt that lay ahead. This usually changed as the night wore on.

The first part was the easiest and quickest. Within minutes after we released the hounds, they had a raccoon treed. Then complications set in.

The animal could be readily spotted in the treetops by the glare of its shiny eyes in our flashlights. But was it a male or a female? No way of telling—the sexes are identically marked. Since the animal had to be taken alive, the next task was get the coon out of the tree; difficult but manageable by giving the tree a good shake and dislodging it with a long pole. When it hit the ground, it took off for the next tree, where the whole process had to be repeated. If it was cornered by the dogs in the open, it flipped over on its back and went at them with its scissor-length, well-honed claws. A tugging match came next, to get five enraged hounds off one extremely aggressive coon that inevitably managed to wrap itself around the nearest dog head. Most often, during this fracas, the coon escaped.

We put a lot of time and thought, and a lot of booze, into moving our prey that last twenty feet, from the top of the tree into the crate—managing it sometimes, but to the end our system needed a lot of refinement. The trapper was an expert shot with a .22 rifle. Aiming only by the glare of our lights, he could just nick the coon's ear so that it would hardly be wounded but the shock would dislodge it. But catching it before the dogs did eluded us. At an army surplus store, I found a camouflage net large enough to stretch under the canopy of an oak tree. My plan was for Rufus and me to stretch this net at shoulder height; then the trapper fires, the coon falls into the net, and we roll it up before the dogs get to it.

The action commenced just as I planned: we stretched the net, the trapper fired, down came the muddleheaded quarry. But our placement was off; instead of the net being under the coon, Rufus was. The animal landed four-footed just on the top of his head, its bushy tail in his face. In the dark, of course, the coon thought it had grabbed the tree trunk, so digging in its claws it slid down—down Rufus's face and down his shirt front. By a miracle his eyes escaped, but his sparse pate, his forehead, and his cheeks for weeks bore eight parallel scars. His shirt looked as if it had been dropped in a paper shredder. Net abandoned on order of project leader.

Meanwhile, a gang of Mexican workers were building fence in our hunting country. They had with them a scruffy little terrier dog and the owner, along with a few of his co-workers, offered to bring in raccoons at a rate of five dollars a head. We laughed, struck a deal, and choked up when they showed up at the headquarters the next morning with five in a box. We paid up, and kept paying each morning, though we were forking over for a preponderance of males.

The rout we were suffering at the hands of those unschooled amateurs and their little dog irritated Rufus—why couldn't we university graduates develop a better plan? On several occasions we had to take a night off and head south to the cantinas in Matamoros, across the Mexican border, to refurbish his wounded ego.

Before the season finished, the workers moved on; we plodded along at the rate of one or two captives a night. At last, by the end of the breeding cycle, Rufus had in the freezer ample fetus-bearing uteruses from each week of pregnancy to keep him happily occupied under the electron microscope for months to come.

Caesar Kleberg on the porch of his home on the Norias division of the King Ranch. Photograph by Brad Smith. Courtesy King Ranch Archives.

The Robert J. Kleberg, Sr., family. LEFT TO RIGHT: Henrietta; father Robert, Sr.; Sarah; Alice; Robert, Jr.; Richard; and mother Alice. Photograph courtesy King Ranch Archives.

Youthful Bob Kleberg with his grandmother Henrietta M. King, Captain Richard King's widow and sole owner of the King Ranch until her death in 1925. Photograph courtesy King Ranch Archives.

The senior Klebergs with their family. LEFT TO RIGHT: father Robert, Sr.; Alice; Bob; mother Alice; Sarah; Henrietta; Richard. Photograph courtesy King Ranch Archives.

Robert J. Kleberg, Sr., with his two sons, Dick (L.) and Bob (R.). Photograph courtesy King Ranch Archives.

Helen Campbell Kleberg in her working habit. Photograph courtesy Toni Frissell Collection, Prints and Photographs Division, Library of Congress.

Dick Kleberg, Jr. (LEFT FOREGROUND), managing the Laureles division of the King Ranch, on a coffee break with his *corrida*. Photograph courtesy Toni Frissell Collection, Prints and Photographs Division, Library of Congress.

A typical King Ranch cow camp in the early 1930s. LEFT TO RIGHT: Santa Gertrudis division foreman Lauro Cavazos; Queensland, Australia, visitor E. E. D. White; Bob Kleberg. Photograph courtesy King Ranch Archives.

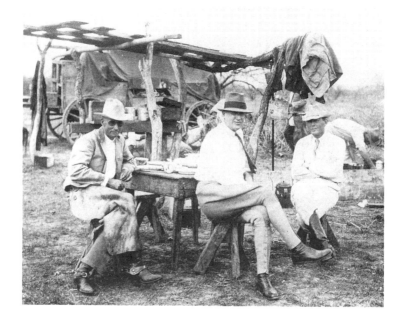

LEFT TO RIGHT: Tom Armstrong, Winthrop Rockefeller, and Bob Kleberg at the annual King Ranch Quarter Horse and Santa Gertrudis bull auction, 1963. Photograph courtesy King Ranch Archives.

Bob's first tour in Spain. LEFT TO RIGHT: the Spanish chauffeur and guide; Bob; Michael Hughes, King Ranch, España, president; Jack Malone, representing the Braga brothers. Photograph courtesy Riondo Braga.

Youthful Bob and Helen Kleberg at a camp house with their daughter Helen, circa 1930s. Photograph courtesy King Ranch Archives.

A herd of imported Santa Gertrudis heifers in front of the main house, Becerra, Cuba. The home is maintained as a museum by the Castro government. Photograph by John Cypher.

A typical cow camp. Left side of table, FRONT TO BACK: Bob's sister, Henrietta Armstrong; Tom Armstrong; Ed Durham. Right side of table, FRONT TO BACK: Bob Kleberg; the author; Bill McBride, foreman, Encino division; Lavoyger Durham, Ed's son. Photograph by John Zimmerman.

Santa Gertrudis, the main home on King Ranch. Bob's cottage in the trees behind the pool on the left; one of the four employee housing colonies above. Photograph by John Zimmerman.

The Thoroughbred Assault, Triple Crown winner, 1946. Photograph courtesy King Ranch Archives.

The annual Quarter Horse and Santa Gertrudis bull auction on Fazenda Bartira, Brazil (auction ring in background). Photograph by John Cypher.

Green Mitchell grass in an experimental plot on the Santa Gertrudis division, King Ranch. The seed was imported from King Ranch, Australia, northern properties. Photograph by John Cypher.

One of the brush-clearing machines used to control the mesquite infestation on King Ranch: two D-8 Caterpillar tractors mounted on one frame, to push the mesquite trees over, funnel them under the body, and cut their taproots with a sixteen-foot root plow. Photograph courtesy King Ranch Archives.

Ninety-day-old *Braciaria* grass on Fazenda Pará, Brazil, demonstrating its tremendous potential on recently cleared high rainfall land. Photograph by John Cypher.

The King Ranch in South Texas, Corpus Christi Bay to the north, Laguna Madre and the Gulf of Mexico to the east. Courtesy King Ranch Archives.

A stand of guinea grass on Becerra, the King Ranch joint operation in Cuba. Photograph by John Cypher.

Santa Gertrudis cattle in a sea of grass on Mostrenco, a King Ranch Venezuelan property. Photograph by John Zimmerman.

Bringing in the herd to begin a roundup, Laureles division, King Ranch.
Photograph by John Zimmerman.

The phosphorus deficiency
experiment under way: cowboys spooning the mineral
into breeding cows. Photograph courtesy Toni Frissell
Collection, Prints and Photographs Division, Library of
Congress.

Bob Kleberg, age 75, cutting yearlings in a Santa Gertrudis herd, Norias division. Photograph by John Cypher.

A Santa Gertrudis herd at roundup, Norias division, King Ranch. Photograph by John Cypher.

Bob in his favorite chair, telephone at his elbow, on the porch of his home at the Santa Gertrudis headquarters. Photograph by John Zimmerman.

Portrait of Bob Kleberg by the English portrait painter Simon Elwes. Photograph by John Cypher.

OPPOSITE: Bob Kleberg working a roundup. Photograph by John Zimmerman.

Bob and Helen together, their resting place on the small island in a lake on the Norias division, King Ranch. The shell leis are a gift of their Hawaiian friend Mona Holmes. Photograph by John Cypher.

CHAPTER FIVE

ON ENTERING
ANOTHER WORLD

EVEN AS THE WORK at home was under way, Helen and Caesar joined to open to Bob the manifold fascinations that Thoroughbred horse breeding and racing could have for a man of his interests and talents. This was not uncharted territory for him; he had already won just about every Quarter Horse race in the Southwest, using a high percentage of Thoroughbred blood to form his Quarter Horse family. Now he ventured into the most competitive and exacting arena in the animal kingdom. Falling in love with the multitude of Thoroughbred records—pedigrees going back to the seventeenth century, with performance data to accompany each generation—he became a student of this magnificent breed.

Since until after World War II racing was almost exclusively an eastern establishment sport, the Klebergs began to travel in the mid-1930s to the breeding farms in Kentucky and to the tracks in the Northeast. New York City and Washington were already familiar to Bob; he had had to spend a lot of time there settling his grandmother's estate. In 1946, he purchased a breeding property for King Ranch just outside of Lexington, Kentucky. Now, with Helen at his side, he began to meet the people in the racing world who were horse owners by avocation and leading investment bankers, industrialists, philanthropists, and government officials by profession. These relationships became invaluable to him, not only as he established himself as one of the most successful owners in the history of the U.S. turf, but for their advice and contacts when he began to expand outside of Texas.

Helen also changed his appearance. Before he married, he traveled in his boots and Stetson. No more. She fitted him in eastern establishment tailoring, persuading him to leave his cowboy gear at the front gate. Though he shed his outer cover on occasion, he was inside forever a cattleman. Pretense was not a part of his character.

BOB HAD EARLIER gotten into the Thoroughbred business in a peripheral way by seeking out mares that could be useful in improving his Quarter Horses. This was in line with his longtime breeding philosophy of concentrating on the distaff side of the animal pedigree. (Remember his remark about his own family: "It's the women who make the difference.") He already had the stallion he needed to infuse more Thoroughbred blood into his ranch horses, a well-muscled, well-bred animal named Chicaro. He began looking for females that would nick well with Chicaro.

If Bob's entry into world-class Thoroughbred breeding and racing can be traced to a time and place, it is the one Tom Lea pinpointed in *The King Ranch*. In 1936 Bob and some friends were driving through the Kentucky countryside when, in a pasture beside the road, Bob spotted a grazing mare. He ordered the car stopped and told everyone with him that he had seen his ideal animal, the one that fitted exactly the conformation he carried in his mind's eye. An instance's glimpse and the direction of his life changed. The mare across the fence, Cornsilk, was the most beautiful he had ever come upon; she epitomized the type of horse he was trying to breed. The episode was a startling verification of his attention to bloodlines, his incredible eye, and his hair-trigger reactions: Cornsilk, Bob later learned, was the daughter of the stallion Chicle, and Chicle was also the father of his stallion Chicaro!

Morton Schwartz owned Cornsilk and Bob eventually bought all the Schwartz mares at auction. In 1936, with Max Hirsch, his trainer and adviser, at his side, he also purchased the Schwartz stallion Bold Venture and he was on his way. By virtue of the time Bob spent with him, Max Hirsch, introduced to Bob by Caesar, became one of his closest associates. They were together each day during the weeks Bob spent in New York, and they talked every day on the telephone when Bob was in Kingsville.

Bold Venture, winner of the Kentucky Derby, sired King Ranch's Assault and Middleground, Kentucky Derby winners in 1946 and 1950. At this writing, Bold Venture is the only horse to win the Derby and then sire two sons to win it. Assault went on to win the Triple Crown. In less than two decades, Bob compiled a racing record that has been equaled by but a handful of breeders in a lifetime.

This was accomplished in part by never-ending homework. Hours that could be spared each fall and winter Bob put into examining pedigrees, comparing track records, tracing performances of near relatives, determining the availability of selected sires—all this before he made the decision on a mating that might or might not produce a live, healthy foal of indeterminate sex. Sitting in his easy chair on the porch, stacks of racing records, sire and dam registers, pedigrees piled around him, he selected the particular sire he wanted to breed to each of his 110 or so mares. When I found him at it, his chin on his chest, his reading glasses precariously at the end of his nose, I prudently did not break in.

THE FIRST DECISION, selecting the proper stallion to breed to a particular mare, usually is the most important the owner makes. While he or she (nowadays there are as many women breeding Thoroughbreds as there are men) is not guaranteed a top racing animal by mating two proven breeders, the sum of breeding a second-class pedigree to an also-ran almost inevitably equals Gainesburger. Herein but one of the triumphs and tragedies so intimately entwined with the sport.

On a trip to England, Bob paid a visit to Knowsley Hall, home of Lord Derby. This was the Thoroughbred equivalent to the Moslem visiting Mecca; for generations the Lords Derby had bred some of the world's finest and most famous horses. A key contributor to the present earl's success was his incomparable stallion. Hyperion, quite likely the breeding sire of this century. On one evening of the visit, quite late, Bob and Lord Derby found themselves seated on the floor of the palatial library, decanters and stirrers spread around them—Mr. Kleberg was teaching the Right Honorable Earl how to mix martinis.

During the course of the lesson, Bob remarked that one of his greatest disappointments as a Thoroughbred breeder was he had never been able to get any mares serviced to Hyperion. He realized the horse was quite old now, and that his book was full for the rest of his life. Lord Derby, who spent a great deal of his time fending off requests to breed his great horse, said that while his book was full, there were always a few cancellations— perhaps he could fit in two King Ranch mares. Bob was most grateful; he would pay any price for the privilege. But Lord Derby did not want money; he had a trade in mind. If Bob could arrange to have two of his mares bred to an American stallion he favored, he had a deal. Fortunately, Bob could and the breedings were carried out; Bob sent two mares to England and John Derby shipped his prospects to the stallion in the U.S.

When it was determined that Bob's mares were safe in foal, they were returned to King Ranch, Kentucky. After the foals were born, Captain Cecil Boyd-Rochfort, the Queen Mother's trainer, visited the farm, examined the young male prospects, and reported to Bob that while each was a fit sort, one was better than the other. Only a short time later, the mare with the better foal was in pasture during a thunderstorm, and she led her baby under a tree. Lightning struck the tree and killed them both. Bob never saw the youngster that had been judged his best Hyperion prospect.

The surviving colt, Zenith, did not race well, but when put to breeding proved his merit in an early crop; he sired one of the ranch's top all-time horses, Buffle. Buffle was an outstanding stakes racer and held promise of being that super breeding stallion that Bob had sought throughout his career. But the game played itself not by man's rules; before he was retired to stud, Buffle developed a strange brain malady, never fully diagnosed, and died within a few days.

This is but another of the wracking disappointments Thoroughbred breeders must endure to pursue their vision of an ideal functioning animal, the image a breeder sees on the screen at the back of the eye. In my view, people who breed animals are at the pinnacle among ongoing optimists; it is always the mating, the next crop of babies, that holds the promise of a lifelong dream.

In 1971, His Lordship and Mr. Kleberg, with Sir Rupert Clarke, the managing director of King Ranch, Australia, formed a partnership to breed and race in Australia and jointly purchased a property, Woodlands Stud, in the Hunter River Valley in New South Wales.

THOROUGHBRED HORSES ARE eligible for registration only if produced by natural mating, so action in the breeding barn in the early months of the year was continuous and a bit wild—horses are about as combative in the sex act as are humans. The principals are corseted up to protect their partners, the mare in a harness so that she cannot kick the stallion at that critical, and vulnerable, moment when he is on his hind legs preparing to mount. The stallion is wearing a headstall with a shank on each side so that two men can guide him home. The foreplay is brief—a few nips by the stallion—then lots of squealing, whinnying, snorting, biting, and in a minute or two the deed is done. Sound familiar?

Eleven months later, barring all-too-frequent miscarriages, a live foal is delivered. For a not-understood reason, the majority of them arrive between midnight and four in the morning; the first thing the wet little bundle of legs hears is the foul language of the attending veterinarian and crew, who have lost another night's sleep. In the next eight months the growing foal, running in pasture with his mama during the day and snug beside her in a stall at night, will have the only carefree time of his life until, and if, he is lucky enough to reach old age.

Even here in the open, on a grassy mat surrounded by a fence that minimizes bruises and abrasions, disaster is only one stride away. This was the case with Assault, the greatest Thoroughbred that Bob bred in five decades of racing. Assault was born in 1943, out of a mare named Igual. As a youngster, he and his mother were running in pasture one day when Assault stepped on a small wooden stake that had been driven into the ground by a surveyor. The stake destroyed the frog, the shock absorber, in his right front foot and came out at the hairline dividing the hoof from the bone structure above. By all odds, the little fellow was destined to grow up permanently lame; thought was given to destroying him. But Assault was beautifully bred, by the ranch's leading sire Bold Venture, so Dr. J. K. Northway, the ranch veterinarian, skillfully designed a special shoe for him with a leather pad where the frog had been, and on it he was able to stand training. Racing history ensued. Assault won the Kentucky Derby, the Preakness, and the Belmont Stakes, becoming the seventh Triple Crown winner on the American turf, and at one point in his career the world's all-time money winner. The sportswriters named him the Clubfooted Comet.

When Assault retired, Mr. Kleberg had every reason to believe he had in his stable one of the country's leading young sires of future money winners, right? Unfortunately, wrong. Disaster again. In Dr. Northway's colorful vernacular, his aim was good for a hip shooter but he fired blanks. Whether it was from the added strain of racing on only three sound legs, or from any other of a thousand combinations of physical maladies, this fine stallion with the potential at breeding service to earn thousands, maybe millions, proved permanently sterile.

UPON WEANING, THE YEARLINGS were separated by sex. They were not yet old enough to reproduce, but they were adolescents with the usual interest in their opposites. A lot of scrapping, biting, and kicking went on at this age, teenagers sorting out their dominance, the origin of the word "horseplay." Their schooling began; they learned to have their feet picked up and trimmed, to lead, to carry a saddle on their backs, to be mannerly.

In the fall, the thirty-five or so yearlings that survived—in health, confor-mation, and soundness—were taken to a barn near the ranch headquarters, adjacent to a training track, a one-mile oval that was as much as possible a duplicate of the turf at Belmont. There they began a more serious train-ing under their tutor, Dr. Northway, the exercise boys (a few of whom went on to make professional jockeys), and the stable hands, blacksmiths, track conditioners, record keepers, etc. Operating a training and racing stable is labor-intensive, which is the principal source of the high overhead con-nected with the sport.

This was a good time of year to be at home. There was a lot of cattle work to do when our long, mild autumn came around. On the mornings when he was not needed in the pasture, Bob was at the track checking the progress of his yearlings. It took about forty minutes to get out a set, exer-cise them over a mile or two, bring them in and cool them down, then saddle the next set, about the same interval as at the races. The time be-tween the workouts was taken up discussing other business. Over the world, walking and talking is the ranching way to decision making.

The youngsters' daily training schedule was the same for the first three months. They were permitted only to gallop in pairs, never to run; growing muscles and tendons could too easily be strained. Even this exercise was not simple or easy. On brisk days when a cool, damp wind blew in on the trades, their instinct was to go all out, and it took a lot of strength and good judgment on the part of the exercise boys to see that they didn't over-extend themselves.

By January the class, now two-year-olds (all Thoroughbreds have the same birthday, January 1, regardless of the day they are actually born), had been schooled to break at the sound of the bell from the starting gate, a contraption in welded pipe, springs, and padded stalls that was another pitfall by which an excitable baby could finish his career—by rearing, or pitching, or bolting, or any number of unanticipated things. If they sur-vived this far, they were ready for a few time trials over an eighth of a mile, first from a running start and later from the gate. On these special days the stable hands gathered at the finish line, the boss on the rail, stopwatches cocked. The pampered youngsters now had to show something—no ex-cuses—Bob would finally get an idea of what they could do after putting so much study, money, time, and effort into them. The exercise boys were as competitive as their charges; saddling the same horses each day, they developed a proprietary interest in them and rode as if the purse were half a million.

"*Hombre!* Did you see the way my chestnut creamed that filly? She's gonna make it! *Chingado,* she's a winner!"

In February or March, at the time Max moved his older horses from Aiken, South Carolina, where he had wintered, to his barns at Belmont Park, especially equipped Pullman cars arrived on a railroad siding outside of Kingsville. They were first-class traveling stables, furnished with the accommodations horses and men needed to make the three-day trip to New York. As the cars rolled out, the yearly cycle began again; the racing season shut down on King Ranch and began on the East Coast.

THE HALCYON SPRING and summer days at the track were the dividends in a risky, roller coaster business that had a few winners and a lot of losers. Consider: the average difference in time in a race on a major U.S. track between the first-place horse and the fourth-place horse is one second. Your horse must be within one second of the fastest horse in the race to earn even third-place money. I doubt that many enterprises in the world are that competitive.

It's self-evident that in a sport where a competitor with the potential to earn several million dollars can in one misstep finish his career, the owner must be an unbounded optimist. Bob was one of these, and his faith that the next season would be the best of his career endured to the end of his life. He seldom spoke of one of his horses that had made a great record in the past; his thoughts were always on the current crop, the one or two that had the potential to be the best he ever owned. That attitude won him a Triple Crown, two Kentucky Derbys, three Belmont Stakes, three Coaching Club American Oaks, three Brooklyn Handicaps, several horse-of-the-year awards, every major race for females in the country, one of the first three places in total money winnings seven out of ten years, and a dozen or two other records.

While the King Ranch stable won races with every class and age of horse, it was unique in the number and variety of races it won with females. The Coaching Club American Oaks is an example. The ranch was the first stable to win this premier race for females three times. The record would have been even better but for one of those flukes that make the sport ever fascinating.

Each year Max came to the ranch toward the end of the winter training season, to look over the crop and make the decisions on their futures and to get in some quail shooting. The best he chose to join him in New York; the next cut, six or eight, went to his son Buddy Hirsch in California; the rest were disposed of, usually at the two-year-old sales. Two things could be depended upon from these selections: (1) very few of the prospects would be sold, and (2) Bob and Max would agree on only a few of the selections.

Bob wanted to give every youngster that had survived training a chance at the track; he had put a great deal into producing them and had watched them nearly daily through the fall and winter. Max's eye was colder, more pragmatic; he wanted to concentrate only on the best and not fill his barns with oat burners that would not earn enough to pay their keep.

During the middle 1960s, there was a filly in training at the ranch named Miss Cavendish. She had a genetic deficiency in her legs; she was splayfooted, that is, her front feet toed out so that she waddled like a duck when she walked. If the condition is moderate, it can be corrected with proper hoof trimming and shoeing. But Miss Cavendish was hopeless; not even the most expert correction could help. Here was a horse upon which the two principals did agree; she should be sold. With her defect, she brought a paltry $1,500 at the yearling sales.

In the summer two years later, Max, Bob, and I were in the box watching the running of the Coaching Club American Oaks; King Ranch did not have an entry that year. Around the final turn and up the stretch came a little chestnut filly, Miss Cavendish, three lengths ahead and going away, running like a paddle-footed duck, a very fast duck. As she crossed the finish line, Bob and Max stood back to back, their hats pulled down to the bridge of their noses; it was a while before they could think of anything to say to each other. Though the stable was about $148,500 poorer than it should have been—the difference between the first-place prize money and the $1,500 sale price—King Ranch did collect a small breeder's purse for producing Miss Cavendish.

THE ONLY CATEGORY in this sport at which Mr. Kleberg felt he did not succeed was in producing a superbreeding stallion such as Bold Ruler or Secretariat or Gallant Man. At one time, late in his life, he thought he had found his perfect horse, and he went to a lot of trouble and expense to acquire him.

In the saddling paddock at Churchill Downs, just before the 1971 running of the Kentucky Derby, he saw a colt named Canoñero II being led around the circle and told himself he was looking at the perfect conformation of the stallion he nurtured in his mind's eye. Confirming his quick impression, Canoñero won the race. Bob entered protracted negotiations with his Venezuelan owner, Pedro Batista, to make a purchase. Meanwhile, Canoñero went on to win the Preakness Stakes, the second leg of the Triple Crown (and become a national hero in Venezuela). He was entered in the Belmont Stakes and ran, but he shouldn't have; a sore hock troubled him and he finished fifth. While he was convalescing, Bob continued to pursue a complicated three-way trade negotiation among Caracas, New York, and Canada.

At one point, urgent business at the ranch called him back to Texas. He telephoned me at home and told me to catch the next plane to New York. I was ordered to sit beside the telephone in the Pierre Hotel apartment and continue talking to the interested parties. I was not to make a commitment of any kind, he was emphatic about that, just talk and keep their interest alive until he could get back to them. His offer was $1 million and it was firm, so I could repeat it if necessary. A hurried trip—a long, dull confinement. The principals called very few times; they were playing the waiting game. After five days pacing the floor, I was going apartment-crazy. By Saturday I had had enough; thinking that the others were surely off on their weekends, I called an Australian friend working in the city and invited her to an afternoon at the races. But first I thought I would impress her by taking her by the barn to show her the wonder horse; I had not seen him either.

We called at Buddy Hirsch's office—he had taken over in New York on the death of his father—and he directed us to Canoñero's stall in a barn close by. Before we even caught sight of the horse, I could smell him. He had a case of thrush, a disease of the hoof that causes a foul odor—it almost knocked me over and gagged my singularly unimpressed date. The hair was nearly gone on one shoulder—the mange—and his right hind hock looked as if a football was stitched under the skin; he could not put his weight on it. A little Venezuelan Indian had him outside his stall and was holding a water hose on the swelling, and this was apparently the only treatment he was receiving. I almost fainted; a million dollars for this! Either I was looking at the wrong horse or my boss had become unhinged. I ran back to Buddy to beg him to get on the telephone and talk Bob out of this nonsense. Buddy was almost, but not quite, as taciturn as his father: "Give me two weeks with him and you won't know him."

Buddy was as good as his word. In a few days a deal was struck and the cripple hobbled over to his barn. Two weeks later, he had him back in training. Unfortunately, this last effort to introduce his mares to a stallion worthy of them was another disappointment for Bob; Canoñero has not been a quality breeder.

FROM THE TIME he got seriously interested in racing until the end of his life, Bob spent a lot of time in New York. Max Hirsch headquartered at the Belmont track on Long Island, vanning his racing entries to the other tracks on the East Coast and as far south as Kentucky. King Ranch horses occupied about thirty-five stalls in Max's barns numbers one and two, barns that his reputation and success as a trainer allowed him to hold for most of his professional life. Bob's investment in the contents of those thirty-five cubicles was a considerable one, so he took an active part in guiding their careers, religiously attending the morning workouts, a daily ritual, and of course seeing the most promising among them run in the afternoon.

Bob was a trustee of the New York Racing Association and had been elected a member of the prestigious Jockey Club, the organization responsible for registering and improving the Thoroughbred breed in the United States. The memberships opened for him the door into the inner sanctum of American racing and were his most valued affiliations.

A day at the races with Bob I look back upon as one of life's fullest times. It generally went like this: At the Pierre Hotel apartment, he kept a Lincoln Continental stored in the garage. The car was waiting when we came down around 8:00 and I chauffeured him on the forty-minute drive to the track. I knew one sure route, but sometimes he wanted to try a new, "faster" way. The instructions came quick and positive: "Left here— right—goddamit—that corner behind us!" And we inevitably got lost. Directions solicited from a Brooklyn street corner type I could barely understand, and we were off again. Each of us had a version of the native's directions—you know who prevailed. More specific signals from the navigator, he kept his left hand between his knees, wigwagging it right and left like a rudder—more unfamiliar vistas. But his directions were positive, concise. Once, halfway through the Queens Midtown Tunnel, he roused himself out of a snooze and ordered, "Go straight here." We always managed to arrive at Belmont in time for the best horses' outings. Max had us figured and held back the ones he knew the boss wanted to see. It was also an opportunity to see horses from other stables work out, King Ranch competitors; the finest racing animals of the year were in the barns around us.

We walked down to the exercise track behind the strings of two to four colts and fillies, usually in the summer sunshine, sometimes in the fall rain and muck. Regardless, the horses had to have their daily exercise. On cloudy, damp days a mist rose in the infield; you had to look sharp to spot your colt breaking in the distance. The lone runner, moving beyond the haze at a gallop that made his back travel in a level line, the little exercise boy hunkered over his withers to form an outline like outstretched wings. In silhouette, the young sprinter transfigured to a dark Pegasus, flying free of the turf, free for a moment of his earthbound masters. Just so, it was the only time of day when the horse was in command.

The workouts were done by 11:30; the last horses were back in their stalls before noon. Then came a critique, in the office attached to Max's living quarters. Here everything was in miniature, the rooms small, the ceiling low, fitting Max's stature. The dingy white frame cottage with green trim matched the barns on each side and barely squeezed in between them; land was at a premium on these immense grounds so close by the city. Max was one of the professional elite; few trainers were able to live at the track surrounded by their charges. Here the boss and Max decided on entries for coming meetings and went into health problems, using racing jargon to go over all the things the sport demanded.

About 1:30, post time for the first race, we drove over to the stands—the boss, Max, his accountant, a fashionable lady named Tad Legere, and I. The traffic directors recognized the Lincoln, waving it through to the members' elevator entrance.

Max usually had business at the pari-mutuel accounting offices; a time or two I followed along with him. I have never seen that much cash anywhere else in my life. There were bins the size of gravel pits filled with ones, fives, tens, twenties, and up, so many they were weighed rather than counted on scales accurate enough to measure a single bill. (Did a stack of forty-nine dirty twenties weigh as much as fifty new ones? I never found out.) The counting room seemed to attract sports celebrities: Whitey Ford, Vince Lombardi. In the 1960s, I suppose they wanted to see where the big money was—things have changed.

Usually, however, I stayed with Bob on the elevator ride to the New York Racing Association trustees' room at the top of the stands. A small, lavish buffet was laid out along one wall, the tables set in tiers before a picture window looking down on the finish line. Above and behind was a sitting area where owners of winners of the major stakes races were invited for drinks with the trustees after the trophy presentations. The room had an accommodation not found anywhere around the track except in the secure business offices: a telephone with an outside line. Offtrack betting had not yet been legalized in New York State; tracks frowned on running bookie shops from pay booths. There under the eaves at the top of the grandstand, sealed off from the din below, this exclusive little enclave was as subdued as a downtown men's club.

After lunch, Bob headed for his box, where his friends knew they could find him. Often his daughter Helen, owner of some fine horses in her own name, and his grandchildren joined him; there was constant people movement. As I said, many of the top names in the American business world gravitated to racing—the Phippses, DuPonts, Whitneys, Millses. It was like a Fortune 500 marathon to watch them make the rounds. One afternoon I was walking up an aisle with Helen's first husband, Dr. Deaver Alexander, when I saw up ahead Bob talking to Harry Guggenheim. I had once applied for a Guggenheim Fellowship to photograph and classify the native cattle breeds of east Africa (I didn't get it), so I was impressed that I was about to meet a member of this philanthropic family. When I said so to Deaver, he laughed, "Harry Guggenheim, my God, look who he's talking to!" Next to Bob was Bernard Baruch.

About the most revered name in American racing is Widener; for generations they have owned and raced the finest. A straightaway track that used to run diagonally across the infield at Belmont was named the Widener Chute. At this time, the patriarch of the family was P. A. B. Widener, an elderly gentleman of spare frame who came to the track only occasionally and when he did was treated like an icon. Bob had a high regard for Mr. Widener. On one occasion, he went over to the Widener box to speak to him and took me along. Introducing me, he said I was a young man he was training. Looking me over, Mr. Widener said to Mr. Kleberg, "Good luck, it's harder to train a man than a horse."

Betting styles were interesting. Bob bet on his own horses unless they were out just for the experience of getting a race behind them. His usual wager was $100; he seldom had anything but a few $100 bills in his pocket. Max bet infrequently, but when he did he plunged; for Max horses were a business. So he patiently watched a sure thing develop and then backed it with a few thousand. Among the variety of systems I came across, I saw only one in play that was infallible. Henrietta Armstrong, Bob's sister, had a bet on the winner in every race—she bought a ticket on every horse.

AFTER THE LAST RACE—we usually saw the whole card through—plans were made with Max for the next day and we headed back to the apartment. There was always a stack of messages waiting at the hotel desk, which for me meant back to work. Some of them were from friends who knew where to find Bob when he was in Manhattan, and they were invited for drinks. The apartment was often crowded by 8:00.

Bob's best friend, brother-in-law, and neighboring rancher was Major Thomas R. Armstrong; Tom had spent his professional career in and out of New York and was often in the city at the same time as Bob. Their relationship was lifelong; they shared great and trying adventures. The son of Texas Ranger and rancher John B. Armstrong, a 1913 Princeton graduate, Tom went into the Army during World War I and rose to the rank of major, the youngest in our Expeditionary Force. The title stuck with him the rest of his life. He returned from overseas to join Standard Oil Company and was posted to Latin America, mainly because of his proficiency in Spanish. An abiding bachelor, in 1948 he made an extraordinarily late and happy marriage to Bob's widowed sister, Henrietta Kleberg Larkin. The Major had, for Standard Oil, dealt with most of the governments of Latin America and had developed a keen reading for people, along with adroit tact and charm, a gentleman in every sense.

Tom's lifelong partnership with his compadre Bob afforded him a clear insight into Bob's psyche. Tom said on occasion, sometimes in exasperation, "My friend Bob has the cleanest mind of any man I know. It should be clean—he changes it every fifteen minutes."

Tom sometimes cohosted the after-races cocktails and dinners, and on one of these evenings he demonstrated his talents. Bob had as a guest another old friend, Shelby Longoria, one of the Longoria brothers who were agriculture and banking entrepreneurs in northern Mexico. Shelby and Bob were just about standoff competitors with the bottle; one time one went down, the next the other. Shelby, well into the evening's elbow bending, invited everyone to dinner. Bob already had his customary reservation at the 21 Club, but for Shelby nothing would stand in the way of his being the host. On this particular evening Bob had hardly touched his glass; he relented and off we went, about eight of us.

When we arrived, Mr. Kleberg and his party were escorted to his table. Before menus were passed around, the waiters appeared with champagne and caviar, a usual Kleberg opener. Shelby, seeing his host's prerogatives preempted, took exception in a voice that could be heard across one of New York's noisiest downstairs bars. He was not going to pay for a lot of silly frills he didn't order. Not even Mildred, his ever-ladylike wife, could shush him down. Then Tom stepped into the melee. He coaxed Shelby out of his seat and over to a bench in the corner, where he stroked the roaring lion in low, soothing tones. Meanwhile, his hand pulled open Shelby's coat and deftly extracted his wallet. Out came Shelby's American Express card, passed to the maître d', and a not wiser but somewhat mollified Shelby was led back to the table. Through all of this, Bob had not said a word, leaving it to his friend Tom to allay the crisis.

The incident had a footnote. The following afternoon at Aqueduct, I happened upon a pretty young lady I had been dating. She was with a vice president of Wildenstein Galleries, Jay Rousuck, and she introduced us. "I recognized you! You were with Mr. Kleberg last night at the 21."

I admitted I was, bracing for a comment on the ruckus.

"And how is Mr. Kleberg feeling today?"

Puzzling question, but I assured him that he was fine.

"Strange, I could have sworn he was sick—he was so quiet."

A thoughtful pause—an afterthought, "By the way, who was the man who took his place?"

WHILE BOB KLEBERG'S racing activities were centered on the East and West coasts, and in Kentucky, when called upon he stepped in to lend his state a hand to legalize pari-mutuel betting, so that first-class horse racing could return to Texas.

While we are the horsiest state in the Union, Texas for the past five decades has had no Thoroughbred racing. During the early 1930s, betting on the tote had been legal. But a reform-minded governor named James Allred, prodded by his strong East Texas Baptist constituency, passed a bill through the legislature outlawing it. The tracks shut down. But a lot of money was illegally but openly changing hands at the thirty-two Quarter Horse tracks holding race meetings around the state. In 1963, the legislature was looking for new sources of revenue; what more painless way to raise state funds than to tax sin, by taking a percentage of these wagers and at the same time giving the racing industry the incentive to expand into big time? A group led by Arthur Seeligson and Hugh Fitzsimmons in San Antonio got together some of the state's Thoroughbred owners and sports lovers to organize a campaign to again legalize pari-mutuel betting at the tracks.

Arthur and Hugh telephoned Bob to enlist his support. He pledged it and called Belton Johnson, his nephew, and me into his office to tell us he wanted us to represent King Ranch on the Executive Committee of the new Texas Racing Association. Under no circumstances were we to commit the ranch to anything until first we checked with him. B. (Belton) and I had heard that admonishment often enough for it to itch like a flea in our ear.

Our governor in 1963 was John Connally, a key player in any state initiative. John was so firmly in his seat that he did not need to depend on a segment of voters for support; he had a statewide mandate. He was a rancher, an owner and admirer of fine horses, and an admirable political risk taker. So early on he announced his support for pari-mutuel wagering. But he was also a consummate political strategist. While he wanted to retain his friendship with the group of deep-pocketed campaign contributors who made up the association membership, he took steps to see that they did not get too much in his wavy, salt-and-pepper, immaculately groomed hair.

Young Bob Strauss, an attorney from Dallas, was just getting off the political launching pad on a career that was to become interstellar, taking him to chairman of the Democratic Party, U.S. trade representative, adviser to presidents, and our ambassador in Moscow. But for now he was in the governor's office and on the governor's coattails. John put Bob Strauss on our Executive Committee as his representative, with back-of-the-hand instructions to see that we did not create any embarrassing conflicts of interest for him. Strauss handled the governor's interests brilliantly, forcefully, and at the top of a voice which—as any number of negotiators, Russian, Japanese, were due to learn—could reach megavolume.

The committee met about once a month; a few minutes into the session Bob Strauss took over. He invariably indicated that there was a hypercritical issue that had to be confronted immediately; our future campaign absolutely depended on it. The governor was doing his part; either we dropped everything and put our shoulders behind implementing his strategy or we let down our only friend—he wasn't about to carry the load alone. What were we, a bunch of social pansies out for a good time? The chips were down, stand up and be counted, get on this when we walked out of the room—the clichés turned the air blue. Each performance was masterful; they got better with practice. We returned to the next meeting, harried and confused and tired but under the impression that by our ceaseless efforts the crisis was averted and the governor was still our friend. Fifteen minutes later, slouched in his chair at the back of the room, Bob Strauss was sending us down another trail, hot after another elusive rabbit. Meanwhile the governor was untroubled in pursuing weightier matters.

When I clued in to the treatment we were getting, my respect for both Bob Strauss and John Connally grew rather than diminished. John was a remarkably fine governor and a remarkably fine man. Since he bred Santa Gertrudis cattle on his ranch, Bob saw a lot of him during his varied public career. He had such regard for him that he would have liked to see him take a responsible position on King Ranch.

One small incident in our long acquaintance gave me an insight into the governor's ability. During the wagering campaign, we organized a media event by holding a luncheon in Houston to present the first annual Horseman of the Year award; Bob was the recipient and Connally was asked to make the presentation. John asked me to give him some biographical background notes; I turned out eight typewritten pages and mailed them to his office in Austin.

On the morning of the luncheon, I went to the airport with a group to escort the governor to the hotel. When he got off the plane, he told me my material had never arrived. Fortunately, I had a copy with me and with everyone around him jabbering and trying to get his attention he was able to scan it during the twenty-minute ride downtown. That was the only look he got; within minutes he was at the head table approaching the podium to acclaim his friend. From the back of the room I tracked him with the paper. Without a note to refer to, he included every single fact on those eight pages, but not in the order that he had read them. Riding back to the airport, I told him what a remarkable performance I thought he had given; his memory was incredible. He thanked me, adding, "I can do it today, but a week from now don't ask me to repeat a word I said."

To SUPPORT THE ASSOCIATION, Bob rounded up friends all over the state, most of whom shared his interest in horses. There was certainly an assortment of individualists among them; an early encounter with one was a harbinger of things to come.

Bob hosted a meeting for the group at the main house and I was the welcome wagon for the ones coming in by private plane. At the time we had a grass-covered runway near the headquarters, and I heard a late arrival circling overhead. At the airfield, a DC-3 taxied up and out stepped a tiny man of wizened countenance, about five feet two, weighing about ninety pounds. Behind large glasses, topped by a Stetson sitting on his ears, he peered out like a little ground owl surveying the pasture from his burrow. He stuck out his hand and informed me, "Young man, my name's Edgar Brown from Orange, Texas, and I'm worth a hundred million dollars."

"Yes sir, Mr. Brown! My name's John Cypher and that's my station wagon over there." (It really wasn't; it belonged to the ranch. But it was the most impressive asset I controlled at the time.)

Mr. Brown had made it big in ships during World War II—he was as flamboyant in his social activities as he was in his business dealings and he had a way of getting everyone's attention. We were approaching an election year, so as soon as he entered the main house he proposed that we drop this racing idea and organize behind running Bob Kleberg for president. Mr. Kleberg gracefully demurred.

On another occasion, a meeting in Houston was hosted by the chairman of Quintana Oil, Douglas Marshall. Doug had an impressive Air Force record during World War II and had married the beautiful daughter of the founder of the company, Hugh Roy Cullen. Doug and Margaret's premier contribution to agriculture in the state was their importing from Egypt some of the finest Arabian horses to arrive in the Western Hemisphere. In an exchange with Mr. Brown, Doug showed us why he was a much-decorated flier—he had guts.

We had gathered after the meeting in the famous water hole in the Lamar Hotel kept by the owners of Brown and Root, Herman and George

Brown, the suite to which Lyndon Johnson was summoned from time to time. Its fame rested on the gathering that was held there each afternoon after five; between them, the men who dropped by for a drink or a card game not only made the political and economic decisions that so affected Houston's destiny, they made some that affected the state and nation as well. A number of them had joined our group.

On this particular night, it was about 2:00 A.M., everyone had had a long day plotting pari-mutuel strategy and was relaxing, perhaps a bit too relaxed. Doug Marshall was sitting in a straight-backed chair at the entrance into a hallway, talking to Bob Strauss and me, crowded in the narrow passage behind him. Mr. Brown, the Orange Brown, walked up to Doug—words were exchanged—an argument of rising intensity ensued. As quick as a seasoned gunslinger, Mr. Brown whipped out a little .38 revolver and stuck it in Doug's left ear. In the din no one even noticed except the principals: Marshall and Brown, Strauss and I—our belly buttons were in line with Marshall's other ear.

Brown: "You son of a bitch, I'm gonna blow your brains out."

Marshall: "You sawed off little bastard, you haven't got the guts."

"Want me to prove it?"

"Go ahead, ya little fart."

Strauss's belly button had been in tight spots before. "Let's ease outta here—down the wall if we can." We flattened against it like the wallpaper.

But Mr. Brown's temper matched one of our Gulf Coast squalls; the sun came out as fast as the clouds had closed in.

"All right, then, I won't blow your brains out. I'll stand on my head." And this little man, he must have been well over seventy at the time, did a perfect handstand, his card case, his bankroll, and the .38 raining onto the carpet around him.

THE WAGERING BILL became the feature event of the 1963 legislative session. By the time it was scheduled to be heard before the House committee to which it was assigned, the voters were in nearly equally divided statewide camps. The capitol parking lots were full of buses that had brought devout Baptists by the hundreds out of the East Texas piney woods; the spectators' gallery was jammed with them. The committee met on the floor of the House chamber to accommodate the crowds. Proceedings began after lunch and ran on until early the following morning, giving everyone who sought it a moment before the mikes.

Mr. Kleberg was the leadoff witness for the proponents; as a trustee of the Thoroughbred Club of America and the Jockey Club, he was able to marshal the income figures that the racing states received from their tracks, and to attest to the agricultural advantages to the state of attracting Thoroughbred horse farms. He was followed by an array of racing notables we had rounded up from over the country. Then the opposition had their shot, but they were left with little to say. Thoroughbred racing had been so well policed and so free of misconduct for so many years that the ministers had to resort to telling stories of old baseball and football scandals. About 1:00 A.M., the bill was passed out of committee to the floor of the House with a recommendation for approval.

When the marathon session broke up, we victors invited the legislators down to the Driskill Hotel for a nightcap. Bob had rooms adjoining a large sitting area; since a majority of the members sided with us and the drinks were on us, we packed them in. One of our guests was freshman legislator Chet Brooks, later the senior man in the Texas Senate. Young Mr. Brooks was a member of the committee that had just heard our bill and had voted favorably. A colleague of his, not present, was Red Berry, a veteran member of the House from San Antonio. Mr. Berry was a Thoroughbred owner, a longtime advocate of racing who even suggested that the state divide itself into five smaller states (a Texas prerogative when it joined the Union in 1845), so that South Texas could go on with racing and the other four states could go to hell.

Mr. Brooks was having a laugh on himself; he told us he had just learned a valuable, emphatic political lesson. Immediately upon the chairman's gaveling the hearing to a close, the opponents had poured out of the visitors' gallery and onto the floor. Enraged, they were telling the legislators who had voted for the bill what their future election plans were for them. There was such a crush that Brooks and Berry were trapped, back to back, against the edge of the hearing table. When he could get a word in, Brooks was pleading for good reason, for an examination of all the safeguards that kept tracks out of counties where they were not wanted, anything he could think of to placate his irate constituents. Jammed against and behind him, he could hear Berry getting his working over, but by contrast Berry said not a word. Rather, he heard his group out, and in the silence as they paused to await his reply, he raised a stiff middle finger, said "F—— ya," and elbowed his way out. He knew he didn't have a vote in the lot of them and never would. Brooks thought it a lesson worth remembering in the futility of trying to recoup the unrecoupable.

Like the rest of us, by 3:00 A.M. Bob was tired and he showed it. It happened that the hearing was called on his sixty-seventh birthday, March 29. In the midst of the din, I went over to him and said happy birthday, adding that I hoped we would spend many more together. He looked me over, put his arm on my shoulder, a gesture he very rarely used, and told me, "I think we will. You know, John, you're beginning to look pretty fit for your age." A part of his strategy in life's tourney was to live forever.

ONE OF THE SAFEGUARDS built into the law that was finally passed was a statewide referendum on pari-mutuel wagering; it was defeated by less than 1 percent of the vote. Bob tried again during the next legislative session; the results were almost exactly the same. He decided King Ranch had the racing it needed on the East and West coasts and withdrew his name from the effort, though he continued to contribute to the association. It took fifteen years, an oil crunch, and a collapsed economy faced with corporate and personal income taxes, before the voters matured enough to add Thoroughbred racing to the state revenue plan.

A PRINCE AMONG LORDS

Near the top of Bob's most valued friendships was Simon Christopher Joseph Fraser, the fifteenth Baron Lovat, Shimi to everyone who knows him. Shimi is a Scot of rare outgoing, international, debonair outlook, the most charming man I have ever met. Lest these traits be mistakenly attributed to a long line of felicitous breeding, the Lovats pridefully point out that the last nobleman beheaded in the realm was a previous Simon, the cantankerous and unpredictable eleventh lord, for his part in the rebellion of 1747.

Shimi is an agriculturalist, overseeing family properties around Beaufort Castle near Inverness. So his interest in livestock brought him to the ranch a number of times, just as Bob visited him in Scotland. Shimi made an effort to import a small herd of Santa Gertrudis to cross with his native Shorthorns, but the British authorities never granted him the permit. Their reasons varied, but the real one was they felt there were already too many breeds of cattle in the British Isles, and they did not want to introduce competition from a Texas exotic.

The last time Shimi visited the ranch while Bob was alive was in the fall of 1968. Bob, Charles Murphy, an associate editor of *Fortune* who was writing a three-part series on Bob, and I were working at Norias, Murphy conducting daylong interviews. Of course, Bob hurried Shimi down to the headquarters; Murphy bristled. He wanted to avoid outside distraction—it was tough enough to keep Bob's attention on the past and away from the telephone, even at this isolated retreat.

In addition, Charles was just finishing his biography of the Duke and

Duchess of Windsor, and his experiences with them had turned him off to all levels of British nobility. But Shimi soon had Charles's attention. When he learned of Charles's interest in the duke, he told us about an experience in his younger days acting as the Prince of Wales's aide-de-camp on a trip to Latin America. The girls swarmed, overrunning them at every stop—the prince needed protection to fight them off. Shimi told me, "Ah! John, I was like the jackal following the lion—picking up the morsels."

The morning after Shimi's arrival, he and Charles and I were at the breakfast table; Bob slept in, as was his habit during his last two decades. He said he had been on the job before 6:00 A.M. enough years for any lifetime.

During World War II, Shimi, a brigadier commanding the Lovat Guards in Norway and at Dieppe, and one of the heroes in Cornelius Ryan's *The Longest Day*, was severely wounded in the hip during the action in Normandy. Phlebitis continually troubled him; he could not stay in one position for long. So he was up and around during the night and in the early morning. Charles turned the conversation toward Shimi's war experiences and for the next four hours he held us enthralled. One account he should record in detail, and I think he has in his privately printed biography; it is vital to the history of the era. Here are some highlights as I remember them over more than two decades.

While Shimi was recovering from his wound, Prime Minister Churchill sent for him. Stalin was pressing Churchill for details concerning the Normandy landing; he wanted to know exactly how it was accomplished. So Churchill was putting together a mission of a field marshal, an air marshal, and an admiral to travel to Moscow to brief him. Shimi was ordered to join them—Churchill had a special charge in mind for him.

The Russians had advanced to the Vistula River south of Warsaw and the signal had been given to the Jews trapped in the city ghetto to rise up and create a diversion. But for thirty days the Russians had halted and regrouped at the river, while the Jews were being pulverized by the German garrison and were running out of ammunition and supplies.

Churchill wanted to fly in an air drop, but the transports did not have the range to take off from and return to England. So the prime minister had asked the first secretary for permission for the planes to refuel at Russian airfields in eastern Poland—Stalin refused.

Churchill instructed Lovat, "Ask him why he has halted on the Vistula."

The party took a circuitous route through northern Africa and Iran to reach Moscow, where they had four or five hilarious all-night eating and drinking bouts with their Russian counterparts. Then one midnight they were summoned into the presence. Stalin's office in the Kremlin was a long, narrow room, as Shimi described it, with a desk at one end. When they were lined up before it, a door opened behind and Stalin stepped out. Shimi said he had two impressions: first, the man was a midget, and second, his fly was unbuttoned. Seated at his desk, Stalin took up a pad and pencil and, with his nose an inch from the paper, began to doodle. The officers, by order of rank, stepped forward and delivered their set pieces. Turning his head to peer up at them, Stalin asked the same questions: how many casualties, in the surf, on the beaches, in the hedgerows?

Shimi, the junior, came last. He had become more and more curious about those doodles and now he was close enough to make them out. They were stick figures of dismembered bodies, with arms, legs, and heads scattered about. He delivered his impressions of D day and the few that followed before he was wounded. Then he put the question: "Mr. Secretary, why are you halted on the Vistula?"

For the first time, Stalin raised his head and grinned. "Let them kill each other off!"

The party was rushed to a waiting plane and nonstop Shimi flew home to Churchill with his one-sentence reply.

By the time Bob arrived at the table, Charles Murphy had become so enchanted he was seriously ready to drop the Windsors, Bob Kleberg, *Fortune*, everything pending, and begin a biography of the fifteenth Lord Lovat.

CHAPTER SIX

GOING INTERNATIONAL:
THE FIRST STEP

IN 1952, MR. KLEBERG made his initial plunge into foreign waters; he did not, however, venture very far to widen his circle. Close by the Texas Gulf Coast lay the largest of the verdant islands in the Caribbean, a rancher's mecca, Cuba. This is where he headed.

Bob had good reason to choose Cuba to make his first foreign investment. Santa Gertrudis cattle had been on the island for nearly twenty years and had proven to be superior to the Brahma and criollo (native) cattle that were the mainstays in the Cuban beef industry. The first Santa Gertrudis bulls taken across the Straits of Florida had been purchased by the E. J. Barker ranch, located on an island called Turigano, just off the Cuban north coast, to breed to his herd of Red Polls. Other breeders followed Mr. Barker's lead until, by the time of Bob's first visit in 1951, Cuba could boast of quality Santa Gertrudis herds that rivaled those in the U.S.

Knowing he had to turn off high-quality animals to compete with the ranchers he had put into business, Bob purchased fifty crossbred Santa Gertrudis/Red Poll heifers from Mr. Barker at $1,000 each to enhance his grading-up program, an impressive price in the 1950s for that large a number of animals.

Cuba was a farming and ranching paradise. The soils were fertile—they had to be to raise the main crop, sugarcane—the temperature and rainfall were ideal. For years, the feeling in the American agriculture community, indeed in the business community in general, had been that an investment in Cuba was as safe as one in the U.S.

King Ranch went to Cuba at the behest of two brothers, George and Riondo Braga of New York, whose family, back to the Spanish colonial era, had been sugar producers in the provinces of Oriente and Camagüey. Forming a joint venture with the Manatí Sugar Company, one of the Braga subsidiaries, Bob set out to create a beef factory in the brushland and forest near the north central Camagüey coast. A ship loaded with bulls and heifers, stallions and mares, fencing and gates, brush-clearing tractors, sailed from Corpus Christi, bound for the port of Manatí. Lowell Tash, the man who had directed Bob's phosphorus supplement research, had as much experience as any American in putting unproductive brush into grassland; he was hired to manage the new enterprise.

Compañía Ganadera Becerra, the joint venture, was a 40,000-acre block of land surrounded by sugarcane fields and other cattle ranches, about halfway between the provincial capital, Camagüey, and the north coast. Fertile land throughout, it could carry the 7,600 head that Bob estimated for it, with grass to spare. Fifteen hundred head of these were purebreds, the remainder crossbreds in the grading-up cycle. While the improvements were utilitarian, they were built to last. There were good stands of hardwood on the property, so the gates, chutes, corner posts, and the like were the stoutest I have ever seen.

By the time of my visit, four years into the development, Tash (only his wife called him Lowell) had nearly completed the pasture work, mainly by bringing a noxious imported thornbush called marabou under control. Marabou covered the ground in an impenetrable mass and grew to about eight feet; it was a terrible pest whose seed had been imported to Cuba in a boatload of hay. Taking hold in this part of the country, it had spread over thousands of acres of good soil and rendered it useless. There was a stand of about 20,000 acres of marabou on Becerra.

In South Texas, Bob had accumulated a lot of experience clearing another pasture debilitation, the obstreperous mesquite. Taking up research begun by his father, he equipped large tractors with plows that destroyed the mesquite's root system, inhibiting regrowth. Eventually Bob root-plowed and seeded over 750,000 acres on the King Ranch. The same mechanisms, combined with herbicide spraying, converted the marabou stands into flourishing green pastures. But maintenance was never-ending. Since high rainfall favors brush as well as grass, the round of clearing and spraying occupied all of the dry season.

Cuba has been in the ranching business longer than any country in the Western Hemisphere. The first cattle entering the New World from Spain were off-loaded here; they formed the nucleus that eventually grew to the millions upon millions of head that now populate the three Americas. While these native animals admirably adapted to the Cuban subtropical climate, they had been selected more for work in the sugarcane fields than for beef. This changed as Becerra made these indigenous animals the building blocks to create a Santa Gertrudis herd.

An early Kleberg priority was to turn off a beef carcass that would cut a steak or roast of the quality and tenderness that the American tourists, a principal segment in the Cuban economy, were used to finding on their stateside tables. For this to be accomplished, a major obstacle had to be overcome. Local packers did not pay a premium for superior carcasses; no matter the conformation or finish, all beef was bought and sold at the same price per pound. The man who was vital to changing this practice was the president of the joint King Ranch–Braga subsidiary, Jack Malone.

George Braga had sent Jack to Kingsville to negotiate a partnership with Bob. When the papers were drawn and signed, Bob turned to Jack and told him he was the new president. Jack protested that he knew nothing about cattle. But Bob cut him off, "I'll take care of the cattle—you take care of everything else."

It was an early demonstration of Bob's ability to make perhaps not the obvious but the best choice to serve him as emissary to foreign governments and foreign markets.

While the herds were multiplying on the ranch, Jack was busy in Havana convincing government officials and meat suppliers that there was no need to squander U.S. dollars importing high-quality beef from the States for the hotel and supermarket trade; it could be produced at home if the incentive, meaning the right price, were forthcoming.

IN 1957, MR. KLEBERG gave me my first foreign assignment, dispatching me to Cuba to make a record of the progress that had been made on Becerra to that point. I accompanied Bob Wells, the tax adviser for the ranch; Jack was our host and guide. We saw a remarkable development: Bob's initial effort was just on the point of beginning to pay. The Becerra development is a vital party of his story. Here he climbed the learning curve by bringing his first piece of raw tropical forest into production.

For several days on the ranch, we rode horseback through the pastures. They had been planted in a grass called *colonião,* a variety of guinea grass imported from Brazil. A remarkably good grazing plant, it produces little stem and is almost entirely green leaf, where the protein tends to concentrate. Needing high rainfall, here in central Cuba it had found an amiable home; the ground was so spongy under the horses' hoofs, their tracks immediately filled with water. While this promoted grass growth, the constant damp caused foot rot in the cattle; preventative treatment was a never-ending chore. But the cattle were doing well; their rates of gain, close to two pounds a day, had not before been recorded in the country.

On completing a record of Becerra's progress, we set off to visit the government and meat-processing people in Havana. It was our introduction to the terrifying intricacies of the Cuban transportation system. There was a small runway on the ranch with a large drawback—the pilot could not see from one end to the other. The countryside was dotted with tall, tough-fibered palms. Rather than trouble to cut them down and dig out the stumps, the men who built the strip doglegged around a grove of them. Why not? They did the same with the roads.

The ranch used a single-engine four-seater aircraft chartered from a pilot in Camagüey, the provincial capital; he knew the strip well. Going in we were lightly loaded and had no problem; departing with a full passenger manifest and excess baggage was something else. Jack Malone and Bob Wells averaged two hundred plus; the pilot and I were skinny but he was tall for a Cuban. The baggage that would not fit in the tiny compartment was piled in my lap—this little flying machine was up to max.

Ready for takeoff—devout Catholic Jack got out his rosary beads—the pilot made the sign of the cross. Just as he went to full throttle I heard him mutter, "We're not going to make it!"

We shuddered and bumped and skidded around the dogleg, then rose a few feet with the stall-warning horn blaring. *Swiiish!* Right through the top of a palm. Fronds flew past my window, pulverized by the propeller, and I felt light in the seat as we began sinking into the jungle. But to the credit of the Cessna Aircraft Corporation, their little machine wobbled, recovered, and climbed; we had an otherwise uneventful flight to the Camagüey airport. On landing, Jack put away his beads and, with a "Thank God," cracked open his door to get some ventilation; it came off its hinges and fell onto the runway. When we finally reached the hangar, we found streamers of palm fronds woven into the landing gear.

The next stop was Havana; our travel adventure was not quite over. At that time, the Cuban national airline flew the British De Havilland Viscount, an admirable four-engine turboprop. Holding reservations, we made our way through a mob of standbys pressing around the gate. I wondered why such a large crowd had not long ago given up on there being that many cancellations and gone home.

Aboard and buckled in, I saw through the port that the gate was again flung open and the standby horde stampeded toward the loading ramp. They streamed down the aisle until the last one was in. A man—a policeman or a conductor—herded them aft, turned, pressed his back against them and inched backward until he had them compressed into immobility, then braced his arms and legs against the nearest seatbacks. The plane taxied out and took off, about as tail-heavy as a transport could get and still fly. Apparently Cuban airliners were treated like Japanese metros at the rush hour.

IN 1957, FIDEL CASTRO and his gang were still in the Sierra Maestra mountains, but they had already captured the hearts and minds of the country peasants and were gaining support in the cities, at all levels of society. On one of our trips around town, Bob Wells asked a taxi driver who was extolling Castro's virtues why he was supporting him. "Señor, this is the first time in my life I've had enough money to take off work and fight a revolution."

For so many, tweaking President Batista's nose was a game, a game that grew to genocide for the middle and upper classes. Of the twenty-one countries in Latin America, in the 1950s Cuba was the only one with a viable middle class, due in part to the large number of people employed in the tourist trade, the country's top-ranking industry.

WE VISITED THE SWIFT and Company packing plant on the outskirts of the city and saw the first beef carcasses graded in Cuba under a new government program called Alta Calidad (high quality). The steers that had attained this grade were raised on Becerra. A milestone in the Cuban agricultural economy, this was the first beef produced under the program to achieve a higher price for its superior quality. Equally important to us, the animals had been able to do it on grass alone, with no grain feed, and they were of Santa Gertrudis blood. Bob had staked his investment in Cuba on getting a higher price for higher quality; Jack and his associates had been able to make that price possible. The years of effort were about to pay off.

OUR ELATION WAS short-lived. Castro seized power on January 1, 1959, proclaimed a land reform program under his Communist government, and confiscated the King Ranch properties. Early one morning, a detachment of troops marched up to the front gate and the officer in charge nailed a copy of the confiscation decree to the gatepost. Manager Tash came out of the house to investigate, leaned down, read the paper. Tash was a taciturn man; he did not start an argument or reproach the captain; he turned and delivered a powerful placekick right between the captain's legs. Needless to say, he shortly found himself in jail, and there he remained for some weeks.

Bob instructed Jack to do everything possible for Tash, in Washington or Havana or Switzerland—whose ambassador, Emil Staddlehofer, represented U.S. interests to the Cuban government. Jack was able to smuggle Tash an airline ticket, with a note telling him to head straight for the airport if for any reason he was released or paroled. One morning, the guard unlocked Tash's cell door and told him he was free—Tash was on the next plane. The door was shut and engines were running when soldiers ran out and put the boarding ladder back in place. They rushed the cabin, seized Tash, and escorted him to a small room in the terminal. There he waited alone while his plane sat at the gate. In about three hours, the soldiers returned, escorted him back onto the plane, and sat him in his seat. The plane took off with its load of frightened, sweating passengers and made an uneventful trip to Miami. Tash got out of the country with the khaki shirt and trousers he was wearing and that was the extent of King Ranch and Braga Brothers' recovery from their Cuban investments.

Unlike most manufacturing, the ranching business is a slow start-up. It takes years to bring raw land to a good grass yield and to breed up a herd to the point of turning off quality and quantity beef. Though the company operated seven years, it was only in the last six months that it generated its first net profit, $600. Total Becerra losses, King Ranch and Braga Brothers', from the Communist theft were $5,719,000. Of this, $3,000,000 was King Ranch's.

CASTRO'S DISPOSITION OF his King Ranch spoils took an odd, dark turn. At a cattle auction in Houston about five years after the seizure, I was approached by a Venezuelan acquaintance who asked if he could speak privately with me—he told me this tale. At that time, the middle 1960s, the Russians were running a propaganda program in Latin America, inviting business executives and educators to tour their country, to show them how they could prosper under the Communist system. A friend of his had accepted one of these invitations and on his tour had visited a collective farm in the southern state of Georgia. The group was taken into a field and shown a herd of red cows. "You will not believe this, John, but those cows were branded with the Running W [the King Ranch brand]."

The friend told my friend that he also saw some young animals, but they had a different brand, one that he did not recognize. I drew on the tablecloth an upside down W with a bar under it, the Becerra brand.

"Yes, that's it!"

To repay the Russians for the aid he was getting to keep his grossly mismanaged economy afloat, Castro was giving them practically everything of value on the island: the machinery in the American assembly plants, the rolling stock, even the Cuban silver coins, and finally our herd of cattle. The Russians fell in love with Santa Gertrudis; they have since dispatched a number of missions to the U.S. to buy more of them.

TO THE END OF his life, Bob did not reconcile himself to this robbery. He was instrumental in getting as many of his Cuban friends as possible out of Castro's clutches, settling and finding employment for them in the U.S. or in Central or South America. He took a hand in the "Tractors for Prisoners" trade following the debacle at the Bay of Pigs, and he cooperated with our government agencies to bring any relief that he could to those being persecuted inside the country.

Over the years since the Communist yoke fell around poor Cuba's neck, I have often thought that the reason the people left on the island have not risen up against Castro for trashing their country is that they have never been pushed completely to the wall. Though their diet is monotonous and poor, they have never gone hungry or suffered the extremes of heat and cold; they have not seen their children shiver and their bellies swell from starvation. The climate does not demand excessive fuel and warm clothes, and they can literally reach out their front door and pick a meal off a tree. The land, even poorly tended, is that kind and fertile.

LES GIRLS

On quite a regular schedule, the boss kept a covey of birds coming up the driveway, the pretty young girls. Bob had a lifelong affinity for them; his solitude after he lost Helen begat an even keener interest in their company. His friends knew this and on his trips away from the ranch they arranged for him to have gorgeous, bright, witty young dinner companions. This almost inevitably prompted an invitation to the ranch, almost inevitably accepted. The young part was important. In his last decades he continued to cultivate his older women friends, the ones he and Helen had made together, but the young ones were a preference—they amused, diverted, and stimulated him.

Bob gave as much or more than he took of their time. Though his companions came from good families in several countries, to be exposed to his lifestyle was a unique experience for them. The ranch, the roundups, the afternoons at the races, the view of midtown Manhattan from the thirty-seventh floor, the jet, the whirlwind excursions to the foreign properties, turned even the prettiest and most sophisticated heads.

When a junket to a foreign ranch was in the offing, a pleasant evening with a pretty young woman often elicited from the boss an invitation to come along. I gritted my teeth—and grinned—those solicitations complicated my life. Schedules and accommodations had to be rearranged; wives of foreign managers had to be alerted so that suitable diversions could be planned. Most of the girls were good sports, but some quickly became bored with the long inspection tours and the cattle talk and would want to set off sightseeing on their own. This called for an escort; a suitable native had to be located. Even the most attractive face and figure could not entice Bob out of the countryside and into a museum or a flea market.

The boss liked as much variety in his girls as he did in his liquor basket—they came in a range of sizes, hair colors, and backgrounds. One of the most in demand, the longest-running of the lot, was a Twiggy type from Venezuela, Diana. An amusing, cricketlike, constantly chattering little charmer, she held him enthralled over a number of years and made Caracas our most frequent stopover. When she was not at the ranch or in the States, they were on the telephone, setting a pace of up to ten Kingsville-Caracas calls a day.

Then there were quite different types: the cool, composed classic beauty from Colombia, related to the president; the sisters, beautiful daughters of a prominent doctor in Houston; two princesses of the House of Savoy; the youngest and most levelheaded, a blonde of statuesque proportions from Paris. On and on, worthy representatives of Mexico, most of the Central American republics, Brazil, Argentina, Australia especially, and the Philippines, France, Italy, Spain, Morocco. They came and went, casualties of marriage or to losing their benefactor's interest. Or to being overconniving—the boss was diverted but not blind. Some were fixtures, a refreshing beguilement to the end of his life.

Particular experiences with them stand out. One long Easter weekend, his guest was a Roman, Gia, who was struggling to make a place in the American interior decorating scene. Saturday afternoon he took her out on a ride. At midevening his cook called to say they were two hours overdue for dinner; did I have any word of them. I told her no but to call me back in an hour if they had not come in. We had had some recent rains and some of the country was boggy; they could easily be walking—Bob had a reputation for putting his cars to the test over untried ground. The cook called back and a search was organized—four of us set out in cars, combing the roads and trails on the two northern divisions. All night we drove—no luck.

At dawn we rolled out the planes; I flew one section and Bobby Shelton the other. By 11:00 we had covered the ground and sighted nothing, so we landed on a road near the Laureles headquarters to rethink what seemed to be a growing emergency. Could they not know where they were (impossible), be rattlesnake-bitten (unlikely), holed up in a nearby motel (possible but unnecessary)? In the midst of going over the scenarios, an exhausted Adán staggered up the road.

Seems that during the late afternoon, Bob and Gia, with Adán in the backseat, had been driving his Oldsmobile sedan overland along the coastline when Bob challenged a sandy bog and lost, again. His heavy car, one he should not have chosen to drive cross-country when he had in the garage several four-wheelers, went down to the hubs. During the night they had jacked it up eleven times, cutting and stacking brush under the wheels—the wheels spun, the car sank. They ran down the battery, making it impossible to close the electrically operated windows—a fresh norther that had just blown in almost froze them to death. At dawn Adán started walking and it took him until 11:00 to reach habitation.

We took off and Bobby was able to land his specially equipped machine on a level stretch near the car, to be greeted by his irate uncle, who had stood on the ground frantically waving a jacket when Bobby had earlier flown over him, twice.

On Sunday evening, Bob called; Gia wanted to go to Easter mass. The three of us packed into a pew; Bob saw the long-handled collection basket coming and poked me in the ribs. "Have any money?" I slipped him a dollar. In a moment he handed it back. "Never mind, I found one."

The next morning, the monsignor came into my office. "There was a Protestant in church last night and I have an idea he was with you."

"How do you know?"

"There was a hundred-dollar bill in the collection plate."

WHY THIS COMPULSION FOR companionship with girls the age of or younger than his granddaughters? I can only guess—subscribing to the De Soto syndrome. Perhaps proximity to a fountain-of-youth wellspring could keep him forever young, or feeling that way. Having no firm conviction about an afterlife, Bob abhorred the word "old." He became unreasonably infuriated when, on any occasion, others implied that "old" might apply to him. Once, at one of our auctions, a dear friend of his, a true love for all of us, Mona Holmes of Hawaii, said to him, "Bob, you look younger every time I see you—what's your secret?" He grabbed the arm of a stunning twenty-two-year-old standing beside him and pointed.

For me, the winsome parade confounded and enriched my life. Like Shimi, I was the jackal following the lion, in my instance the grizzled monarch of the pride. Nature makes a place in her scheme for each of her creatures. Hooray for the rewarded jackals.

CHAPTER SEVEN

INVENTING A BEEF FACTORY—VENEZUELA

EVEN THOUGH HE had lost his investment in the first Latin American country he had ventured into, Cuba, Bob Kleberg kept alive a lifelong interest in the hemisphere down below. He had grown up among Spanish ranch companions and spoke their language well. Some of his closest family friends lived south of the Rio Grande, back to his parents' and grandparents' time. But above all he saw opportunity in the vast tropics and subtropics; his experience on the hot, humid Texas coastal plain, his breed of tropical climate-adapted cattle, uniquely put him in position to tackle the problems in the vast, largely undeveloped, partly unexplored continent.

BOB HAD EQUIPPED himself to cover the distances involved. Even before he took up overseas travel as a routine, he had made a deal with the Humble Oil and Refining Company to share a half-interest in an airplane. Their first joint purchase was a DC-3. Humble had a fleet of aircraft; when he put in a request for his plane, Humble accommodated by sending it down from their aviation center in Houston. But Bob was not an easy birdman; the low-flying, lumbering, swaying old kite made him sick.

When the turboprops came on the market, he and Humble invested in a Grumman Gulfstream I, with its superior speed and altitude capabilities. South America and Europe were within range; it was far more useful, but it could not cross the Pacific to Australia. This did not suit Bob, who wanted eventually to have a plane that would take him to anyplace in the world where he did business. He had to wait for the next generation of Grummans, the Gulfstream II.

Bob carried on an extended debate with himself over putting up his half of the cost of such an expensive airplane, priced at that time at around $10 million. The factory turned up the heat by arranging a demonstration; the Grumman crew picked us up at the ranch for a trip to New York. The statistics the salesman gave the boss were impressive: navigation computerized, certified to 42,000 feet (weather problems were thereafter beneath him), speed approaching Mach 1, two-way passenger-ground communication. This twin-engine jet was a globetrotter; it could deliver him to any point on earth he chose. While it was equipped to carry thirteen passengers and a crew of three, rarely were there more than five or six aboard.

The passenger cabin was an airborne apartment. The writing desks were against the forward wall, then two chairs that made into a bed, a couch-bed opposite with another chair, then the dining table seating six, a galley complete with cooking facilities, and, aft, the dressing room. A convenient door in the dressing room bulkhead gave access to the baggage compartment, making it possible to change between stops. Often we boarded at one of the ranches, sweaty and mud-caked, washed down in the lavatory, changed to city clothes, and were ready for a meeting or a dinner when we landed.

On the demonstration flight, we went into Washington National Airport to drop off a passenger. As we taxied out, the factory representative came back to Bob. "You have small airstrips at most of your ranches, don't you? Watch the distance markers out the window as we take off." We were airborne in 1,000 feet. The boss mentally finalized the sale before we crossed the Potomac.

On the way home, he told me, "This is a hell of a lot of money to spend, but an airplane like this will extend my working life another ten years." He used it almost exactly that long, and he used it well. The first year the ranch owned it he was aboard over seven hundred hours.

BOB'S WIDENING CIRCLE of interests had spread considerably since he had launched his nearby Cuban operation in 1952. One of them was not too distant from Cuba's shores, in southern Florida just south of Lake Okeechobee. The lake is, in fact, the northern anchor of the vast Florida

Everglades. The high rainfall on this pancake-flat land flows south into the swamp, in a river eight inches deep and forty miles wide; it is the principal water supply for the continuous strip of cities on the east coast. To utilize the rich soil, a giant reclamation project has channeled the flow into canals, and the properties through which these canals pass have certain water rights.

Bob's interest in ranching in these unusual surroundings came about in a roundabout way. One of his neighbors in Camagüey was a sugar producer, mill owner, and the finest Santa Gertrudis cattle breeder in the country, Alvaro Sanchez. Next to Bob, Alvaro had the best eye for cattle of any man I have met.

Castro stole everything Alvaro owned; his extended family became penniless refugees in New York City. His son joined the Bay of Pigs expedition and was captured on the beach—Alvaro turned his entire attention to freeing him. He was one of the principals in the Tractors for Prisoners deal. One of the men who joined him in the effort was Walter Beinecke, Jr., a descendant of the founder of S & H Green Stamps, the trading stamps that were so popular in the 1950s and 1960s. Walter also owned a commuter airline with routes along the East Coast, and had other interests in Florida.

Beinecke acquired 40,000 acres of unimproved land in the Okeechobee region, intending to develop a sugarcane farm utilizing Alvaro's expertise. But sugar production is a closely regulated business and they were unable to gain all of the rights necessary to put such a large tract into cane. Alvaro's first love was cattle; together they made an offer to Alvaro's friend Bob to create Big B Ranch, in a state that already had a high Santa Gertrudis population.

The soil was called muckland; it was hardly soil at all but decomposed vegetation overlaying a limestone base. The capital costs to put the land into improved pasture were high, but the access to nearly unlimited quantities of irrigation water mightily attracted Bob. When planted in Saint Augustine grass, the pastures had a high carrying capacity, on the order of a cow to every 2½ acres.

But Big B was never a Kleberg favorite. Despite the fact that Alvaro graded up a fine herd of Santa Gertrudis, there were bothersome health and nutritional problems that were never completely overcome. Normally he would see these as a challenge, and he did; but the underlying reasons for his not finding Big B attractive were aesthetic. For one thing, the ranch was two-dimensional—out on the land the tallest thing you saw was the backs of the cows. Trees could not be planted in the pastures. The cows tended to rest in their shade, digging out and packing down the muck, and forming a water hole. Bob loved trees and missed them on Big B.

While he was a frequent visitor, stopping off on his trips to and from South America, he stayed only for the day or overnight and we were on our way. As high a regard as he had for his friend Alvaro, he seemed to find the ranch dull.

DRAWING ON HIS land-acquiring experiences in his own and in foreign countries, Bob had put together and honed a set of guidelines that he inevitably followed before he committed the King Ranch to an investment in a foreign country. They were simple and few. He sought countries that had a viable ranching industry, that had an ecology that gave his Santa Gertrudis an advantage over the traditional breeds, and that had promise for marketing purebred and commercial cattle. He wanted his properties to be of a size that could support good numbers of beef animals while the herd was going through the four-generation, twelve-year process to breed up to purebred Santa Gertrudis. And he wanted intelligent management that he could teach and trust and that would stay with him over the long pull. Economically, he needed a business and government climate that supported a reasonably stable currency and that had a history of long-term dollar repatriation.

Bob's goal was twofold: to produce quality beef in tropical and semi-tropical environments while building a demand among local ranchers for his Santa Gertrudis. He realized that the cash that was accumulating from the South Texas mineral royalties could not lie idle in the U.S.; by our laws even overseas it had to be invested in the corporation's primary business—ranching. But once the investment was made, profits could be put into related and nonrelated enterprises: real estate, minerals, fertilizer plants, nearly anything that showed promise and was acceptable to a foreign government.

In the core business, building a demand for purebred Santa Gertrudis was the key. After three years of operation, a ranch could turn off a considerable number of fat crossbred steers that sold at beef prices in the local market, usually about $250 a head. But a purebred breeding bull of similar age and weight, costing little more to raise than the steer, might fetch a minimum of $2,500 or as high as $50,000. The profit motive was important here, but Bob had a broader, more ethereal goal. His bulls, distributed among surrounding ranchers, would do more to increase the quantity of high-quality protein available to the country than any other agricultural introduction that could be made. Consequently, the general economy would improve, creating a more stable climate in which to do business. His plans were long-term, very long compared to most business investments, but the rewards over time could be considerable.

Tom Armstrong, an old hand at negotiating with Latin American governments, was one of the people who tutored Bob in dealing with the officials in the countries where he eventually located, a prerequisite for anyone who plans to own or lease foreign real estate. Land ownership is about the most emotional issue running through the veins of any national body, regardless of its political stripe. This was especially true in Latin America, where so much of the best agricultural land was already in the hands of absentee landlords. So another foreigner, no matter the sterling reputation that preceded him, had to be assured that the administration foresaw his entry into their agricultural economy as an asset to the country.

When I began traveling with Bob, Major Armstrong was also my coach, on survival: "John, when you're invited to a public gathering where the president is appearing, for your own good health don't stand near him."

With these basic precepts as a guideline, Bob developed a personal strategy for setting up a foreign operation. First he arranged introductions to a few leading agriculturalists in the country, and they in turn made arrangements for him to meet the leading people in the financial community and to see the kinds of properties that interested him. He studied the climate, soils, infrastructure, market potential, and at the same time he widened his contacts, studying people, on the lookout for compatible, knowledgeable local partners and managers, men who would stay with him over the time it took for the cattle generations to multiply.

When he decided that investment conditions were favorable, he sought an appointment with the president or chief of state. Only when he was assured by the top man that his enterprise would be welcomed into the national economy did he pursue a land purchase or lease. Later, when his company hit a rough spot in its dealings with a state or financial agency, he took advantage of his rapport with the chief executive to straighten it out. It was a pragmatic, one-on-one approach.

Bob did not invest in every country that attracted him. When later he began considering moving into Europe, he took a look at Italy and Greece and backed away. He did not feel he could comfortably work with the government or the people with whom he was dealing. His excellent inside contacts also forewarned him that the Sicilian Mafia was active in the meat-distributing trade.

THE NEXT CIRCLE IN Bob's spreading activities, measured by its distance from Kingsville, rippled across Venezuela. The Venezuelan investment was an outgrowth of one of his many efforts to help his displaced Cuban friends. Here is the roundabout way he found himself in business there.

Gustavo de los Reyes, the scion in a founding colonial family in Cuba, had been a neighboring rancher and friend during the 1950s. In 1959, when Fidel Castro seized the government and threw out the dictator Batista, he was welcomed by almost the entire Cuban population and by our own government. Gustavo was one of the first in his country to recognize that Castro was secretly a Communist; he began working against him. Gustavo had gotten his information from an officer in Castro's forces, a Colonel Morgan, an American adventurer and double agent for the U.S.

George Braga, King Ranch's partner in Cuba, arranged an appointment with Allen Dulles, director of the Central Intelligence Agency, so that Gustavo could lay out for Dulles proof that Castro was an undercover Communist lackey. Dulles heard him out, said he knew that the things Gustavo was telling him were true, but U.S. policy at that time was to back Castro. Dulles had no option but to support that policy.

When Gustavo returned to Cuba and reported this to Morgan, Morgan saw that he had lost his support in the U.S.—he informed on Gustavo to Castro. Morgan, popular with the troops, was in a secure military position that put the army in the palm of his hand. Castro told Morgan he was making him a national hero and heaped honors and praise on him. But gradually he eased him out of the command chain and isolated him from his men. Then he had Morgan shot.

Meantime, Gustavo was arrested, forced to defend himself in one of Castro's famous soccer stadium show trials, and sentenced to four years in the dungeons on the Isle of Pines. His confinement was the Gulag type: overwork, undernourishment, no medical facilities, constant harassment. Periodically, Gustavo was dragged out of his cell in the middle of the night, stood before a wall with searchlights trained on him, facing a firing squad. The squad reached the point of aiming, then the commander dismissed them and returned Gustavo to his cell.

Despite this sort of treatment, he and his companions managed to steal odd parts and build a radio to listen to the "Voice of America" from Miami, and to publish a clandestine newspaper to give the other prisoners the news reports they were receiving. Gustavo had a lifelong problem with his eyesight; with no medical treatment it began to fail and his health along with it. Finally he was paroled to his family home in Havana, under house arrest.

Then one day Castro sent word to him—he had a deal in mind. Finding himself in a monetary bind because of the American embargo, Fidel was strapped for hard currency. He wanted Gustavo to go to Washington, to the secretary of state's office, and tell them that if the U.S. would restore the sugar quota to Cuba, he, Castro, would pay to American owners whose properties had been seized in Cuba $1 billion in reparations. Further, Gustavo must go on a U.S. lecture tour, promoting the idea that the U.S. government should accept his proposition. Gustavo agreed to carry out the first part of the mission but not the second; he would not be a mouthpiece for Castro's propaganda. Castro accepted Gustavo's reservation and Gustavo was freed to fly to Mexico City.

Gustavo fulfilled his part of the bargain by going to Washington to call at the State Department. He was shown into the office of the Cuban affairs officer, where one of the staff—Gustavo remembers his name as White— took down his story. He then flew to Palm Beach, Florida, to the home of his daughter, Christina Fanjul, where he was reunited with his wife and family and got the medical treatment and rest he so sorely needed. Nothing came of Castro's proposal. Years later, when I told Assistant Secretary of State for Latin American Affairs William Rogers this story, astonishingly he was not able to find even a memorandum in the State Department files recording Gustavo's interview.

From Florida, Gustavo came to the King Ranch to visit Bob and this is where I met him, on Bob's porch. He was a shell of a man, suffering from malnutrition and the effects of his failing eyesight. Bob told him, "Get your health back. Then travel until you find a place where you would like to ranch. I'll back you and we'll go into it together."

When Gustavo was sufficiently recovered to put his life together again, he chose to go to Venezuela, where he had friends and relatives, Cubans, who had already established themselves. With their support and advice, he explored the country until he found an undeveloped piece of property that suited his needs.

The land was unique. It was a rain forest located in a valley opening on the Caribbean, about 150 miles west of the capital city of Caracas. In rain forests, it normally rains about half the year and is dry the remaining half. While this valley received only sixty inches a year, relatively low for a rain forest, it rained three hundred days a year. Showers drifted in off the Caribbean at about 2:00 every afternoon, dropping a little moisture. The fact that it was green in March and April when the rest of the whole country was dry, including the conventional rain forests, was crucial to the plan developing in Gustavo's mind.

This rare climatic condition, year-round rainfall, was discovered in a clever way. A pilot with the Venezuelan airline wanted to go into the ranching business when he retired. At that time, the company was flying DC-3s that bumped around below the clouds, in visual contact with the ground. He kept an eye out for a place along his route that stayed green when the surrounding country was brown, and he eventually spotted this remote valley, on the coast fifty miles northwest of Valencia, about half-way between Caracas and Lake Maracaibo.

Gustavo explored the forest, riding horseback over the rolling hills and under the steep valley walls, and he decided this was the place for him. Negotiating an agreement with the owners to buy 35,000 acres (the airline pilot was never able to finance his brilliant idea), he returned to his friend Bob. Bob approached this investment the same as the others he had undertaken, by going to the president of Venezuela and to the minister of land reform to see if he would be welcomed in the country. His reception was cordial; the initial purchase was made in 1966 and the project was launched. King Ranch retained an 80.5 percent interest in the organization, Gustavo came in for 10 percent, and the remainder was taken up by Venezuelan business associates.

Bob had his initial experience clearing rain forest to develop pasture-land on Cape York Peninsula in northern Queensland, Australia. By 1967, the work was essentially complete on the 50,000-acre Tully River ranch, so the clearing machinery, the accessory equipment, even the Australian machinery manager, were shipped to Mostrenco, the new Venezuelan ranch, to begin work.

THOUGH I REALIZE I FLY IN the face of popular ecological thinking, to my mind the jury is still out on the issue of the rain forest—we have yet to put the rain forest and our place in it in proportion. It is seldom even spoken of by its name; for years it has been the "endangered rain forest" or the "imperiled rain forest," to the point where the words will eventually become hyphenated. This sort of hysteria overlooks the massive strength and resilience that is endemic to this primeval ecosystem, strength that has so far been triumphant in reclaiming its own. Amid the almost daily accounts of the amount of forest that is being destroyed, I have not yet read a figure on the acres that regress with almost equal alacrity from agriculture enterprises, or roads, or airfields, or even villages, to the rain forest from which they were formed. The battle to keep rain forest land in continued production, of either grass or foodstuffs, has seen just about every skirmish go to the forest.

One of the most oft-quoted attributes given the rain forest is that it is the major supplier of oxygen to our atmosphere, a gigantic photosynthesis factory for converting the world's carbon dioxide. Balderdash. The supplier of 90 percent of our oxygen is the oceans—mature rain forests consume about as much oxygen as they produce, through the process of reducing litter on the forest floor to the compost that eventually makes up its soil.

Converting forest to traditional row cropping is detrimental to the fertility of the normally shallow topsoil—and it is shallow, often on the order of three to nine inches. Microbial activity is adversely affected by the tropical sun reaching the bare soil between rows and between crops.

In King Ranch experience, putting high-rainfall forests into permanent grass pasture creates maintenance problems that we do not yet know how to deal with economically; the forest is too strong a competitor. We were beginning to get a handle on the regrowth; eventually the techniques will come to hand to control it with the balance necessary to maintain fertility. Our grass selections appeared to be the right ones. The fast-growing tropical perennials of the genus *Guinea* or the running grass similar to the Bermuda family called *Braciaria* are able to put an almost immediate uniform cover over the ground and to keep it constantly shaded, even under heavy grazing.

Consider that in a rain forest most of the trees are mature; their growth has come to a virtual standstill and their ability to convert carbon dioxide to oxygen has slowed with it. Compare these trees with the fast-maturing grasses that within three to six months reach a height of eight to nine feet, are grazed down to ten inches, and then regrow, three or four times a year. This phenomenal photosynthesis is converting enormous amounts of carbon dioxide. On an acre of ground, which is supplying the most oxygen to the atmosphere over time, the grass or the trees it replaced? Thus far, the limited research gives the nod to the new growing plants, but more needs to be done. Meanwhile, I cannot accept that the forests, the flora or fauna living within them, have already been devastated to a point that the damage is irreparable. Damage has been done, but to an extent far below the forests' immense powers of recovery.

In these regions Bob's foremost object was to protect the land, to keep it at its optimum, not its maximum, production. Where rain forest pastures have been damaged, it has been from overgrazing, a short-sighted sin that equally destroys fertility in all other types of environments. Bob's enduring creed was to protect the land. The cattle were a passing thing, the converters of the produce of the land into food for human consumption. The land, for him, was forever. Properly cared for, it would sustain and even increase its yield over time.

Someday we will learn to make this enormous asset, the forests, a partner with us in a continuing, reasonable quest to live in harmony with our surroundings.

THE CLEARING OPERATION, properly done, is a study in precision. The soil cannot be left barren; nature does not permit it. As soon as the mature trees are logged and hauled to the mill, the debris must be stacked and burned so that the sowers can get over the ground with their bags of seed. They winnow it into the onshore breeze and it falls in receptive crevasses; within days a green carpet blankets the humus. On Mostrenco, Gustavo cleared 21,000 of the 34,000 acres, leaving the forest on the hilltops and ridges to control erosion, to give the cattle a shady place to rest, and to add a third, a vertical, dimension to the surroundings. The trees were an aesthetic as well as an indispensable part of the ranch, maintaining a habitat for the monkeys, the giant macaws, and the myriad other birds that lived among them.

ONE OF THE CHARACTERS Gustavo inherited with the property was a retired local cattle buyer named Celestino. He was over seventy years old, but as stout and resilient as one of the tall mahoganies. Gustavo kept him around because he knew the lay of the land; he was the self-appointed inspector and the nemesis of the tractor drivers. Celestino's vocation was walking; day after day he covered miles through the dense undergrowth, discovering small valleys, running streams, limestone caves, small springs that no one knew existed. And he checked on the clearing operation.

In the heat of the day, the drivers had a habit of finding a secluded spot, parking their tractors in the shade, and taking siestas. Celestino, hiding among the trees, often spotted them and reported to the boss. The drivers caught up with the stool pigeon; they kept an eye out for him and when Celestino was sighted in the vicinity, they passed a code to each other by revving their engines up and down, bore down on him, and tried to shove the biggest tree they could find over on him. But Celestino was too agile; he played games with them and then disappeared in the protective undercover.

WITH THE HELP OF people like Celestino, Gustavo put a great deal of study into laying out his pastures, 160 of them in all, forming them in pairs that could carry equal numbers of cattle. Each pair was given the same name, e.g., Palo Verde 1, Palo Verde 2. The cowboys, mostly native Indians, then knew that when they were told to move a herd, it was always to the pasture of the same name.

The fences were living testimony to the soil fertility. Barbed wire was strung between stout hardwood posts, then in between slender stays from a tree called *cola de ratón* (rat's tail) were tied to give additional rigidity. Within a few weeks, these stays took root; two years later they were trees, providing a living fence post that never rotted and furnishing an additional supply of stays from their new growth. This same tree grew in Cuba; fences using *cola de ratón* were sometimes over a hundred years old, with posts that had never been replaced.

Managing tropical perennial grasses is an art requiring a gifted eye, diligence, and a lifetime of application. Gustavo grew up practicing it in Cuba and he applied his experience to Mostrenco. The cattle must be moved when the guinea is grazed down to a height of ten inches, or half-way down the lowest leaf. If they are taken out of the pasture too soon, grass is wasted. If they are left too long, they pull up the succulent plant by its shallow roots and destroy it. When they are moved, they must go into a pasture that has reached its maximum growth but has not yet begun to put on seed. Seeding is a trauma for a plant; it takes nutrients from the leaves to supply the bloom. Consequently the grass loses a great deal of its protein value, protein that puts pounds on a steer.

In the process of nurturing these fast-growing grasses, the soil gives up a great deal of its nitrogen, the most vital element for plant growth. A family of plants called legumes are nitrogen fixers—that is, they increase nitrogen in the soil by producing it in their root systems—but none of these are native to tropical rain forests in Venezuela. King Ranch, Australia, management had been successful in introducing legumes from New Guinea onto their rain forest ranch, so Bob ordered me to arrange for a supply of seed to be shipped to Mostrenco. Gustavo tried it near the tops of the hills, where the soil was most likely to leach, and the vinelike plant took hold. It was an example, one of many in the King Ranch organization, of taking advantage of an experience in one country to solve a problem in another.

Only when the clearing was well along, the fences and roads in place, and the water tanks located and dug, did Gustavo turn to building homes. The men were provided for first with a housing colony; then came the main residence. In a Spanish Colonial style, it stood on a hillside overlooking the Caribbean at a distance to the north, surrounded by waving grass and fat cattle on the other three sides.

THE COMPANY WAS JUST reaching this point in its development when the King Ranch organization, and particularly its boss, received an untimely, irreparable loss. Jack Malone, who was, among so many other things, the King Ranch intermediary with the Venezuelan company, suddenly, tragically died. Jack had been a longtime friend of Gustavo, back to pre-Castro days, making him the logical man to oversee Bob's interests.

Bob appointed me to replace Jack. He did not undertake to give me a title and bind me even closer to his elbow without polling his relatives on the ranch, sounding out their opinions on having someone outside their family in intimate, daily contact with him and privy to closely held corporate business. Some of them did not give me their endorsement—I was not surprised. A close-knit group like this, whether blood-related or in-laws, often becomes territorial, building fences to keep at a distance those outside their pedigree, perpetuating their exclusiveness. In their place, I might easily have had the same reaction.

FROM ITS INCEPTION, Mostrenco was planned as a fattening ranch for steers purchased from other ranchers, a veritable beef factory. In the late 1960s and early 1970s Caracas, a three-hour truck ride away, was on an economic roll fueled by the oil boom and was short of beef; the country's ranches could not provide the 2,000 head a day the capital alone needed. So Venezuela was forced to import. A market with a high demand was waiting, especially at the end of the dry season when most ranchers had sold their steers and there were few fat cattle available. At the time it was developing, Gustavo and Bob agreed that Mostrenco could grow enough grass to fatten 4,000 steers a year and that the ranch could make money at that rate of turnoff. Their estimate was slightly awry. Some years as many as 19,000 head were sold, and still the cattle could not keep up with the phenomenal grass growth.

Truly Mostrenco became the beef factory that Gustavo envisioned and the most profitable venture in the King Ranch foreign operations. It was also well within the framework of an old, well-tried formula that Bob applied, one way of assessing his investments—i.e., land is worth twice the value of the cattle it will carry:

Land, price per acre plus improvement costs	$ 52
Cost, 700-pound steer @ 32¢ per pound	224
Land cost per animal unit (1.5 acres supported one animal)	78
Gross profit per steer, per year	126
Gross return per acre, per year	84
Maintenance cost per acre, per year	20
Net return per acre, per year	64

It is glaringly apparent that land is not available in the U.S., anywhere, that fits this equation—thus another motivation for Bob's venturing overseas. But other considerations come into play in our country that mitigate

the difference between the price of rangeland and the protein it will produce. The most recent and fallacious one in the western U.S., and in Texas
especially, is the revenue generated from leasing the land for hunting.
Game management does not necessarily carry a high overhead, making
leases a substantial profit generator, sometimes even higher than the cattle
turnoff on the same acres.

WHEN MOSTRENCO REACHED its full carrying capacity, it became apparent that Compañía Venezolana de Ganadería, the parent organization,
could not buy enough young steers in Venezuela to assure a steady inflow
to Mostrenco, where the plan called for a complete turnover every twelve
months. During the wet season, when ranchers were holding on to their
steers because they had lush grass, large numbers of thin cattle were
smuggled in from Colombia for sale to the fattening operations. But purchasing these common steers was an erratic, risky business for a high-
exposure foreign company. Gustavo was forced to go into cow/calf ranching to supplement his purchases.

By 1970, a search for new breeding properties was under way. Gustavo
traveled to the south central part of the country, where land was undeveloped and cheap, looking for the type that suited his needs. When he found
a prospect, he asked me to pass the word to the boss and we flew down to
have a look. A number of prospects passed under the wheels of the Toyotas
before both he and Bob agreed on their first purchase. Their choice was a
132,000-acre ranch south of the Apure River in open country, the Venezuelan llanos. At that time it was beyond the frontier; there was little or no
settlement south of the Apure, which roughly divides the northern one-
third of the country from the southern two-thirds. The ranch was near the
northern boundary of a great grassland plain that extends into the Amazon
basin.

When we landed on the property, El Cedral, in a twin-engine charter, I
poked my head out the door, looked around, and quietly, very quietly,
voted to get back aboard and leave—I could not visualize what Gustavo
saw in it. Located between two tributaries of the Apure, during the wet
season the entire ranch, excepting a few low hillocks, went underwater.
Fences did not exist; the territory was open range so the cattle, horses, and
burros that drifted on and off it were a mixed lot of El Cedral and neighboring animals.

The cattle were not a bad type, a mixture of criollo and Brahma, but
the horses were something else. They were scrawny little things hardly
weighing 600 pounds; worse still, there were 3,000 of them around and

they were mixed with 700 burros! When the purchase was finalized, Gustavo told the boss, "Congratulations, Bob—when you bought this place you became the biggest jackass breeder in Latin America." Fortunately, when the livestock was finally sorted out, Gustavo's neighbor took both the horses and the burros off his hands.

The manager, who visited El Cedral only periodically, had six of these runty horses saddled and waiting for us to make an inspection. As we were preparing to mount, he sidled up beside me and whispered, "Pick one with no hair in his tail."

Three of the six had tails like rats, bare, scraggly, and pointed; the others were bushy. In South Texas we have a parasitic disease that causes horses to lose their tail hair; since I was the junior member of the party, I thought he was trying to pawn off a lice-ridden mount on me. But he was doing me a favor. On open range like this, the only way to catch an animal is to rope it; they did a lot of roping on Cedral. If the cowboy cinched his rope to the saddle horn, in the normal way, and roped a 1,300-pound bull from a 600-pound horse, it was no contest—the bull took charge. So they adapted; the rope was tied at the base of the tail, the tail hair was woven into it, and the horse was taught to turn away from the animal rather than face it, so the horse could spraddle its hind legs and pull with its tail without being thrown off its feet. A horse with no hair in its tail had had it pulled out by the rope. A bushy tail indicated that the little outlaw had not been ridden recently and the man who mounted up was in for a rough, uncertain ride.

GUSTAVO'S MINUTE INSPECTION of the gentle rise and fall of the contours convinced him that the water could be controlled, not dammed up and held on the land, but diked so that the flow slowed, the silt settled out, and the water moved to the next set of dams, where the process was repeated. The rate of water movement was the key; if it stood on the pasture too long it inhibited grass growth, and if it flowed too swiftly it eroded but did not soak in. The pasture then lost its nutrients, turning to a dust bowl in the dry season. Native to the property were varieties of grasses that had adapted to growing in standing water, the best among them a tall succulent called *lambadora*. It furnished 60 percent of the grazing during the wet season.

Bob had experience controlling water flow on near-level land on the ranch in Texas, so he understood and appreciated the plan Gustavo had for Cedral. The purchase was finalized and the bulldozers moved in. Creating the water management system was expensive, but the results began paying off as soon as some of the dikes and channels were in place. On a visit a year later, in August 1971, we saw a different ranch; even though we were in the rainy season, the pastures for the most part were above water, green and lush.

Work went on in the wet, but it wasn't easy. We began this rainy season tour in small boats, putting along behind the main north-south dike that controlled the easterly flow. During the construction work tiny islands, about the size of small rooms, had been thrown up by the bulldozers every few yards behind the dam. On each of these, one or more alligators had set up housekeeping—as we passed, they slithered into the water and followed us a way.

Taking no chances on bogging down when we went ashore at the south end of the dike, Gustavo had four jeeps and a tractor waiting for our party of four. He wanted Bob to see some scrub clearing and a new outstation and corral he was building on the south boundary. Off we went in line, with the tractor bringing up the rear in the event one of the four-wheelers got into trouble. One did—then another—and another. The grassy muck had no bottom; we lost the first vehicle in just a few hundred yards, not so much by having it bog as disappear. Sloshing over to the next in line, we kept going, but within a mile we were in trouble again. The tractor arrived and I was fingered by the boss to dive under the muddy water with a chain, to find the bumper somewhere down there. The tractor grunted and threw up twin plumes of water and mud and joined the Toyota.

Gustavo had experience in this muck; he ordered a log cut and tied across the tops of the tractor's back wheels. When the machine was put in reverse, the log would rotate, strike the mud, and lift the two main wheels, or so it was planned. Instead, the log acted like a scoop—the tractor dug its own grave, leaving only the tall exhaust pipe showing above the grass. A trip that would have taken twenty minutes in the dry season took five hours—we sloshed into the new campsite with one jeep still aboveground, the remains of the caravan spread out in a line of watery bog holes behind us.

THE ALLIGATORS THAT overran the canals were not a menace; they lived off the local wildlife and did not bother the cows or calves. But El Cedral was home to another ill-famed predator—the piranha fish. They were native to the rivers on each side of the ranch, and they swarmed into the lakes and canals during the wet season. Again, there was no evidence that they attacked the cattle; there was plenty of wild food for them also, in the form of other fish and the remains of carcasses left behind by the alligators. I expect that they bored in when the alligator caught its prey and helped themselves right out of its jaws, but I never saw this.

One midafternoon, we were inspecting a weir under construction in one of the dikes. The construction crew had sharpened the ends of concrete reinforcing rods and were spear-fishing in the torrent that flowed through the open gate. Just as we arrived, one of the Indians jabbed a large piranha right through the middle and held it up for Bob's inspection. The thing certainly had an impressive set of teeth; it snapped at us like a rattling machine gun.

Back at the headquarters after dinner that evening, we were sitting on the screened porch around a Coleman lantern, our only light; the power plant had not yet been installed. A group of men walked by and Gustavo made out that one of them was carrying the fish over his shoulder, still impaled on the spear. He called to him to bring it to the light so that we could get another look. The lantern was on the floor and as he tilted the spear down, the piranha flopped off and began dancing in a circle, its teeth chattering as viciously as when it was caught. In a flash the fish had the porch to itself. It had been out of water with that rod stuck through it for six hours, yet it was ready to tear our feet off. Its reputation seemed deserved.

THE WORK OF THE MOMENT was sorting out the herd. On the open range, Cedral cattle were running with cattle from neighboring ranches; they had to be separated according to brand and the neighbors' animals put outside the newly erected boundary fence. So the next day we watched a roundup that was unique to Bob's ranching experience. He always enjoyed watching trained, competent men handling livestock; he really got a boot out of this one.

The cowboys were Indians, natives of the region. All their lives they had lived in this wet country and had never worn shoes, a practical expedient since they would have immediately come down with foot rot. Their saddle stirrup, rather than triangular to accept a rider's boot, was a small brass ring into which the rider stuck his big toe. Mounted on the little native horses, they had gathered the cows and bulls and were going through them looking for the strays. When one was found with a foreign brand, it was roped and towed out of the herd—the horse, legs spraddled, rump low to the ground, pulling with its tail.

When the animal was in the clear, another man jumped off his mount, raced over to (in this instance) the bull, grabbed him by the tail, and, with a mighty heave, threw him on his side. As the air whooshed out of the poor animal and he lay for a moment stunned, the heaver darted around to his head and stuck his big toe in the bull's eye! The theory here was, if the bull couldn't see, it wouldn't move. It worked! The bull lay there until another cowboy, on foot, took up a position between the bull and an opening in the fence about a mile away. He whipped off his poncho and went into a matador's stance, his makeshift cape taut down the length of his arm. The man with the big toe retrieved it, flew around to the tail, and pulled the bull to his feet. Using the tail as a rudder, he pointed the bull toward the matador. The abused and enraged animal charged, the matador swirled his cape in a passable paso doble, and the bull, with a swipe of his horns, kept to his escape route. The *corrida* kept at this exotic cattle handling all afternoon.

THE HERD INSTINCT is one of the most dominant influences on bovines; they tend to stay together. But there are a few exceptions, and one of them made a local name for himself. He was an old black bull of considerable size and intimidating horn. Dry season or wet, he was always found in the water, meandering around up to his belly getting his fill of the tender *lambadora*. When he grazed out a pond, he apparently had the good sense to move during the night—he was never spotted on dry ground.

Gustavo ordered his men to bring in the rogue, and the contest was on. When they rode their horses into the pond to herd him out and rope him, he charged, hooking at bellies and flanks and putting everyone back on the banks. Next came a small boat: they roped him and he gave them a surfboard ride until he tired of the game and shook off the lariat. Mainly because of this cantankerous animal, which by this time had become a Cedral cause célèbre, Gustavo asked me to ship him two airboats, powered by small auto engines driving airplane propellers. By swooping in, getting the bull between them and lashing him to both boats, the hands were finally able to manhandle him ashore. He had evaded his captors for over two years and when he was finally hauled away some of the fun went out of the cleanup operation.

ON THE WHOLE, the Indian hands took with aplomb to the civilizing accoutrements Gustavo provided them. For instance, they had previously slept in hammocks that they swung in a circle, placing an oil drum packed with green leaves in the middle and each night setting a fire under it. The smoke warded off the hordes of mosquitoes that after dark feasted on every living thing; they were the worst I had seen anywhere, even in South Texas after a hurricane. Gustavo screened in their living quarters, relieving them of the choice between asphyxiation and anemia. Hammocks are state-of-the-art in Venezuela. One oversized job was called a marriage hammock, designed for couples. It helped to be a contortionist just to sleep in one alone—only a pair of acrobats could have performed their conjugal duties. But they must have been diligent learners; the place swarmed with children.

Among the novel new additions, by far the feature attraction was the flushing toilets. The Indians were fascinated by the water rushing through the bowls, and they crowded around, flushing them by the hour until the water reservoir ran dry. But all their lives they had gone to the bathroom squatting under a tree; it was physically impossible for them to perform seated on a stool. Try they did, but within a week Gustavo had on his hands the worst case of mass constipation in the history of the llanos. He was able to get to the bottom of the problem when he coaxed a shy explanation from them, and came up with a happy solution.

Venezuela imported its plumbing fixtures from Europe, among them the old-fashioned toilets that were round bowls set flush in the floor, with two small porcelain, foot-shaped platforms in the middle, called *toilettes à la Turque* by the French. I remember seeing them in the rest rooms in the lower-class Paris bistros I frequented in my youth. Gustavo replaced the sitting type with the squatting type and the problem was solved; the Indians still had their swirling water and Gustavo had a healthy, cramp-free *corrida*.

ALL OF THE LLANOS, El Cedral especially, are a naturalist's dream. Myriads of birds flocked there in the wet season—black-bellied tree ducks, scarlet ibises, the giant soldier crane, one of the largest birds in the world. As we had seen on our boating excursions, the alligators that had lived along the rivers had moved into the canals and onto the islands behind the dams, within three years breeding into the thousands. Gustavo obtained a government permit to harvest 1,500 a year; you could not tell they were missing and their hides, taken by professional hunters, generated an overhead-free supplemental income. The alligators did not bother the cattle; they had a more accessible food supply. Most of the swampy land in eastern South America is inhabited by a native aquatic mammal that looks like a cross between a nutria and a pig. They vary slightly in type and are called by different names; in Venezuela they are the *chigüiris*.

A *chigüiri* born and raised on Cedral must have thought it had found paradise, pre–Adam and Eve. The ponds were dense with water grasses and reeds and were so numerous that each family group had its own aquatic

apartment. Under these ideal conditions, they too multiplied at an un-
canny rate; we were never out of sight of them. They were the daily alligator entrée, but they outbred their only enemy. Prepared fresh, their meat
is inedible, but when salt-cured, as are hams, it has a distinctive flavor that
is especially prized as the Venezuelan Easter Sunday dish. Each year in the
early spring several thousand were harvested on Cedral, providing another
source of bonus income.

Bob was an expert pistol shot, quite good enough to enter serious competition, though he never did. Getting ahead of him in a match was well
nigh impossible and I never did, except once, and it involved a *chigüiri*. We
had been driving all morning inspecting the levees along the river; they
were the *chigüiri* sunbathing beaches. Constantly they were rolling over
and scurrying away from our slow-moving jeep. The manager who was
chauffeuring us had a .357 magnum pistol holstered on his belt and Bob
asked if he could try it. The cowboys were delighted to have a *chigüiri* for
its meat and hide, so he lined up on one in a nearby swamp, but he didn't
come close. The pistol sights were away off, and I could see the bullet
cutting grass a few feet above the animal's head, an almost impossible
thing for the shooter to spot from behind the blast.

He tried several more times and finally gave up in disgust. A few minutes later, we sighted another one, a large male, standing on the opposite
bank of a small pond. I asked if I could have a shot, and to compensate for
the faulty sight aimed about five feet low. The bullet struck the water,
ricocheted, and hit the animal square in the head! Bob whirled in his seat,
pointing his finger at me. "Bet you a hundred dollars you can't do that
again!" Need I say I didn't press my luck?

The next day, the top gun was able to refurbish his reputation. From
the outset of this particular trip, Bob had along in his baggage a cooler
loaded with five bottles of his best Dom Perignon champagne. I was assigned to look after it, keep it iced, and tote it about with the rest of our
luggage. Partly to rid myself of the chore, each evening I suggested that the
moment was perfect to salute the ranch, or our hosts, or whatever, with a
few glasses of the Dom's nectar. But relief eluded me; I just got another
order for a Scotch and soda, or more likely a daiquiri, the unofficial national drink of Venezuela.

Now we were leaving Cedral to return to civilization in Caracas. There
was a small asphalt airstrip at the end of the paved road—and the end of
civilization—about eight miles from the ranch; in the wet season we were
forced to use it rather than the grass strip at the headquarters and we had
arranged for the pilot to meet us there at midday. We were on time, but a

weather front delayed the plane; it began to pour. The Mantical airport terminal was a lean-to with no walls, just a palm-thatched roof about eight feet square, where we sat out the squall huddled together in a useless effort to keep dry. All of us—Bob, Gustavo, his son Gustavo, my wife Patricia— were drenched, fighting off mosquitoes and pretty miserable; then Bob thought it time to pop open the Dom Perignon. Thus commenced one of the more memorable impromptu parties in my experience.

We had put away the first bottle when out of the downpour a dilapidated pickup truck appeared, sloshing in the twin ruts leading from the highway. Out climbed a broad-shouldered, bandy-legged man of medium height and powerful build. He was a mestizo with red hair, light green eyes, and fair skin that the tropical sun had turned to blotchy medium-rare beefsteak. A cheery fellow, an acquaintance of Gustavo, he shook hands all around and ordered his Indian helper to bring him a stool from the truck. The Indian fetched a doll's seat, an old-fashioned thing with a woven rawhide bottom and a straight back which completely disappeared when the man sat down. But he didn't stay there long; Bob, who rarely saw anything smaller than a ranch that he wanted to own, fell in love with the seat. He thought it the perfect gift for his little friend Tom Armstrong, so he set about taking possession.

When the stranger heard Bob admiring his beat-up relic, he offered it as a gift, but Bob would have none of that. The owner was also wearing a pistol, a hog leg with about a twelve-inch barrel, a real cannon. Bob proposed a pistol match, the chair against a hundred dollars for the winner. The redhead thought he was being kidded and laughed and asked Gustavo for a translation, but finally upon him dawned the vision of a very profitable day. The rules were drawn up; the target was the empty champagne bottle at about thirty-five yards, best two out of three.

The pistol owner wasn't a bad shot, but he had trouble with his handicap—he had never had champagne before. He nicked the first bottle before Bob became accustomed to the weapon; we drew the cork on the second to provide the next target. Our friend threw his head back and downed his glass in a gulp—when the gas exploded in his stomach, his face took on an even richer hue. He laughed along with us, but I think that he thought he had been poisoned by this strange thing the gringos drank. From the second bottle on, it was no match and within a short time, near the bottom of the fourth bottle, the chair changed hands.

Someone said something about lunch and our mellow new friend jumped into the breach—he would provide it. He and his Indian set off for the village of Mantical, several miles to the east. I had noticed that Gustavo had been quiet during the shooting match. Now he told Bob, "You have to watch that fellow, he's a cattle rustler and a thief, the most notorious in this part of the country. The local militia spends most of its time trying to trap him in the act."

That sobered us a bit but not much. The four-wheelers that had delivered us to the airstrip had returned to the ranch; we were stranded. While we outnumbered him and his Indian, he had prudently taken the hog leg with him. The rain had slowed to a drizzle by the time the pickup reappeared. We had done our host an injustice—he brought out a box loaded with sandwiches, whole loaves of country bread split across the middle and layered with slabs of beef and sliced tomatoes. And he brought along a drink more to his liking: warm beer. By the time we had finished off everything, the sandwiches, the champagne, and most of the beer, the plane landed. We thanked our patron; he promised to call when next we were at the ranch. On the way out to board, Gustavo asked Bob how he liked the beef. "Hope you found it OK, it was probably one of yours."

THE KLEBERG HEADQUARTERS in Caracas was the Tamanaco Hotel, one of the better ones in Latin America. All of the suites opened onto large terraces, and it was in this outdoor setting that most of the ranch's business and entertaining took place. The hotel even turned over to Bob a waiter-bartender named Alfredo who was so devoted that during our stays he remained on duty around the clock.

One of the reasons Gustavo settled in Venezuela was that he had a host of relatives and friends there, some Cuban refugees, others from the old Venezuelan families that had intermarried with their Cuban landowning counterparts. All of them became friends and they vied to have Bob in their homes when he was in the city. Of the national societies in Latin America, Venezuelans seemed to be the most open and cordial. They had our custom of entertaining in their homes, unlike the Argentines and Brazilians, who invited their friends or business associates to restaurants, clubs, or hotels.

These friendships inevitably led to business arrangements; King Ranch took minor interests in a few Venezuelan enterprises—real estate developments, feed processing and storage, fertilizer production—and they took minority shares in the King Ranch subsidiary. Generally these were profitable for the partners. By saying this I imply that Bob went from success to success in his ranching, agricultural, and business dealings. This, of course, was not the case. One venture, into which he put years of time and a great deal of corporate money, involved his Venezuelan partners.

In the mid 1960s, a friend on the East Coast introduced Bob to a man of scientific background named Dr. Joseph Kazickas, and arranged for Dr. Kazickas to visit the ranch to brief Bob on a process to liquefy natural gas. There was an untold quantity of it in the mineral reservoirs under the ranch in South Texas that was underpriced, partly because of its limited means of distribution. Liquefying it was a way of putting it into containers for overseas shipment in international trade. The idea of making the gas that the ranch owned a more valuable commodity, to compensate for the dwindling oil reserves, caught Bob's attention.

I was instructed to pick up the doctor at the Corpus Christi airport, drive him to the main house to spend the night, and the next day deliver him to Norias, where the boss was working cattle. During our forty-five-minute trip to Kingsville, I caught occasional glimpses of him in the dash lights—I had never seen a more nervous, agitated man. I learned from him only a little about the mechanism he was scouting the country to raise money to support; he told me it was not yet patented and I gathered his state of mind was at least partly attributable to the risk of having a relatively simple, inexpensive process get away from him.

Kazickas came to Bob recommended by Bob's friend, and that was a warrant that he was the genuine article and that he would get a sympathetic hearing. Such was Bob's confidence in anyone who had gained his trust. The doctor convinced him that he had access to a process that would liquefy gas at five cents cheaper per thousand cubic feet than any other process in use at that time, which, as it turned out, was true. Given that kind of saving, it seemed that there was a bonanza ahead for the group that controlled the patents. Bob agreed to join Kazickas's other investors and entered the up and down, down, down world of entrepreneurial pioneering.

Bob's first setback was his most devastating. He contacted his friends at Exxon to bring them into the newly formed organization, Ocean Transport; they had discovered one of the largest gas deposits in the world in Libya but had no access to a market. Bad timing; Exxon had, just a few weeks before, signed a contract to use another liquefaction process. Had Bob landed Exxon, the venture would have stood a chance of success—without that, it teetered with a fingerhold at the top of the cliff but eventually fell into the chasm. The investor group forged ahead, relying mainly on developing a market with the large pipeline companies that distributed commercial and household gas in the Northeast, going so far as to build a pilot plant and a model gas container that was loaded with liquid gas and put aboard ship for a sea trial. But restrictive regulations rose like great walls in their path. Liquid natural gas is under extreme pressure, making it highly volatile; one misstep, a faulty weld in a container, a bad valve, and the ship or the unloading system or the storage tanks become giant bombs. The ports in the urban areas were not willing to risk having liquid gas terminals in their complexes.

One by one, the investors began to back away from putting funds into further research and development. They represented public companies and were spending stockholder money, the most vocal of whom were often environmentalists. Bob believed in the basic concept and was not hampered by having to answer to a public body. As his partners fell away, he assumed a larger and larger share of the expense. Toward the end, Joe Kazickas joined the exodus and began looking for other speculative opportunities. He never told Bob he was pulling out, but it became more and more evident that his interest was flagging.

Venezuela had the same problem as Libya. Along with their oil, which was their only appreciable source of foreign exchange, they had large deposits of natural gas and were not developing domestic industries at a rate to use even a fraction of it. The gas was being flared, wasted, in the big fields such as the one in Lake Maracaibo. One of Mr. Kleberg's closest friends in Venezuela was Eduardo Mendoza, a younger member of a prestigious family—one older brother had been the interim president of the country, another an ambassador. Eduardo traveled often to the States and had seen the uses to which we were putting our natural gas deposits. He undertook to organize a Venezuelan subsidiary of Ocean Transport to market gas outside the country, to the U.S. and to their neighbors in Latin America. An ownership plan was developed, with 30 percent of the shares held by Ocean Transport, 30 percent by the government-controlled oil company, Petroleos de Venezuela, and 40 percent by private Venezuelan investors. Exploratory talks were arranged with the ministry and plans were formulated.

On one of our trips in mid-1970, Bob invited Dr. Kazickas to fly down with us to talk with these groups, men who were in a position to negotiate a long-term gas purchase contract with the government. In the only discussion Joe sat in on, I thought he was withdrawn to the point of turning them off. He stayed in Caracas only overnight and was on his way, leaving it to Bob's other partners to send their people from the States to follow up. It was the last time I saw Dr. Kazickas. Again, the roadblock was handling the cargo in stateside ports; nothing ever came of the Venezuelan participation.

The determination in Bob's character that in the past had driven him to overcome obstacle after obstacle to eventually achieve his goal proved in this instance to be his undoing. He stayed with the thing longer than he should have, much longer than his more pragmatic associates. In the end, he was virtually carrying the enterprise alone. The company was eventually dissolved, the patents passing into the public domain. Ocean Transport was one of Bob's few ventures outside of agriculture, and his most salient business failure.

WHEN BOB STAYED WITHIN his ranching domain, his successes were a revelation. On my first visit to Mostrenco, the property was developed enough so that the first land that had been cleared was covered in mature stands of guinea grass. About halfway through our drive I told him this was the most beautiful ranch I had ever seen. On the valley floors where the cattle tended to congregate, they disappeared—the grass was taller than their backs. The herd made its presence known by the movement of the supple green spears—they swayed in waves as if a submarine were cruising just under the ocean surface on a calm day. The steers lived in a sea of nutrients and they gave back what they took in, gaining from one and a half to two pounds a day, only a little less than they were able to put on in a feedlot in the States.

There were problems, of course: foot rot on the damp ground, hoof-and-mouth disease—*aftosa*—the scourge of Latin America, pasture maintenance (when the grass grew, everything grew, noxious plants included), the cost of applying fertilizer (guinea grass is a fierce soil depleter). But all of these could be overcome with experience, diligence, and money. Even though the development work was continuous, causing the subsidiary company to be a constant borrower from the parent, year after year Mostrenco made a profit on operations. More than once, its worth was assessed by other landholders in Venezuela. Judged in acres, the King Ranch holdings were the fifth-largest in the country. From time to time the four larger ranch owners—the English Lincolnshire Investment Company, Daniel Ludwig's $38 million ranching development, and the Rockefeller brothers' interests—came to Gustavo with propositions to trade acreage for an interest in Mostrenco. It was the only developed ranch in Venezuela with abundant green grass the year around.

In addition to its purely business worth, it was a credit to the relationship between Bob Kleberg and Gustavo de los Reyes, a mutual respect and abiding trust, each in the other's judgment.

THE WORCESTER BULL

Doris Lindner was not quite a visitor; she came to the ranch to work. But in the attention it was necessary to give her, the interruption she caused in the ranch's routine, her sojourn qualifies her to be included here.

During the 1950s, the Royal Worcester Company, makers of some of the world's finest porcelains, undertook to produce replicas of some of the more noted individuals among the world's breeds of horses and cattle. Miss Lindner's first commission was to sculpt the queen mounted on her Guards' charger. It got such a good reception that for a number of years Royal Worcester kept her moving about the world modeling other outstanding animals.

Stanley Marcus, a marketer of Worcester china through his Neiman Marcus stores, was a friend of Bob's. He sought Bob's consent to include a King Ranch Santa Gertrudis bull in the series. Bob was hesitant; others had tried to sculpt one of his animals but had never been able to put it together to his satisfaction. Further, Marcus wanted him to sign the first one hundred of the five hundred porcelains that were fired, thus putting his imprimatur on something he might not want associated with his name. But Marcus was persistent and convincing, sending along photographs of Lindner's work, and Bob relented. Of course he delivered Miss Lindner to my hands, with the admonishment, "I don't want to see the thing until she's finished. Then I'll decide one way or the other."

Miss Lindner looked as if she did most of her work in marble—she had the shoulders and forearms for it. Marble was, in fact, her preferred medium. Past middle age when she visited the ranch, she had had a fine career in her own right. But the body of her work had been in modern art; though she had exhibited widely, she had not made those really big sales. So doing this series was a financial windfall for her. Lindner was something of a maverick, even for her London pre–World War II art circle. She raised a son without a father—the son had migrated to Australia and she was proud of the life he was making for himself.

Doris arrived late one night, eager to get to work first thing the next morning. A shady, quiet location had been chosen for her, and a bull named Prince, a fine mature animal with a great disposition, was her model. As we were laying out her simple table and her tools, Bob drove up. He stayed long enough for introductions and to see that she had everything she needed, but not long enough to become entangled in any commitments, even tacit.

Our artist was a dedicated worker; she was on the site every day, morning and afternoon. Her sessions were limited only by the ever-patient Prince's eventually becoming restless. Adhering to the rule that no one sat at the main house table without a host, I broke into whatever I was doing and fetched her for lunch and dinner. Though Bob had planned to keep his distance, he discovered that they had a mutual affinity for martinis and that Miss Lindner could keep pace with him, pitcher for pitcher. So he had her over to his home a number of evenings, spelling me.

Finally, after a month of work on this eight-inch-high little replica, one noontime Doris said, "Enough. If I do any more the thing will become slick, overfinished."

I made a date with Bob for the final, critical inspection and collectively Miss Lindner and I sucked in our breaths. He was at the modeling stand in the hour, with a serious mien and a gruff greeting, "Give me a few minutes." Quietly he circled the model, then the bull, then back to the model. Ten minutes passed, a quarter of an hour.

I don't remember how he broke the silence; it was with something like "It'll do." A half-hour's discourse followed, pointing out a skin fold on one side, the fraction turn of a leg on the other, from the head to the tail. Doris circled beside him, ticking the Plasticine at the questionable points. Afterward she told me, "Wonderful! He didn't say a word until he had thought the whole thing through."

Another day's work and she was back on the plane to London, holding her treasure in a box on her lap, a nervous wreck over what might happen to it before she delivered it to Worcester.

THE STORY HAS AN afterword, an insight into the British artistic versus the commercial approach. Less than a year later, I was in Australia and I made a date with Miss Lindner to meet her in London on my way home, so that together we could go to Worcester to see the first of the bulls come out of the kiln.

We arrived in Worcester in time for lunch. Headed by Managing Director J. F. Gimson, a large, florid man of an expansive nature, the whole board was assembled in the directors' dining room. Doris was so taken by this demonstration of the merit they gave her work that she got right into her pre-lunch martinis, joined by Mr. Gimson. By the end of the two-hour repast, we were a happy, misty lot.

Next came the highlight, the bull inspection. The chief engineer and I were ahead of the group when we walked onto the floor housing the great kilns. On a table nearby stood the first six little bulls to come out of the first round of firing; there were eight additional firings to follow. One look and I felt the blood drain from my face. From between the shoulders to the tail of each of them, their backs made a downward arc that left their bellies on a level with their knees. It was the worst possible conformation a bovine can have. What the hell had gone wrong and what was I to say? Obviously the whole project would have to be scrapped, but how could I get this over to this phalanx of hardheaded businessmen who had authorized a considerable development expense?

As it turned out, I didn't need to open my mouth. Up came Miss Lindner on the arm of Mr. Gimson.

Gimson, clearly no cattleman: "Aren't they lovely?"

Lindner: "My God! What have you done to my bull? You bunch of nincompoops, I told you not to touch my model! Where is that mold-maker?"

The shock induced sobriety all around and the levelheaded engineer stepped in. The ceramic was hollow; when it began to cool, the outside and inside temperatures went down at different rates. The air trapped in the core succumbed to the exterior pressure and forced the back down. The solution was a simple one: cast a small hole between the front legs, let the pressure equalize, seal the hole.

Then Mr. Gimson demonstrated why his lifelong business acumen had propelled him to the chief executive's chair. "But what shall we do with these six? I know! We'll ship them to Australia."

CHAPTER EIGHT

MEANWHILE, BACK AT THE RANCH

RECALL THAT IN THE Foreword I warned that to describe Bob Kleberg's life, often I would have to "jump across time zones and continental boundaries in not seeming but actual disarray." Disarray for his associates, perhaps, but well ordered in his mind. While he continually had a number of projects whirling around him, he had the ability to concentrate on them one at a time, blocking out extraneous interruptions that crept in.

Another facet of Bob's makeup: He was a traditionalist in one of our most tradition-bound businesses. He believed that some ranching practices had endured for centuries because they were the right practices; he had to be shown a very good reason indeed to change them. But at the same time, he was open to innovation. As we have seen, at times in his life his receptive mind set him on courses that carried him past his profession's frontiers.

These two attributes came into full play in the early 1960s. While embroiled in the confrontation with Castro over the Cuban confiscations, and in the midst of developing ranches in Latin America and other parts of the world, he undertook a scheme at home that attracted inordinate public attention.

IN 1946, IN HIS FIRST purchase outside of Texas, Bob began buying land in southeastern Pennsylvania. It long had been a practice for southwestern ranchers to send steers to rented pastures in the Midwest for final fattening before slaughter. However, for the King Ranch product, the eastern market was better than the midwestern one. The beef-eating population was concentrated there and the restaurant and hotel trade was an outlet for slightly heavier carcasses. By acquiring a permanent range in the Northeast, Bob was able to fatten close to the best market centers and avoid the shrinkage (the weight loss animals incur in transit) and bruising that were costly to the producer.

His newly purchased fattening range, Buck and Doe Run Valley Farms, was located in Chester County, sixty miles west of Philadelphia. Farmed for generations by some of the early Dutch settlers to this region, the soil had been exhausted. But when it was properly limed and phosphated, the grasses thrived and it developed into some of the best pastures in the country for growing out steers. Buck and Doe was the fox-hunting domain of Bob's friend Plunket Stewart; Bob agreed when he bought it to maintain the timber jumps between pastures so that the locals could continue to ride to the hounds.

Each spring, 5,000 steers were gathered in the pastures near the railroad loading yards on King Ranch. As soon as the grass was up in Chester County, the signal was given and the largest annual cattle movement since the trail drives of the 1870s began. It took about five days to load them out, a trainload a day, so they arrived at Buck and Doe within a week, first to last. The trip was a hard one on the cattle. By law, they had to be unloaded to water and rest; each loading and unloading entailed a lot of jostling about. They arrived bruised and exhausted, and it took them about thirty days to return to the fitness they had reached on leaving Texas. But when they were marketed in the fall and winter, they were on the trucks just over an hour and were delivered to the packer in top condition, bringing a premium market price for their grade.

Little by little, during the 1950s, as the packing business became more dispersed and cattle were fattened in feedlots closer to the market centers, trucks took over the hauling from the railroads. Finally, in the early 1960s, the railroads went out of the business of transporting livestock. But the trucks that served the smaller producers so well did not fill King Ranch's need. The Texas-Pennsylvania haul was too long and the same railroad watering and resting regulations applied to the trucks. No practical means was at hand to move 5,000 head in so short a time, and the short growing season in Pennsylvania made time critical.

BOB HAD A FRIEND, Gerard Harrison, who ranched south of Houston. Gerard had a mind at the apex of a whirlwind; he was the entrepreneurial type that had a dozen ideas a day, of which two or three a year might prove workable. Gerard saw the innovative pond-raised catfish business developing along the southern banks of the Mississippi, bought some vacant riverside land, excavated ponds, and went into fish farming.

In another far-off world, the General Motors Corporation was having difficulty getting enough space on railcars and trucks to deliver their new cars to dealers in the fast-growing southern and southwestern markets. They experimented with alternate transportation by constructing a string of three triple-decked barges to river-transport new cars from their plants in the North down to New Orleans. For some reason, it didn't work out; the project was abandoned and the barges were put up for sale.

Meanwhile, Gerard was keeping some of his cattle from Texas on the land in Mississippi that he was not using for his catfish business. He too was looking for a way to move his fat steers south to the Louisiana market. Learning of the barge sale, he bought one of the three, the bow section, and converted it into a floating feedlot. The two upper decks were partitioned into pens that held about a dozen head each, with alleyways in between, each pen with its water and feed troughs. The lower deck, in the body of the barge, was used for feed storage. Gerard made several hauls along the lower river, but he didn't have the volume of cattle to keep his new contraption busy. He rang up his friend Bob just at the time when Bob was puzzling over how to get his steers to Buck and Doe for the coming season. The upshot was Gerard loaned his barge to King Ranch free of charge to make a try at solving our problem. Bob handed the organizing over to me.

The concept was ingenious—the doing was something else.

Helen, Bob's daughter, lived on Buck and Doe from the time of her first marriage and had raised her family of six children there. While the ranch manager, Sam Wilson, was in charge of the day-to-day operations, Helen took an active hand in running the farm. Her parents visited Buck and Doe almost as often as they were in the East; they even had their own home close by their only child and grandchildren. Bob had passed happy times on Buck and Doe with both his Helens, and he wanted to see it continue in the productive way he had originally intended.

I WAS NOT AWARE of the magnitude of our country's inland waterways system until I got involved in this exercise. The Mississippi, the vertical trunk, is supported by lateral branches, the Tennessee and Ohio Rivers to the east, the Arkansas and the Missouri to the west, along with other tributaries. Connected by a series of canals constructed over the years by the

U.S. Corps of Engineers, they form a vast network that ties the Great Lakes to the Gulf of Mexico.

Most of the Texas mainland is separated from the gulf by a barrier island, a long sandbar that has been built up over the eons by the advancing coastline. The internal waterways were extended, beginning in the 1920s, by dredging a canal behind this barrier island to create a secure passage for shallow draft barge traffic. It's possible to cruise from Brownsville, at the southern tip of Texas, via the rivers and the Great Lakes, to Newfoundland without entering open ocean water.

HELEN'S FATHER ASKED her to find the closest port to the ranch where the barge could unload. She was able to locate a dock south of Pittsburgh, within 150 miles of Buck and Doe's front gate.

I contacted our friends at the Port of Corpus Christi. In 1926, Bob's father, Robert, Sr., had been instrumental in founding the deepwater port; there was a close association between its directors and the ranch. They provided us a mooring site with a sufficient dockside parking and turning area for cattle trucks to maneuver up to the loading ramp. They also found us a towing company that could see the barge to its destination in Pennsylvania.

Bob reasoned that if this idea had a future, we needed advice from a naval architect, so I retained a young engineer from New Orleans named Arthur Grant, a riverboat specialist, to observe the first trip and assess our future needs.

Our ranch feedmill mixed the bulk feed and sacked it in fifty-pound bags. The daily routine of opening those sacks in the dark, unventilated hold and dumping them onto the auger that delivered the feed to the upper decks was a grind that took its toll on the hands who made the trip. There were no crew quarters on the barge; Gerard just pitched a tent on the roof for his river cowboys during his short runs on the lower Mississippi. I made a deal with the tug captain to permit our men to eat in their mess and use their extra bunks.

A thousand details had to be attended to that had not occurred to anyone; all of us were breaking in together. Longshoremen, for instance— their union representative appeared at the loading ramp just as we were backing in the first truckload of cattle. Apparently nothing moved on or off the docks without their moving it. Oddly, they had been nowhere in sight when our boys were manhandling the feed sacks into the hold. Now they wanted to take charge of putting the cattle aboard. I told the man our cargo was self-propelled; what could a bunch of no-experience cattle handlers do? It turned out they didn't have to do anything, they just had to be there—those were the regulations. We negotiated. I rebutted with this not being a commercial operation but an experiment in a new form of livestock movement. If we were successful, new vistas in intracoastal transport would open, with consequent long-term profit for the stevedores. He bought it and our cowboys went to work.

The floating feedlot had a capacity of about 750 head. We were able to load on the ranch, truck the forty miles to the port, and get all of them aboard between dawn and sunset, even though we had to put up with a lot of interference. The newspapers showed up, and the TV stations. This attracted the people working around the docks and crowds began to form, crawling over, under, and around the trucks and coming over the side of the barge to spook the already jittery steers. The harbor police were called in to cordon off the lot of them.

At last the steers were penned, watered, fed, and settled down; the crowds had lost interest. Since the tug planned to pick up the barge before dawn the next morning, everyone was sent to their rooms to rest. At sundown I was on board alone, standing on the roof of the top deck overlooking the dock, when a ship rounded a turn ahead. I walked across to the water side to watch it pass, and as I did the barge did a slow roll from starboard to port. I couldn't believe it! My weight, 146 pounds, had tilted a floating feedlot with a full load of cattle and grain aboard.

As fast as I could I raced to a telephone and called Bob Grant at the motel a few blocks away. He and Gerard sped up a few minutes later; the three of us climbed to the top deck and walked from one rail to the other. Tilt—and then a slight bump—it did it again.

Bob Grant's first words were, "Let's get offa' this thing!"

From a more pragmatic viewpoint, dockside, he jiggled his slide rule, made some calculations, and came up with an estimate of just how top-heavy a full cargo had made Mr. Harrison's rig. Apparently the lighter, bulkier feed in the hold and the heavier animals and the water tank above had upset the General Motors formula for a uniform weight distribution. We were in no danger of capsizing here in the shallow backwater of the upper harbor; all day long, the barge had been rocking back and forth, settling one corner and then the other into the silt just three feet below the hull. But out in the channel crossing Corpus Christi Bay, where forty feet of water separated the barge from the bottom, she could turn turtle, taking the tug and the herd with her.

Mr. Grant got out his navigation charts and his calculating instruments and earned his retainer. The only part of the trip in deep water was the first fifteen miles; once the barge entered the Intracoastal Waterway on the east side of the bay, the water in the canal and the river system would not be deep enough to be a hazard. Also, the barge would be traveling in a train, lashed to adjacent barges, so that they would form a stabilizer around it. The only problem we faced was the immediate one, getting across the bay. A call to the harbor master located two loaded oil barges set to sail. They were snugged up to ours, and with this secure escort the feedlot was on its way, on schedule.

I rode along for a day to see that things settled in, then dropped off at a little port a hundred miles up the canal. Even as we cruised past this sparsely populated part of the coast, small planes and helicopters carrying news crews buzzed around overhead. When the train left the Intracoastal and entered the Mississippi above New Orleans, it turned into a circus parade; small boats appeared in such numbers that the river patrol had to regulate traffic. During daylight, aircraft made continuous circles overhead. When the barge approached a large city, my telephone in Kingsville would begin to ring—reporters wanting background for stories; I had no difficulty pinpointing its hour-by-hour progress.

At the junction of the Illinois and Kentucky state lines, the train left the Mississippi and entered the Ohio, and our troubles began. Each morning, the men hosed down the decks and washed the manure overboard. Of course, manure is a form of fertilizer; we put it in our lakes and tanks to promote algae growth, which in turn feeds the fish, just as we use it on the pasture to promote grass growth. The environmental people along the Ohio played their game by a different set of rules, the ones in their book— they began writing citations for polluting.

Passing Cincinnati, we became an even bigger media event. The patrol officers kept pace with the barge—each time a steer kicked a splatter of manure over the side, they began to write, with the TV cameras peeking over their shoulders. This on a stretch of water that I understood periodically caught fire, so heavy was the waste disposal. Sounds unbelievable, doesn't it? But in the bygone unregulated days it happened in some of our Texas rivers and harbors too.

At last the tow arrived at the unloading dock on the Monongahela south of Pittsburgh. Helen had the trucks waiting, and the steers were grazing on Buck and Doe pastures the following day. For them, it was a twenty-nine-day cruise on a rock-steady ship with all the food and drink they could wish. They had gained an average of 2.8 pounds each day they were aboard, a total of nearly 59,000 pounds of beef added to the cargo during the journey.

We had the barge returned to the Harrison Ranch in Mississippi for cleaning and minor alterations, while in Texas we organized another trip. The pattern set by the first voyage seemed OK, except that Bob changed the feed formula. He did not think it necessary to spend the money to fatten the steers while they traveled. His goal was to keep them from losing condition so that they would be ready to gain on grass, a far cheaper form of feed than the sacked rations, when they reached Buck and Doe. This time only roughage was put aboard, in the form of the hulls that are removed from the outside of the cottonseed. A bovine will eat nearly any kind of fiber, as long as it can be digested. For maintenance only, cottonseed hulls are an adequate feed for a limited time.

The first three-fourths of the trip went swimmingly, smoother than the first one, except for one gut-wrenching incident. Cruising an unpopulated stretch of the Intracoastal Waterway late one night, the tug lost the packing around its propeller shaft and began to sink. The captain cut the barge loose and beached the tug on a mudbank—the barge continued its journey, silently, smoothly, without lights, on up the waterway. The captain radioed for assistance and reported the barge's position, or lack of it— neither he nor anyone else knew where it was. At dawn the search began. The wayward feedlot was soon spotted resting against the shore a few miles north of where it had been cast off. When the hands boarded, they found the steers contentedly munching away, the only ones that had kept their cool during a panicky night.

Then the barge rounded into the Ohio again. In order to keep the environmental people off our backs, we had installed splash boards to keep the manure aboard during the seven days it took to traverse the river. But the feed was both lower in nutrition and bulkier, so the steers ate more of it and produced a lot more than the anticipated quantity of manure. When they arrived at the unloading dock, they were knee deep in the stuff and exhausted from the effort to get to and from the water and feed troughs. On the trucks, some of them lay down and the others ran over them; we had a number of injuries. By the time they were turned into pasture, they were no better off, perhaps worse, than they would have been traveling by rail or road.

On this trip, the barge had struck something that had opened a small rift in the hull. Gerard took it back down the Mississippi to a boatyard equipped with a floating dry dock, unfortunately suited for a tug but not for a contraption the length and light weight of the barge. Only about half of it would fit inside; when the water was pumped out to raise the dry dock, the barge broke in the middle. Realizing that it was beyond repair, Gerard had it cut up for scrap.

LIKE SO MANY innovations in the traditional ranching business, where livestock practices have stood the test of millennia, this one was brilliant of conception but fraught with unexpected hazards of accomplishment. We should know our animals by now, but we don't; they continue to surprise us by performing the way they are born to do, not the way we think they should.

Everyone, the boss included, was disappointed that our barging venture had not worked out; it seemed to hold promise, since so much of the beef produced in the U.S. comes from the states that are served by our inland waterways system. We place a lot of emphasis on food quality; this was an opportunity to deliver beef to the packer in better condition than it had left the ranch. But Bob was pragmatic. "There is always a reason," he told me, "why we do things the way we're used to doing them."

THE HOME OF THE BRAVE

On a social occasion in the East, Bob and Helen became acquainted with a young and comely European of distinguished heritage, Princess Maria Gabriella de Sevoia, daughter of King Humberto II, the deposed king of Italy. They invited her to the ranch for a visit; she arrived accompanied by her cousin, Princess Catherine de Cröy. The de Cröys, of French-Belgian background, had a lineage that was one of the oldest in Europe, and from their family tree hung the sweet fruit of talent and accomplishment.

One of their ancestors, Prince Benoit Azy, was caught up in the French Revolution. Disguised in rags, he joined the mobs in Paris's Place de la Concorde to watch the guillotine blade fall on the necks of most of his relatives. But he survived the genocide, reclaimed his family lands near Nevers, and created one of Europe's most productive breeds of beef cattle, the Charolais.

Bob developed an early interest in Charolais; the King Ranch became the first importer of the breed into the U.S. when he brought a small herd up from Mexico in the early 1920s. Though he never saw the de Cröy herd, he learned a good deal about their background from his visitors. Four of the family of seven sisters and a brother traveled to the ranch over the years.

The Klebergs, de Cröys, and Cyphers developed a long-term friendship; but only when the ranch entertained another visitor, an Englishman named Robert McCready, did I fully learn of their unique, noble attributes under stress. He told me this story.

From the era of Prince Benoit Azy, who journeyed to England to purchase Shorthorns to breed to his native cattle, the family had Anglophile leanings. All of the children of Prince Leopold and Princess Marie spoke

English as well as they spoke French. Their nannies were English. During World War II, McCready was a lieutenant in the British Special Forces, assigned to lead a group of forty officers and men far behind enemy lines in occupied France. His superiors instructed him to contact the family de Cröy.

On station, the squad fell into a reciprocal routine with the enemy. In the air war, the Allies had gained complete control, so the Germans were forced to move about only at night, hiding in the villages or forests to sleep during the day. The British slept at night and had the freedom of the countryside in the light, setting off their lovely fireworks to blow up enemy supplies and generally disrupt services.

Many times McCready led his men to the château at Azy, near Nevers, where the de Cröys shared their meager rations with them and provided the officers beds. The enlisted men slept in the hay in the barns. On one of these overnight bivouacs, the British were up and out at 6:00 in the morning. Almost immediately, the de Cröys learned of a German patrol headed their way. They had time only to gather up the cigarette butts and clean the dishes, not to change the beds, before the Boche arrived.

Prince Leopold handed his two youngest daughters, Catherine and Emmanuella, about ten at the time, two brooms and dispatched them out onto the front driveway, to sweep away the tracks left in the sand by the British jeeps. They were at it when they looked up to find they were surrounded by German soldiers. The soldiers could not understand what two little girls were doing, out nonsensically sweeping at 6:00 in the morning. The girls told them they were playing dolls—the Germans believed them. So the Germans trooped in and ludicrously bedded down on sheets left warm by the departed enemy.

McCready and his men roamed the forest of Nivernais, one of the largest in Europe, until the Allied forces overran the region and the Germans retreated. He told me that during the entire operation he lost only one man. A sergeant got drunk in the village, crashed his jeep into one of the stout gate pillars at the château, and broke his neck.

THE DE CRÖYS SHOWED their mettle at their last contact with the retreating Germans. The Germans came into the village at dawn, preparing to bed down. The village baker foolishly fired through his window, killing one, and a shooting, grenade-throwing fight broke out. Two little baker's apprentices raced to the château to alert the prince and princess. They ran to the village to find the Germans rounding up the peasants and herding them into their homes, under confinement. In one of their kitchens, Princess Marie came upon a white apron and a bit of red cloth. She donned the apron, made a crude cross of the cloth, and plastered it on her chest.

In the village square, the German commander had arrested twelve men and had them standing against the church wall, facing a firing squad. The princess stood in front of them and demanded of the commander why he was doing more killing while his own troops were wounded and dying around him. He replied that he had no doctor or medicines; there was nothing he could do.

Princess Marie told him she was a nurse and that she had medicines at the château—if he would spare the men, she would treat his wounded. A deal was struck and the princess took a motorcycle to the château, where she enlisted one of her daughters, Marie-Dorothée. Back on the motorcycle, they returned to the village and spent the day patching up the enemy.

At nightfall, the German officer decided he would not shoot the hostages after all. They would march up the road ahead of his men, targets in the event they were attacked by more of the partisans. Prince Leopold hurried his daughters Marie-Dorothée and Claire on bicycles, ahead of the retreating troops, to warn the guerrillas in the woods that Frenchmen were shielding the Germans—don't fire. One of the resistance fighters was their brother, Leopold; he was a member of a group of Communist guerrillas. His nom de plume among his comrades was Le Prince Rouge.

Princess Marie had always been the matriarch to the locals—forevermore she became their Joan of Arc.

The thing about this incident that most impressed the princess's daughters was seeing their mother, their model of decorum, speed off down the drive astraddle a motorcycle, her skirts flying.

THROUGH THE KING RANCH gates nobles of nearly every stripe have passed, none more noble in their hearts and by their conduct than the de Cröys.

THE EPISODE HAS A tragic epilogue. Years after his visit to the ranch, Robert McCready was appointed a supreme court justice in colonial Kenya. While serving his country at that post, he was murdered.

CHAPTER NINE

BRAZIL, A MULTIFACETED ADVENTURE

AT THE PERIMETER OF the next concentric circle beyond Venezuela lay the King Ranch do Brasil properties, one of Bob's earliest forays in his ring of expansions into Latin America.

Keeping to his credo of going first to the men who knew the country, in 1953 Bob took up the offer of an old friend, A. Thomas Taylor, to join him in looking at the possibility of setting up an operation in Brazil. Taylor was chairman of the board of International Packers, a subsidiary of the giant meat-packer Swift and Company. In the U.S., Swift had long been the principal King Ranch fat cattle buyer; Bob and Tom had an ongoing relationship.

Tom was a Yale graduate, a football standout who had married Geraldine Swift of the Chicago family that descended from the company founder. Tall, broad-shouldered, ruggedly handsome despite a prematurely bald pate, Tom had a resonant, commanding voice that could convince his employees and associates, by persuasion or intimidation, to do just about anything. The Kleberg-Taylor association, beginning here, wove a thread through the King Ranch multinational complex.

Tom invited Bob down to look around, escorting him on an extended trip through the south central states of São Paulo, Mata Grosso, and Minas Gerais. Companhia Swift do Brasil, an International Packers subsidiary, was already in the ranching business in the Presidente Prudente area, about three hundred miles west of the city of São Paulo, mainly fattening steers for their packing operation. Bob found that part of the country, on the western frontier of Brazil at the time, well suited for his Santa Gertrudis. Its rich red soil, high in iron and balanced in the other minerals, received a fifty-inch rainfall. He became a partner in a joint venture with International Packers by purchasing two properties near the two owned by the company. They then bought a property jointly, merging the five— Bartira, Larenga Doce, Formosa, Mosquito, and Brasilandia—into a unified ranching operation of 147,000 acres. Four of the properties were adjacent, or almost; Mosquito, King Ranch–owned, was about ten minutes' flying time to the south.

KING RANCH DO BRASIL officed with Swift do Brasil in the country's leading industrial city, São Paulo, an overcrowded, underserviced, smog-choked wasteland that made it a pleasure to get out into the country; the flight to the ranches was a hygienic relief.

Clearing, the first step in the chain of developments leading to creating a ranch on a frontier, was done in two ways: the time-honored and the Bob Kleberg–efficient. In the first, Indians moved in, hand-chopped and burned, and planted a crop of sorghum. By contract, they had the right to stay on the land for three crop seasons. On harvesting the third crop, they planted perennial grass seed furnished by the owner and then moved on to another location to repeat the process. The government smiled upon this form of putting to work as many *colonos* as possible. Over time, owners got their land cleared; at the end of three seasons tenants were ready to move anyway. If they stayed any longer, they would need to spend money on fertilizer. The three-year planting and cultivating rid the land of regrowth, leaving behind a clean bed for the new grass.

But this hand grubbing and sowing was too slow for Bob's taste. He had acquired unimproved land as his portion of the combined ranch at around nine dollars an acre. By getting in with his heavy tractors and plows, he recovered the purchase price from timber sales. So he used his clearing technique in tandem with the traditional Brazilian one.

The King Ranch headquarters was on Mosquito; the home was the most beautiful of Bob's foreign lodgings. Designed by his daughter, Helen—though her plan unfortunately had not been faithfully executed—

the house had a long, open pattern with broad porches typical of the region. The garden made it unique. Laid out by Roberto Burle Marx, the landscape architect who planned the new capital, Brasília, it was a year-round rainbow of the ornamental plants of the region, grouped around a pool and a running stream.

The combined properties also formed one of the best breeding ranches of the King Ranch international chain. The soils and climate were so amenable that the 147,000 acres could carry about the same number of cattle as the 825,000 acres in South Texas.

Mosquito had a unique feature. There were a number of small springs that outcropped within its boundaries, which were fenced in such a way that the springs furnished all of the drinking water for the livestock. A number of diseases were endemic to this region, as they are to all of eastern South America, and the principal way they were spread was by infected animals drinking from brooks or rivers that then carried the pathogens downstream to a neighboring ranch. Since Mosquito's water was self-contained, the breeding cows were isolated from this source of pollution.

This hygienic novelty was especially important to Bob; he had spent his life and a great deal of money combating communicable infections that reached his herds from outside sources. Largely through his efforts, the hoof-and-mouth outbreak that ravaged Mexico in the early 1950s was prevented from spreading into the U.S., sparing our bovine herds incalculable damage. So he was agreeable to paying a premium for a property that afforded protection from outside contamination.

Mosquito was bordered on the south by the Paranapanema River, a tributary that flowed into the mighty Paraná, which in turn emptied into the Río de la Plata west of Buenos Aires. Along the river was a rain forest of ancient origin; some of the trees were gigantic even for the tropics. Beside the eroded banks, roots were exposed, pitching the trunks over at bizarre angles. Orchids and bromeliads, thriving in the humid shade, encrusted the trees' near-horizontal trunks and branches. While Mosquito was cleared to put the pastures in grass, to the state's credit this 5,000-acre glade was under the protection of the National Reforestation Bureau and was fenced off, left untouched, a cool, quiet riverside haven where we stopped every day for a camp lunch.

King Ranch's agreement with Swift do Brasil placed management in the hands of our local partners. An American, Francis Herbert, was the president of the Swift affiliate and the overseer of the ranching properties. Francis—the only United States citizen heading a King Ranch foreign operation after Lowell Tash was forced out of Cuba—had brought his wife,

Martha, to Brazil after World War II and they had adopted the country, raising their four sons there. A fast-talking, fast-moving Mississippian with a broad southern Portuguese drawl, he is the best bird shot in heavy brush I have ever seen. His ranching outlook was oriented toward the packing business—a tough, competitive, low-profit-margin trade. Francis did not waste money on anything, but he did take kindly to Bob's admonishment to build and improve the comfortable pair of foremen's homes on Bartira, where he often put up during his visits. Francis was a most enthusiastic salesman for Santa Gertrudis and Quarter Horses; as soon as he had the numbers to do it, he began making purebred animal sales by private treaty and at auction. He was also a leader in the Brazilian Santa Gertrudis and Quarter Horse breeders' associations.

Having passed his entire professional career in international business, Francis knew the ins and outs of dealing across borders as well as anyone in the King Ranch organization. Early in our association, he gave me some advice: "John, in a business like you're getting into, you can expect that about 20 percent of it will be in trouble all the time. It won't be the same 20 percent, but somewhere out there about that ratio will be causing problems. If you can't stand that kind of heat, this kitchen isn't for you." There were times when as high as 50 percent of King Ranch's operations were generating pain in Kingsville, but over the course of my career Francis was near the mark.

THE FOREMAN IN day-to-day charge of the Brazilian ranches at the time King Ranch formed the partnership was a formidable, venerable character named Monte Irwin. Monte was a pioneer U.S. cattleman in Latin America, going down in his youth to work for one of the large English land companies. On his record was a feat I can hardly comprehend: sometime after World War I, he rode horseback from Buenos Aires to Caracas! It took him about two years, as I recall; though I never got him into a mood to tell me about it, in that day before roads and before much bushland law and order, it must have been adventuresome. Monte was schooled by taskmasters who believed in taking everything out of a property and putting the minimum back in, a credo among many absentee English landowners. He brought his flog-the-land philosophy to the King Ranch organization and over it he and Bob came a cropper.

Like any thinking businessman, Bob identified and hewed to his mission: to convert grass, the world's most abundant living substance, into high-quality human food. He accomplished this by converting a coarse, fibrous protein into a palatable, high-quality one, by passing it through an animal. During his work in developing the Santa Gertrudis breed, he experimented with importing exotic grasses to South Texas to determine if he could find one that was a superior performer to the nearly six hundred local varieties. Among the natives, he attempted to select and improve the more promising. This was a preoccupation during his whole life; he was constantly on the lookout for a grass that was better than the ones he was planting. So he gave a lot of time and thought to nurturing to full production his new pastures in Brazil.

Monte, on the other hand, looked out over this abundant stand that Bob had recently planted—and had ordered to be left alone to seed and multiply—and saw the quick profit he could turn by packing in the steers. To him, grass not eaten was wasted, so he grazed the not-quite-established pastures down to a point beyond their ability to recover. The grasses disappeared, weeds and scrub took over, and the pastures virtually went out of production. The money went into the bank all right, but the manufacturing plant had been devastated in the process.

On Bob's next trip, he became grimmer and grimmer as he rode from gate to gate, seeing the tall, rank weeds and spreading brush swaying above the brown stubs of his once verdant stands of bunchgrasses. At the end of the ride he exploded. Monte had, in the eyes of a man whose lifelong guiding tenet was to protect and to nurture the land, committed the cardinal sin—he had overgrazed. Either Monte followed Bob's instructions—managing grass in a constructive, ever-renewing way—or he had to find other grass to manage. Monte relented and did his best under Francis Herbert's tighter rein, but it was the old story of the difficulty an old hand has learning new ways. In a relatively short time, Monte passed into honorable retirement.

After Monte, there was another management turnover, caused by a difficulty we had on all our foreign properties: the young American foreman was working and occupied; his young American wife was lonely and bored. Then, in one of the very few instances in my experience where a couple joined together to make a worthwhile, dynamic life in a remote setting, Pete Emmert and his wife, Mary Lee, carved out a career on King Ranch do Brasil. For twenty-one years, these two native South Texans stayed with it on remote Bartira, acclimatizing to Brazilian ways, raising and educating three children. When they returned to the States, they left a multitude of Brazilian friends behind.

IN THE JOINT VENTURE with International Packers, part of King Ranch's capital input was the nucleus Santa Gertrudis breeding herd. As with the other foreign operations, these were crossed with local cattle to create the herd that eventually stocked the ranches. The Brazilian cattle population is made up primarily of the Brahma breeds, originally imported from India; while we call them Brahma, their proper name in the land of their origin is Zebu. There are over twenty different Zebu breeds in India; in Brazil the most numerous of these by far are the Nellore.

The grading-up program on King Ranch do Brasil began on a base of Nellore cows bred to Santa Gertrudis bulls. Though there were some who were skeptical, feeling that the Santa Gertrudis already carried enough Brahma blood, Bob was confident that his breed would dominate. Four generations later, he was vindicated: the purebreds on the joint-venture ranches were some of the best in the Santa Gertrudis world.

IN TANDEM WITH the grading-up process, the pastures had been re-planted and were again coming into full bloom; all seemed well, but there were always problems waiting behind a problem. The next one that confronted King Ranch do Brasil pointed up for all of us the benefits of taking advantage of work done in one location to solve a problem in another. The background is this:

Early in the 1900s, Robert, Sr., Bob's father, obtained a small seed sample of a grass native to South Africa, a perennial called Rhodes grass. Named for the entrepreneur Cecil Rhodes, this waist-high bunchgrass was an outstanding protein yielder in the semiarid regions in South Africa; the climate and terrain of South Texas are often considered comparable to those of South Africa. The grass took hold on King Ranch in a spectacular way; by the 1930s, tens of thousands of acres had been established in both heavy and sandy soils. The feeling at the time was that the grass problems on the Gulf of Mexico coast had been solved; it was now possible to turn off one-third more beef on Rhodes grass than on unimproved pasture.

Then, with the swiftness and devastation of a plague, the grass withered and died. As nearly as the research scientists were later able to determine, someone in the Rio Grande Valley, on the South Texas border, imported a barrel of dishes from Japan. They were packed in straw and the straw was infected with the Rhodes grass scale. This scale is actually a parasitic insect that feeds on the basal crown and nodules of the grass, extracting its juices and killing the plant. It leaves behind clumps of whitish residue, hence the name "scale."

The straw was apparently dumped in a refuse pit, and the scale began to spread, first locally and then, via the railroad and highway right-of-ways, north to the ranch. Within two years, the Rhodes grass was wiped out. Equally devastating, the scale attacked the native and the other imported grasses, eventually lowering the pasture yields in South Texas over 30 percent.

It was typical of Bob that, rather than throwing up his hands at a seemingly insurmountable problem, he enlisted the assistance of every plant and range scientist at his disposal and went to work to find ways to both combat the scale and develop crossbred grasses that would resist it. It was a long, costly search lasting over twenty years, but eventually his tenacity paid off.

In Hawaii, an almost microscopic wasp had been imported from the Far East to combat a scale in the sugarcane plantings. Its diet was very specific: it fed only on the scale. Through the Texas A&M University Experiment Station, Bob had the wasp imported and propagated at the university's research center in the Rio Grande Valley. When sufficient numbers were available, the little critters, encased and thriving in the nodules of infected grass, were taken up in small aircraft and released by the hundreds of thousands over the pastures. The wasp brought the scale under control, not just on King Ranch but along the length of the coastal plain as well.

In Brazil several years later, we were having lunch at a cow camp where a herd was being sorted through a corral. I was sitting on a carpet of parra grass and, just doddling, I pulled up a runner beside me. There, on the node where the grass branched from the root, was a clump of Rhodes grass scale. I showed it to Bob and Francis, who were seated nearby. The scale, though not as virulent as the strain that infected the U.S., is endemic in Brazil, but no one realized we had it on our properties. Bob gave instructions to have the A&M people send a supply of wasps to the ranch as soon as possible.

Here we have a situation that points up the advantages of using experience from one part of the world for solving a problem in another. A grass was imported from South Africa to Texas; it was wiped out by a scale from Japan; the scale was brought under control by a wasp originally from India, which in turn was exported to Brazil.

ON AN AFTERNOON in 1967, Bob and I were in the apartment in New York when Tom Taylor called. He needed to talk urgently—Bob invited him right over. For the first time in our acquaintance, Tom was flustered and upset. He had just come from an International Packers board meeting where the directors had voted to sell the company to an international conglomerate, Deltec Panamerica. A tool of the American investment banker Clarence Dauphinot, Jr., Deltec was particularly active in Brazil and Argentina, gobbling up undervalued companies or raising equity capital for strapped utilities and other businesses. It appeared that Mr. Dauphinot did not particularly care what type of enterprise he bought, as long as it could be turned over, usually short-term, for a profit. This was the opposite of what Bob looked for in a partner: an abiding interest in ranching that kept the partner hitched over time.

Bob acceded to Tom's plea to buy into Deltec, so that Tom—with Bob's backing and his family's stock—was able to retain his seat on the board. Bob was represented on the board by Leroy Denman. From the beginning, it was not a happy union. Dauphinot had no interest in the packing business or in the ranches—and no interest in learning about them (particularly from his partners)—even though he was now one of the largest ranch owners in eastern South America and in Australia. At each of the stockholders' meetings, he confronted a disgruntled but impotent ranching and meat-packing segment that could take little contrary action in the face of his major personal and proxy stock holdings.

On an October afternoon in 1973, we flew from São Paulo to Rio de Janeiro so that Bob could attend a Deltec board meeting. It's hard to believe, but even when traveling on a private plane you can lose your luggage. The pilots failed to put aboard one of Bob's cases, the one containing his suits. On their return to São Paulo, they discovered their error and put the suitcase on the next commercial flight to Rio, a hop of about twenty minutes. That was it—the bag sailed off into that never-never land where the streets by now must be paved with assorted hard-sided suitcases. I learned later that it was off-loaded in faraway New York, but from there the trail played out. So Bob spent three days in a blazer and khakis among some of the hautest of the haute monde. Then at a dinner for the board and their guests, at the Rio de Janeiro Museum of Modern Art, he had a run-in with Dauphinot's wife, Penny, so his aggravation climbed as the meetings progressed.

The morning following the run-in, the business session opened. Though of course outsiders were not admitted, Bob asked me to join him at the break, mainly to report on that goddam bag. I found him and Tom Taylor and Billy Prince, the principal heir to the Swift fortune, in a huddle in one corner. Bob was in a fury over something that had developed in the meeting and was adding up shares among the three of them to see if they could oust Dauphinot. He seemed to think that they had the number needed to take control, and maybe they did. But Tom and Mr. Prince—a genial, unflappable sort of man—were reluctant to act. If they ousted the management, what the hell would they do with the company? It was a sensible, pertinent question. Bob cooled down, as he usually did when he had had an opportunity to vent his spleen, and the meeting went through to conclusion without undue interruption.

THE DELTEC INTERLUDE had a happy, a felicitous, ending. Mr. Dauphinot did exactly as he had planned from the beginning. He sold International Packers, in both Brazil and Australia, to local buyers. In Brazil we found ourselves associated with a man who I have felt was the finest partner King Ranch had in any segment of its domestic or foreign operations, Dr. Augusto T. A. Antunes. The son of humble rural schoolteachers, Dr. Antunes began with nothing and built Companhia Auxiliar de Empresas de Mineracão Internacional (CAEMI) into one of the world's leading ore extraction companies. When George Moore, the chairman of the board of First National City Bank, learned that Dr. Antunes had become Bob's partner, he told him, "Dr. Antunes is the finest businessman in the world."

Bob's first meeting with the doctor was on the porch of the guest house at Bartira. First off, Dr. Antunes made it clear that he did not plan to take a hand in managing the company; he was leaving all the International Packers people in place and he expected them to continue the things they were doing. "I only wish to come out to the ranches occasionally to see the pastures and the trees and the cattle. I do not intend ever to set foot in one of the slaughterhouses."

He talked with us for several hours that evening—it was an unusual time for Bob; he sat almost mute, assessing his new partner. The doctor's interest in the ranches was in their ability to produce high-quality protein, a dietary requirement he felt a majority of the Brazilian people lacked. He went on to discuss his plans and his aspirations for his compatriots, several times saying that he sought for them social justice. Abbott Reynal, the young president of King Ranch's Argentine subsidiary, had come up from Buenos Aires to join our party, and he asked the question that had been puzzling me: "Doctor, how do you define social justice?"

Without hesitation, Antunes replied, "Social justice is the process of giving everyone an equal opportunity to become unequal." He went on to explain that to his mind it was society's responsibility to see that all citizens had good, equal health care to nurture their bodies, and a good, equal education to nurture their minds. Then they could build on these two resources to rise to their full potential.

Turning to Bob, he said that in a partnership such as theirs, the partners should know the plans the principals had made for their succession. His agenda was in place: he had created a foundation controlled by five or six of his business associates. Further, he had cut his family members out of the line of succession, but he planned to give each of them a chance to prove their worth in the business. Having said this, he came down on Bob for not preparing for his retirement or death; apparently he had done his homework on King Ranch. Bob could not answer; he kept his silence.

At a follow-up meeting in his Rio office, the doctor arranged for our party to meet the key people in his company. He explained each person's responsibilities and directed us to the proper one to see when we had a question or problem. It was an indication of the CAEMI management style that, on their home ground, there were more of us sitting on our side of the table than there were of them on theirs.

DURING THE ADMINISTRATION of Brazilian president Emílio Garrastazú Médici, a government plan was initiated to open the Amazon basin to settlement and development. The first phase called for building two parallel roads, one north and one south of the river, a gigantic undertaking in the wilderness, possibly the most ambitious ever in Latin America. But it was a relatively short-lived dream; only an eastern segment of the southern highway was eventually completed. Under the Superintendency for the Development of Amazonia (SUDAM), the state offered tax incentives, including incentives to develop land, to encourage businesses to move into the region.

Bob was interested in putting together in Brazil a fattening property on the order of Mostrenco in Venezuela; Francis encouraged him to investigate a SUDAM proposal; each contract with SUDAM was drawn up to fit the circumstance. Under the one Francis eventually negotiated, half the land we acquired for a fattening ranch was to remain in natural forest.

Finding the government's conditions attractive, Francis located a 176,000-acre tract in the state of Pará—about two hundred miles south of the river-mouth city of Belém—that had the potential to fatten our steers bred in the south. It was in the Amazon basin but on the tributary Rio Gurupi rather than on the main stream. Fat steers could be barged out to the packing plants in Belém about nine months of the year. A major advantage of this location was that the processors in Belém were five days closer by ship to the European and U.S. markets than those of any other port in Brazil or Argentina.

When João Goulart was president, the Communists were a potent force in Brazil, and they opposed the development on the premise that foreigners should not be allowed to invest in land along with Brazilians. But Goulart had been ousted by the senior military officers and President Médici had his mandate from his brother generals; he felt no need to placate the opposition. The negotiations over transferring a clear title to the land were prolonged, but at last Francis had everything in order, and in August 1970 we flew up from Argentina to the new capital, Brasília, so that Bob could meet President Médici, outline his development proposal, and formally accept the deed.

On approaching the Brasília airport, I had the impression we were landing on one of the plateaus of the moon. In this extremely dry climate few plants grew; the barren, light tan soil was exposed to the eroding wind. From the air, the city looked symmetrically surreal, laid out in a pattern of swirling avenues and arcing lakes. But at a distance Latin American reality intruded. In a barrio nearly as large as the city huddled thousands of shanties, homes of the workers who were constructing the model capital.

Exploring Brasília is worth the trip to its remote locale. "Futuristic" best describes it; the designers tried for a quantum leap into modern architecture. With some of the buildings they made it; with others they fell into one of their dry gulches. The churches I found especially curious, one a gigantic cube of steel girders with walls entirely of blue stained glass. The national cathedral was underground, yet it was surmounted by a dome with an opening at its apex, giving the interior a light, airy feel.

Mr. Marx, the landscape architect, did an inventive job of laying out the government centers and the streets connecting them. He had lost a child in a traffic accident; the street intersections are such that the pedestrian does not cross at traffic level.

BOB GOT ON FAMOUSLY with the president; apparently the government was pleased to have a foreign company with the reputation of King Ranch make an early investment in the Amazon. General Médici had assembled his ministers involved in the SUDAM project; the minister of agriculture reported to him: "I have studied Mr. Kleberg's work around the world and I think he is the kind of man we want to develop the Amazon region."

The president then asked the assembly if all of the paperwork had been completed so that at this moment he could hand Mr. Kleberg a clear title. The minister of Indian affairs replied that only one document was missing—an agreement guaranteeing that the ranch was not disturbing Indian hunting grounds. The president dismissed this, waving his hand: "Oh, let them hunt Santa Gertrudis." This was another rare occasion when Bob was speechless.

King Ranch do Brasil's new, unexplored rain forest was ninety kilometers from the Brasília-Belém highway, a gravel-surfaced, all-weather road that made it possible to truck cattle up from the southern properties. The country was typical tropical forest: a dense stand of mature trees and undergrowth flourished in the 120-inch annual rainfall. Oddly, the humus on the forest floor had not decomposed to form the depth of soil usually found in stands the age of this one. Digging into it, we often measured only about four inches. Also, the ranch was dotted with gravel outcroppings where nothing grew.

The first task was to build a road from the highway to the head-quarters. It was a slow, laborsome undertaking; every nail and bolt, every tractor part, was hauled in from the south, myriad streams had to be bridged, bogs filled with cross-laid logs. The work progressed apace—until the contractor was surprised in bed with a policeman's wife. Upon putting to rest his riddled remains, Francis had to find a replacement, a time-consuming delay.

When clearing began, King Ranch do Brasil bowed to the state's re-peated request and hired a large labor force to do the work with axes and power saws. This was one of the poorer regions of the country, and the government people saw an opportunity to decrease unemployment at no expense to themselves. Eventually about seven hundred Indians were on the payroll, and with this horde came problems.

An immediate, pressing one was their high incidence of malaria. Ma-laria is endemic in the Amazon region, reducing these poor people to a lethargic crawl that makes them incapable of putting out more than a few hours of physical effort a day, if that. Francis devised a program that brought what appeared to be an insurmountable affliction under control. First, he limited access to the property to the main road leading to the headquarters, located near the main gate. Then he set up a clinic, a hospi-tal, and a research and testing laboratory. His company doctors and medi-cal technicians blood-tested every worker on the ranch and assigned each one a number. Every morning the foreman called off the numbers of those who were to have blood drawn that day, in a rotation that assured that within thirty days everyone was retested. Those who reacted positive were quarantined from the rest, put to bed if they were running a fever, medi-cated until they had a negative test.

It seemed to me that the Indians, perhaps not fully appreciating the treatment they were getting, might resist coming into the clinic once a month to be punched with a needle. I raised the point with the doctor; he replied that if the daily card check showed that one or more had not ap-peared, "We send the chaser."

Chaser? To me that was the swallow of beer that follows a shot of tequila. To answer my next question, he called into the next room and an

Indian of singular stature appeared: six feet six inches or so, bullet-headed, broad-shouldered, thin as a sapling. The doctor explained that this man was given the number of the errant worker, and off he went to run him down. After making a trip to the clinic tucked under the chaser's arm, the man usually appeared voluntarily at his next appointment. Francis's program was so successful that SUDAM described it in a pamphlet to guide other companies that were entering the region.

SINCE THE CLEARING was accomplished by hand, there was no heavy equipment in place to remove the logs. In any event, it would not have been possible to get them out, either by road or by water, since there were no mills in the area to process them. They were left on the ground and most of them, along with the undergrowth, eventually went to humus. But the larger logs were strewn through the pastures, presenting obstacles to gathering the cattle. On my first evening on the ranch, we were sitting on the verandah at sundown when a group of cowboys came down the road, headed home. All of them were riding mules—I almost spilled my drink.

"Francis, why is it that while we are out all over the world touting the virtues of the Quarter Horse, on our own property you're using mules, of all things?"

"Well, John, you've got to understand that you have to adapt to your country. In this high-rainfall climate, the pasture's always wet; a horse will get foot rot in no time at all. But a mule, nothing can hurt its feet. Also, a mule is the most sure-footed animal in the world. Run a horse through the grass littered with those logs and it'll kill you in no time. A mule will feel its way along, never stumble or fall. The men know what they're doing—they wouldn't ride anything else."

Bob just laughed. In his youth, he had had a lot of experience breeding mules in Texas.

THE PARÁ RANCH WAS difficult to inspect; there were only a few unimproved roads, graded trails, and the logs and debris on the ground made it difficult to ride or even walk over it. On a visit in 1973, Francis had two helicopters sent out, and Leroy Denman, his wife, Diana, and I were passengers together on a look over the forest that the company did not intend to clear. The pilot was flying at treetop level, between the towering hardwoods on both banks, following the twists and turns in the river. When we had seen enough, he made a climbing 180-degree turn to retrace our course back to the headquarters. We never saw that river again. Circle and zigzag as we might, only tall, dense jungle spread out below us. I was in front, eyeing the gas gauge, and I could see Leroy, a lifelong pilot, leaning forward to get a glimpse of it. As it nudged toward empty, he made a suggestion: "Everyone take off their shirts before the motor quits. On the way down, as we reach the tops of the trees, throw them out. They'll hang there and the other heli will be able to spot them from the air."

Brilliant! I suggested Diana go first. But just as we were about to unbutton, the pilot spotted the other aircraft on the ground. It was a near thing, and taught us another lesson on how little we were able to read the jungle.

BOB INTENDED THE AMAZON development, like the rain forest property in Venezuela, to be a beef factory to fatten the steers bred on the southern properties. But by the early 1970s, the ranches in São Paulo were growing so much grass that they could fatten all the animals they bred. Only a small surplus was available to ship to the north, so to stock the Pará ranch, steers were purchased locally. Around the mouth of the river, other developments were under way that influenced the Pará ranch. More and more people were moving into the region, creating a local demand for beef that consumed all of the Pará output. King Ranch do Brasil did not ranch on these pastures—so laboriously improved—long enough to determine their full potential. Shortly after Bob died, the directors judged that it was in King Ranch's interest to part company with Dr. Antunes. In the property division, the Pará ranch passed to him.

In my opinion, this was a mistake; our partner was possibly the most influential man in the country. A good partner is of inestimable value—as the following instance shows. The most trying thing Francis had to contend with in projecting his budget and cash flow was the capricious way the government put price controls on beef at one moment and took them off the next. When the voters got restless, beef price was used as a political carrot to lower the cost of living, at the rancher's expense. At one point, he was in the ridiculous position of having a price control on the hindquarter of a steer and a free market on the forequarter.

At a Deltec meeting, I was visiting with one of their directors, longtime friend Oakley Brooks. Dr. Antunes had been our partner for over a year, and I remarked to Oakley that in that time we had been fortunate that price controls had not once been imposed. Oakley grinned a crooked grin; had Dr. Antunes not joined us in the beef business, the price situation would have been quite different, he surmised.

THE SUDAM INCENTIVES focused worldwide attention on the Amazon region. One of the developments initiated under the plan was the most ambitious land-utilization program undertaken in modern times, and it was conceived, financed, and directed by one man, Daniel K. Ludwig. For Mr. Ludwig, agriculture was an avocation; his fortune was amassed in the shipping business—amassed to a point that in 1982, when *Forbes* magazine began publishing its annual list of the four hundred richest Americans, he was number one.

Mr. Ludwig acquired a concession of 3.5 million acres on the Jari River, a tributary of the Amazon branching to the north, about 250 miles upriver from Belém. A man of cantankerous reputation that almost equaled his deep pockets, he was chary of entertaining visitors. But Francis Herbert had done consulting work for him in the livestock part of his venture, gaining an entrée that permitted him to take Bob and his party up for a look around. Also, Dr. Antunes and Mr. Ludwig were business associates and friends; Ludwig ore ships hauled the minerals CAEMI mined along the waterways on the east coast.

The strip at the Jari development could not accommodate the G-2, so at the Belém airport we were escorted to the door of an ancient DC-3, the front of the cabin packed with freight. While we stood around waiting to board, Francis told us, "When you pass through that door, I want you to think of yourselves as Alice—you're off to Wonderland."

On takeoff, we had a panoramic view that gave us an indication of the difficult-to-comprehend size of the Amazon. From the waterfront in Belém, one sees only what appears to be the ocean. But the other bank of the southern branch of the river is out there, over the horizon. From the air we could see, across forty miles of water, the island of Marajó in the middle of the Amazon delta. Completely surrounded by the river mouth, this is the largest of a cluster of hundreds of islands—large enough for over a million cattle and water buffalo to graze on it.

As we turned downwind to the airfield at Jarilandia, the headquarters of the Jari Company, we passed over a block of jungle where clearing was just finishing. Using the largest bulldozers available, the workers had piled the debris into a huge cone in the center of the open space and had doused it with diesel oil or some other combustible, setting it alight just as we circled over it. In the still air, an orange column of flame instantly shot skyward, higher than our altitude, and began to rotate—in a few seconds it was an orange and blue tornado, a twisting fire storm that disappeared in the clouds above us. It was a sight to heat the point of an environmentalist's pen, degradation a thousand squatters could never match. The pilots prudently kept their distance; still, the unusual weather pattern gave us a good shaking before it died down and we turned in on our approach.

The first thing we saw as we drove into the outskirts of the head-quarters community of 50,000 workers was a city block of concrete homes going up, all of them at the same time. Steel forms were in place to make a two-bedroom house in one pour, and parallel lines of these forms stood ready to fill that same day. Swimming pools, stores, schools, and churches sprang out of the ground along with the houses, a complete city block a week. While Mr. Ludwig was frugal with his personal accoutrements, such as that DC-3—at the time he was still riding the commercial airline from New York to Belém—he did not stint with his people. The Indian labor force had never before seen accommodations or services like these.

The manager, Clayton Posey, met us at the airport and took us to the guest house for lunch. It was located on a cliff overlooking the river, beau-tifully designed, furnished, and landscaped. From the garden, I looked straight down on a ship unloading at a dock below us. Even on the Jari tributary, the river was navigable for oceangoing vessels.

During the afternoon, we toured Wonderland: Mad hatter, walrus and a swarm of carpenters, cats and bats—the lot. The forest was being cleared and replanted with a variety of tropical pine native to Honduras. This fast-growing conifer was mature enough for a first cut in three years, the second in seven, and a clear-cut in ten. Mr. Posey showed us a demonstration harvest. Sitting before a hectare (2.47 acres) of planted trees was a small stack of logs, about four feet high and five feet long. The stack represented the average amount of wood one hectare of land will grow in one year in Canada. At the next plot, we saw a stack the same height and about thirty feet long, the amount a hectare will grow in a year in Georgia. The final stop was before the stack that had been cut off the hectare behind it, one year's production. It went down the road, over a slight rise, and disap-peared—two hundred feet or so distant. It was a graphic example of the production potential that appeared to make it worthwhile to develop this remote outpost.

A sidelight to this demonstration touched on a matter I had raised earlier: the relative amounts of oxygen released by growing plants and a mature forest. Mr. Ludwig must have had this oxygen depletion issue thrown at him. I was told the scientists here at Jari had made measure-ments and found that the growing pines produced a higher volume of oxy-gen per hectare than the mature stands of native forest.

The plan was to convert these pines into plywood and paper, mainly cardboard. To facilitate this, a state-of-the-art mill was fabricated in Japan and mounted on a giant barge. It was towed across the Pacific and around Cape Horn, up the east coast, up the Amazon and the Jari, to a location that had been dredged out for it in the bank of the river. When the barge/ plant was in place, the mooring was diked and the water pumped out, so that the barge sat on dry land until the timber in the vicinity was harvested and processed. Then the mooring was reflooded and the barge floated out and moved to a new location, where the process was repeated—an ingenious setup. On a subsequent visit, I toured the plant; it was so large that it was difficult to haul in enough timber to keep it running at full capacity. I am not certain they ever did accomplish that.

We drove through palm oil plantations and past cattle pastures to a 4,000-acre rice farm, where we met a Texan who had been involved in developing a new strain of rice on the Gulf of Mexico coast. He had brought the first seed to Jari and was trying it out in model flooded fields— the first crop was about half-mature when we saw it. The Wonderland here was down the road about two miles—a new, complete, $15 million rice-processing plant, ready to receive its first grain. This staggering investment had been unequivocally committed before determining if rice could be grown at all in this region.

FRANCIS TOLD US THAT, some months before, Jari had been having problems with their cattle program and Mr. Ludwig had retained him to make some recommendations. While they had a number of breeds in their pastures, they had staked their production plans mainly on the Charolais, a French breed that is outstanding in temperate zones but not well adapted to the tropics. When Francis completed his survey, Mr. Ludwig called together his managers to hear his report. Francis began by listing all of the fine features they had going for them. Ludwig broke in, "Mr. Herbert, we know all of that. Tell us what we are doing wrong."

Francis replied that he was being asked to be candid and he would be. The whole setup was an unbelievable waste of money; they were expecting to accomplish in one breeding season what they should be testing and researching over three or more generations. Mr. Ludwig cut him off: "Mr. Herbert, I am seventy-three years old and I intend to see this project completed. Good day, Mr. Herbert."

BY THE TIME WE returned to the airfield at nightfall, we were off-balance, dollar signs swimming before our eyes. Bob could only shake his head. Never before had he seen a more graphic example of the violation of one of his most basic tenets—never, never overcapitalize a property.

Jari, though still operating, is headed to a sad, fizzling end—the jungle will someday take back its own. Sad, because Mr. Ludwig sincerely tried to make his dream a reality for the country that had done so much for him. True, he planned to build a $2 billion pyramid to himself, but he also wanted to create a model that would trail-blaze a path into Amazonian Brazil. The SUDAM people kept pressing him over the secretive things he was doing in their bailiwick, not realizing their benefactor had a low tolerance for pressure of any kind. He walked away, leaving it to them to run, and they do not have the expertise, the wherewithal, or the motivation to run it.

ALL OF THESE EVENTS—the setback his pastures had suffered, the ins and outs with his partners—at times had given Bob a stormy voyage in Brazil, but it seemed that at last he had reached calm water. In September 1970, the two of us were ending an evening at Bartira; we had bid good night to the others and were walking together from the main house to the guest quarters. I remember the air was heavy and still; during the day the clouds had begun to roil, the thunder trumpeting the curtain rising on the rainy season. To me and to the night around us he said that the King Ranch was the world's best agriculture organization. "Someday it will create contacts for my family all over the world."

It did for a while—a scant breath as history passes.

THE PRESIDENT'S CAPRICE

In 1963, the State Department put Bob and the King Ranch in an awkward position. In defiance of the military junta that had ruled the country, Vice President João Goulart, through a series of contorted political maneuvers, succeeded to the presidency of Brazil. Goulart, though not an avowed Communist, espoused their doctrine, especially in the matter of land ownership. U.S.-Brazil relations were in shambles, and Goulart had scheduled a visit to Washington to repair Brazil's standing with President Kennedy. Before he left Brazil, he put forward a request to visit the King Ranch in Texas.

In the thick of an ongoing battle with Fidel Castro, Bob almost bolted his traces at the idea of having a Communist on his property—not only because of his own ideological views, but because he knew his moderate-conservative Brazilian friends would look askance at his entertaining their political enemy. But his government was entertaining the man, and a snub would further expose King Ranch to the possibility of having its Brazilian properties seized under a leftist land reform program that was in the making. So a compromise was reached. He would invite the man and his party to Kingsville for as short and as low-key a visit as possible. Bob absented himself from the ranch—he was already scheduled to be away—to avoid any contact that might lead to misinterpretations.

When the party arrived, it was evident that Washington was also playing it low-key. The security was minimal; the State Department had even brought the chief of the small Secret Service detail out of retirement for a few days to make this trip. There was little advance preparation, and the publicity and press releases that usually rained down upon us dwindled to a sprinkle.

President Goulart was affable, agreeable; he seemed to understand the ranch's position. Middle-aged at the time, slight of build with a pleasant, open face, he was lame to the point of dragging one leg—we were told it resulted from a political fracas. His energy must have been indefatigable for him to have campaigned as relentlessly as he did with that handicap. To his credit, during his stay his demeanor was flawless—he seemed to enjoy everything he was shown and in the end graciously said that Brazil was fortunate to have King Ranch as a partner.

The thing that made this rather routine visit freaky in the extreme was Mrs. Goulart—as presidents' wives come and go, she was idiosyncratic, in spades. Either eighteen or nineteen years old at the time, this Aphrodite-shaped beauty was quite like her sculpted counterpart: her head was missing. We were told she had had a brief career as a showgirl in one of the clubs in Rio before just recently marrying Goulart—they were practically on their honeymoon. Rarely in my experience have I come across one so adolescent, even for her tender years.

Apparently the president had noted this in his bride; he had equipped her with a chaperon, a middle-aged woman who quite possibly had been a beauty in her youth but had hardened and weathered under the strains of her livelihood: satisfying the whims of her capricious charges. In the first two hours of our outing, Madame Goulart decided she had seen everything rural she cared to see and wanted to go shopping. Shopping—in Kingsville! Arrangements were made to show her around the Running W Saddle Shop and Ragland's, the community's only department store. A half-hour's walkthrough and she was back at the ranch with time on her hands; thankfully she passed the rest of the daylight hours at the pool.

The second and last night of the visit, a formal dinner was planned; some of the local and state politicos were invited. Just after dark, our group returned from the pastures and were filing into the main house front hallway when we came upon the first lady, just as her companion was telling her it was time to dress for dinner. Madame went into an unbelievable screaming, crying fit—she wanted to go to a drive-in movie! Apparently she had heard of them in Brazil but she had never seen one; now was her chance and a presidential formality was not going to stand in her way. This time her friend could do nothing to calm her—the volume continued to rise. At last Goulart appeared, opened the bedroom door, shoved her in, and marched in behind her.

Apparently the bride still held marital sway. A short while later the Secret Service chief, a 350-pound Irishman with tender feet and a short temper, let me know that the president had relented; we needed to get a party together to head out to the nearest outdoor theater. So in place of sitting through a two-hour dinner with my colleagues and friends, I found myself sitting beside a security man in the front seat of my station wagon; sandwiched in the back were the chaperon, Madame in the middle, and the enormous, grumbling Irishman. The movie was some sort of comedy, I remember. Madame giggled and squirmed and hugged her friend's arm all the way through it, even though she didn't understand a word that was spoken.

In April 1964, João Goulart was forced out of office by a union of the state governments and the armed forces and fled to Uruguay. Later he settled on a ranch in Argentina, in the northern province of Corrientes where the King Ranch also owned properties, and died there in 1968. I wondered when I read of his departure from Brazil if he took Madame Goulart with him.

CHAPTER TEN

ARGENTINE PROBLEMS, PEOPLE PROBLEMS

WHENEVER BOB GOT AS far south as southern Brazil, he continued on to Argentina if he could. The Argentine operation was a relative latecomer to the King Ranch South American group; the four ranches forming the company were purchased from 1958 to 1967. The delay lay in waiting for a more favorable post–World War II political climate—one that would make it possible for a foreign firm to do business in the country without being subjected to the caprices of Juan and Evita Perón. But venturing into Argentina must have been on Bob's mind from the time he began thinking of ranching outside Texas. In the mid-1920s, one of his and Helen's early overseas trips was a cruise to Argentina—they wanted to see, as Bob succinctly put it, "the best damn cattle country in the world."

From the end of World War II to 1955, when Juan Perón was overthrown, he and Evita managed to wreck the beef business, the country's leading exporter. The *estancieros* formed a small, elite group in Argentina, set apart from society's mainstream. Holding titles to the vast acres the peasants worked, they made a large, inviting target for liberal populists like the Peróns. Beating up on them deflected heat from the country's many problems.

Bob watched this development, stayed in touch with his friends who were suffering under the dictator's deliberate attempt to annihilate the ranching community, and waited. Following Perón's ouster by the army, the country began to stabilize, and Bob headed again for the land that had so long attracted him. For Bob, Argentina was the supreme challenge—to his ability as a rancher and for his Santa Gertrudis cattle. It also proved to be a supreme frustration.

Tom Taylor was again a pathfinder, arranging introductions and trips for the two of them and sitting in on negotiations with the owners when Bob selected properties that interested him. Bob told me that he and Tom for thirty days stayed holed up in a suite in the Plaza Hotel in Buenos Aires, bargaining with a parade of local ranchers. When Bob had the essentials for his new structure organized, he arranged a meeting with President Arturo Frondizi. Frondizi welcomed him into the Argentine agricultural community with the wish, "I hope you succeed as well here as you have in Texas and in Australia."

But Frondizi was puzzled over the plan Bob had developed. Bob had told the president he intended to buy properties both in the Buenos Aires region—in their world-famed pampas—and in the north near the Brazil-Paraguay frontier. Frondizi had been briefed; he knew the advantages Bob's Santa Gertrudis had over the traditional cattle in tropical and semitropical climates, where Argentina's leading breeds were not acclimated.

For two hundred years, the Argentine *estancieros* had journeyed to England to buy the grand prize winners at the Royal Society shows, bringing home the world's best British Herefords and Shorthorns, the Scottish Aberdeen Angus bloodlines, to graze and multiply on their incomparable alfalfa pastures. The upshot was, the finest beef cattle in the world were in Argentina. Frondizi logically asked why Bob wanted to place his Santa Gertrudis in the temperate pampas, alongside these formidable British competitors.

Bob had an answer. He planned to buy the best British females he could obtain and crossbreed them, in their climate, to his bulls, thereby producing offspring that would be acclimatized to the northern Argentine semitropics. He also wanted to be able to transport his crossbred steers from the northern ranches to his own verdant alfalfa fields in the pampas, for fattening near the market centers. That made sense and it was in line with the plan he had implemented in Australia and Brazil.

But behind this reason stood another—a characteristic reason for a man of Bob Kleberg's makeup—and he kept that reason to himself. He sought the challenge of taking his Santa Gertrudis head to head with the best, on their own ground. He was confident his cattle could establish a production record in Argentina's temperate zone that would equal that of the world-renowned British locals—and he had bided his time for over thirty years, waiting for the right opportunity to prove it.

KING RANCH, ARGENTINA, was chartered with the parent company owning 85 percent of the stock and the managing partner, Juan Reynal, 15 percent. The Reynal stock was later purchased by King Ranch, Argentina, making it a wholly owned subsidiary of the Texas corporation. Three properties were purchased. Two were a few minutes' drive from each other on the border of the provinces of Santa Fe and Buenos Aires, two hundred miles west of the city of Buenos Aires. The third was in the province of Corrientes, five hundred miles to the north.

In the south, El Abolengo was the headquarters. Its 18,485 acres were mainly heavy black soil that could support either pastures or row crops. The region had a thirty-four-inch rainfall, limiting agricultural plantings to wheat and corn, sorghum, soybeans, and sunflower seed. The home was a large, comfortable, rambling building in the English style, the garden extensive and well tended. Of all the countries where King Ranch operated, Argentina was the one where ranchers had the most livable quarters; their homes were usually large, well constructed, and surrounded by well-tended gardens. I think one of the reasons for this was that, though nearly all of them had homes or apartments in the capital, they entertained quite frequently at their country places.

THE NEARBY PROPERTY, 24,213-acre Carmen, was slightly larger than Abolengo, but with soil and topography of not quite the same quality. There was more sandy loam land here, and the slightly rolling fields contained low spots where water collected in the rainy season, drowning the vegetation.

More lavishly planned than Abolengo, at one time it was perhaps one of the more ostentatious, ad-lib freaky, rural homes in the province. The man who developed it was not a rancher by profession; he was a Norwegian who had made his fortune in the shipping business. He wanted a showplace more than a cattle property, so he built a very large, rambling, Italianate home surrounded by a park modeled on the one at Versailles. The tree-lined paths were decorated with marble pedestals surmounted by larger-than-life statues of voluptuous, inadequately draped ladies in a variety of interesting positions. A large lake had been excavated at the foot of the slope leading away from the house, and here he fashioned a Venice-like lagoon, with piers, mooring pylons, and a fleet of imported gondolas. By the time Bob acquired the property, the gondolas had rotted away around the skeletons of their docks. But in its bloom, it must have hosted a colorful series of outings.

On these two southern ranches, the purchased British-breed cow herds were put together. Again, a small Santa Gertrudis nucleus was exported from Texas to initiate the crossbreeding program. By 1958, the South Texas herd had multiplied considerably over the numbers Bob had to choose from when he first went abroad; the young bulls and heifers that sailed for Buenos Aires were the best ever to leave the home ranch. Bob was off at a fast start to catch up with and surpass those magnificent British animals.

The small, lush pastures on Abolengo permitted keeping the herds close by the headquarters, making possible an artificial insemination program to accelerate the use of the better bulls.

The northern ranch, Aguay, was almost as large as the other two combined—40,215 acres. Although its forty-two-inch rainfall was higher than that of Abolengo or Carmen, its soil was light and sandy, with rocky outcroppings, not suitable for row crops. Aguay was well developed for a property its size, with a comfortable though simple main home and sturdy outbuildings.

Aguay had always been a good sheep ranch, and it had on it about half the number of sheep that it had cattle. Two of the outbuildings were shearing sheds; all of the capital outlays were in place to carry on the wool production. But woolgathering was not a Kleberg forte. Even though King Ranch had a history of wool growing—Captain King ran large flocks of sheep in the 1880s—Bob had an ingrained prejudice against sheep, and on the other foreign ranches he had ordered them sold. But this time he relented and allowed Aguay to keep its flock.

The province of Corrientes—in a region oddly called Mesopotamia—was lightly populated and had not been developed to any extent. In this respect, Aguay was the most similar to South Texas of all our foreign properties, and of course Bob had a feeling for that. The two regions even shared a number of native animals: skunks, wildcats, snakes, hares, tortoises. Prairie bird life thrived; a dove quite similar to our mourning dove gave Bob and his party good shooting. But the most spectacular bird on the place was the rhea, a South American ostrich. Slate gray and about half the size of the African variety, it blended well with the landscape. A sharp eye might catch three or four together at sundown, loping away from the car.

IN FOUR GENERATIONS, the Argentine Santa Gertrudis herd justified Bob's confidence; he was turning off steers of the weight and finish of those his competitors bred. But he did not make inroads into the established

British breed herds on the pampas; the conservative *estancieros* stayed with the animals that had served them so well over two centuries.

Still, in the face of these biases, Bob's cattle had a dramatic, lasting impact on the Argentine industry. By the late 1960s, he was turning off 5,000 weaned steers in the semitropical north, trucking them down to Abolengo and Carmen, where their gains equaled or excelled those of locally raised steers. But the price of the Aguay land had been about one-third the price per acre of Abolengo. His innovation—breeding steers on cheap land in the north and fattening them in the high-priced fields in the south—changed land values in the country: the selling prices of the ranches in the north began to move up on their distant neighbors in the pampas. Thus in the time that Bob ranched in Argentina, the value of the King Ranch properties there doubled.

THROUGH THE NEARLY thirty years that King Ranch owned these Argentine ranches, the problems were numerous and varied, but at their root just about all of them were people problems. In the beginning, Bob chose a local partner and longtime acquaintance, Juan Reynal, to head the company. Juan had been in agriculture, in one form or another, all his life. Resident in Buenos Aires, Juan and his wife, Jeannie, an American from a prominent San Francisco sugar family, were active in the city's social life. Juan was a polo player, an outstanding ten-goal one in his prime, a winning attribute in the leading polo country in the world. A handsome, broad-faced man with a beautiful shock of white hair, Juan had an engaging personality; everyone who met him liked him.

As well connected as he was, Juan had a problem. Whether or not it was actually the case, he was perceived to have been in league with Juan Perón during the years Perón was in power. For the old families, the landowners, this was an unforgivable betrayal of class. When Juan took charge of King Ranch, Argentina, setting up the ranch operations and buying the cattle to stock them, he became King Ranch in the country where ranching was the leading industry. Perhaps he felt a need to reassert himself—to escape the stigma—so sometimes he went his own way, disregarding the instructions Bob had given him. Eventually the boss would learn of these things and call him to account. The Reynals would make a trip to Norias for a few days' roundup or shooting with the Klebergs—Juan with his explanations prepared—and mutual assurances and affections were exchanged. The chain of events was repeated from time to time.

Understanding its origin, Bob tolerated this behavior; he genuinely liked Juan and kept to his credo of trying to change him, to get him to do what he wanted him to do. But sometimes he despaired. On a night in Brazil, where we had just arrived from Argentina, he told me, "The most valuable thing in the world to me is a man who will do what he is told. Lauro Cavazos would do what I asked him, Monte Irwin and Juan Reynal would not."

IN 1964 JUAN MET Bob in New York, lobbying him hard to add a property to the northern operation. Oscuro, 82,745 acres, was located in the province of Corrientes, about forty miles west of Aguay. Sitting in on their conversations, I gathered that Juan had an interest in Oscuro, but it was never clear to me what that interest was. At first Bob was a reluctant purchaser, but when he visited the property, he saw another challenge. The ranch was undervalued because of its dismal past performance; it had never been properly managed. Bob was confident he could turn it around and bring it to its full potential.

Located in a lowland area, on the banks of a tributary that fed into the Paraná River, about two-thirds of the pastures went underwater in the rainy season when the river overflowed its banks. The other third, on higher ground, was covered with brush. One of the reasons the property was underpriced was the calving percentage. The cows produced very few calves, and the previous managers thought this was due to some mineral deficiency—that the flooded land was leached out. Not so. At the beginning of the rainy season, when the river rose, the cows grazed in the water, feeding on the first tender plants that emerged. They could handle water two or three feet deep, but their calves following them could not—they were carried downstream and drowned.

Mr. Kleberg had had experience controlling water flow on the level land in South Texas. He ordered a dike built along the upstream property line that would divert most of the water back into the river. Openings were made at intervals that allowed some of the water to irrigate the lowland pastures without flooding them.

Shortly after the purchase of Oscuro was completed, Juan Reynal had a sudden, massive heart attack that quickly took him. Training under him was his youngest son, Abbott, and Abbott succeeded his father as president of King Ranch, Argentina. Abbott was quite young at the time and had not had the opportunity to accumulate experience in the cattle business. But he had equipped himself by attending Texas A & M University, had an intelligent, level head, and was as prepared as any young man could be in this tragic circumstance.

Abbott's first undertaking to improve Oscuro was to hire engineers to design the dike; he got it constructed in good time. On my first visit to Oscuro, tractors were scooping up the last shovelfuls of earth to complete a ten-mile mound. Bob had explained to me the type of diversion dike he had in mind; one of similar length had proven itself on the ranch in Texas. It varied from three to six feet high and was built with motor graders.

As the plane descended over Oscuro, the boss became more and more puzzled. The dike was visible from quite a distance, an immense slash on the horizon. On the ground, he found a fifteen-foot-high Great Wall of Argentina, massively overbuilt and of course excessively costly. Mr. Kleberg couldn't wait to be face-to-face with those engineers, and when he was, back in Buenos Aires, he turned both the air and their complexions blue. They had not only overengineered, they had staked out the dike in the wrong place.

Faulty as it was, the structure admirably served one of the purposes for which the boss had envisioned it: the cows put it to immediate use. They went to it to bed down at night, delivered their calves on it, and left them with their sisters who babysat (cows have this habit too) when they went out into the water to graze. In one year, the calving percentage rose to a normal number.

Oscuro was acquired with a herd on it, but the numbers were low and they were principally Herefords, not suited to the climate. Abbott was ordered to purchase cows to stock it, local animals with a percentage of Brahma blood. They had just been delivered at the time of our visit. Abbott had them trailed in for Bob's inspection, 3,000 animals strung out below the dike. It was the largest herd of cattle I had ever seen. (When my rancher friends read this, any number of them will look me up to tell me they have seen herds that were larger—"During the blue norther in '20, when all them cows drifted off the Staked Plains," and so on. We cattle people are like that.)

ON HIS INSPECTIONS, Bob liked to have at least one meal a day out in the camp. Abbott did not let him down—the cooks on the Argentine *estancias* were some of the best in the ranching world, and their outdoor *asados*, or barbecues, were their premier culinary achievement. Like our own, they were usually daylong affairs. If the crowd was large, an ox was spitted and roasted whole.

For a smaller number of diners, a calf got a unique Argentine treatment. Unskinned, it was spread out flat on a corrugated tin grill with the hide down, nearest the coals. The gaucho cooks took great pains to see that the heat was never high enough to even singe the hair. The roasting lasted all day, with frequent inspections and criticisms from the guests, self-acclaimed experts every one. The hide gradually stiffened and rolled at the edges, creating a shallow bowl to hold the juices. When the meat was finally done, the guests that were left on their feet were treated to some of the tenderest beef in the epicurean world.

On Oscuro, two of the cooks lived in an outcamp near the riverbank. During the rainy season, their transportation to and from the headquarters was of an unusual sort. The knoll where their homes were located became an island during the months when the river was in flood stage. The water was two to three feet deep for several miles back to the higher ground, isolating them and their families. A horse could wade across the flooded country, but riding him was dangerous—he might bog under the weight or stumble in a hole. So the animal was fitted with a buggy harness and a tow line, running to a small canoe. The passengers steered with a pair of long reins. But the horse needed little direction; going in he headed for the end of the road and going out he homed in on the distant island.

ABBOTT ENTERPRISINGLY DEVELOPED an alternate source of revenue on Oscuro; he diked sections of land on the riverbank and planted rice. Even though Bob had little faith in grain and cereal crops, thinking them in oversupply worldwide, rice had a good market both in Argentina and for export. When the property was eventually sold, the new owners bought it for its proven ability to grow rice.

BEGINNING IN THE MIDDLE 1960s, the Argentine military government began losing its hold on the economy; inflation became rampant and civil disorder followed right behind. Trotskyite groups, uniting with the Peronistas, began a kidnap-and-kill campaign, culminating in the assassination of Bob's friend Pedro Eugenio Aramburu, an ex-president. The military government acceded to the radical demands and called general elections. The unthinkable happened—Juan Perón was returned to power. During these tumultuous years, the CIA and the State Department advised Bob to stay out of the country; he had too high a profile to be exposed to the *Montonero* guerrillas and their kind. We had on our hands a frustrated man. From Brazil he was only an hour's flight to the northern Argentine properties, yet he was forced to endure years without setting foot on them. He did not suffer in silence. But the security of every form of communication in and out of Argentina—the post, telephones, and cables—had been breached. There was no way to get him in and out of the country with any reasonable measure of safety.

Meanwhile, the Argentine beef market was taking a bashing. The 1974 oil crisis raised the price of petroleum products to a point where the Western Europeans, Argentina's best customers, could not afford to import its beef. With the flow of foreign currency into the country drying up, the Peronistas slapped on a prohibition against foreigners remitting profits. During this time, the King Ranch subsidiary continued to make money—not a lot, but it was holding its own. Abbott had increased the grain and cereal acreage to offset the income loss from the falling meat prices.

So the Argentine problem and our problem continued to be a people problem. I have never been able to understand—and many sociologists are equally puzzled—why a country whose population is nearly 100 percent European, made up of peoples whose ancestors brought to it from their homelands, their traditions for self-rule, cannot govern itself. During the years he could visit in the country, Bob followed his habit of giving a cocktail party at the Plaza for his friends; there were a lot of them. They were as distinguished a group as I have ever been among, men who headed the country's largest corporations, many of them in international trade. Most of them had been educated in England or in the States; they had been exposed to the foundations of the democratic process. Yet when I questioned them about their political future, almost unanimously they shrugged. None of them seemed inclined to risk soiling their hands by taking an open part in steering their country toward even a degree of social stability, nor in uniting as a group rather than pursuing their own agendas.

OUT OF THE BUSHLAND — THE MASAI

For decades, the ranch has been a popular watering hole for our U.S. State Department. The western movie, mythicizing the cowboy for all of the world's cultures, developed among foreigners a fascination for our peculiar ways and dress. So the diplomats zeroed in on us as the "typical" spread to show their visitors when they scheduled tours for them around the country. Disneyland was their other choice—it outranked us.

Depending on the visitor's standing—his value in our foreign policy scheme of the moment—he got treatment ranging from an all-out escort, government airplane, Secret Service protection, every honor rendered, down to "Sir, your airline ticket, your itinerary, bon voyage."

One of the most diverting, most exotic, of these Kingsville stopovers was made in September 1962 by Edward Carlow Mbarnoti, chief of the confederation of Masai tribes of central Africa. Chief Mbarnoti's home was in Tanzania, where he was also a member of Parliament. The antithesis of the mental picture I had of these tall, spare, stately people, the chief was short, broad of face and frame, Cambridge-educated, impeccably English-accented and -tailored—about as urbane a visitor as we had entertained. In his party were three of his chief ministers and his State Department escort, a bright, handsome African American who was assigned to the Africa desk.

To put a kind light on it, the other three Masai had the appearance of spending as much time becoming westernized as it took them to pack for the trip. In particular, one of them had my sympathy. Though he was of typical Masai stature—tall, long-headed, fine-boned—every other tooth in his upper jaw was missing. On the quiet, the escort explained to me that these missing teeth had been sharpened. The chief decided it would set back his image in the U.S. to be seen around Washington in company with these barbaric dentures, so just before they embarked he ordered them pulled. Perhaps the teeth had been a badge of office. The State Department briefing paper gave him the title of the chief's disciplinary officer. Actually, I was told, he was the tribal executioner.

The Masai are herd keepers; their livelihood gave them a valid reason to be interested in ranching. But their management outlook was quite different from ours—to them only numbers counted. When they were shown some of our better breeding cows on our first morning out, they were astonished. "Why do you let your animals grow to such monsters! You could feed three cows with the amount of fodder it takes for this one beast." I launched into my beef quality and production lecture—it went right past them. Their credo was, you milk them every day, bleed them once a month, trade them for wives, and cut their throats only when they are too old to produce a calf or to use for barter.

Milk was the staple in their diet; they consumed quantities of it at the table and carried thermoses of it around with them. At home they enriched its protein content by mixing it with blood. This tended to simplify the menu. Our meticulous State Department people routinely furnished us lists of the dietary preferences and prohibitions our guests shared and we planned around them. In this instance, the list of staples was short and the items—meat and milk—readily available, literally on our doorstep. The staff elected to forgo the warm blood.

This I passed on to the manager of the main house, Leroy Curry: meat and milk, plenty of each. But habit dies hard; Leroy was accustomed to putting at least three courses on the table—fewer than three were, by his definition, not a meal. So at our first lunch together, the comedy of clashing cultures began.

I seated the chief on my right and the escort on my left, with the others scattered down the rather long table. A consommé was set before us, along with a King Ranch condiment called picante. This sauce is made by grinding a native pepper, chilipiquin, with a sprinkling of tomatoes and spices. We pride ourselves in claiming that this chili is the world's hottest, and that we are able to down it—in small doses. It was unfailingly served in a divided dish, jam in the other half.

When the picante came around, I warned off the chief and he passed it; apparently the gap-toothed sword swinger did not hear or did not understand me. When it came his turn, he ladled three spoons of picante into his cup, along with the same amount of jam. I was wide-eyed, mesmerized into immobility, like a ground squirrel in that instant before the rattlesnake strikes.

He tried the first spoonful. Little wonder this stoic could survive having half his teeth pulled at a sitting. He bolted upright in his chair, his eyes bulged, his complexion went from chocolate to deep blue, but he uttered not a sound. Rather, mournfully eyeing the chief, he slowly and methodically downed the cupful, spoon after spoon. My face ached at the thought of the effect the picante was having on those recently vacated jaw cavities—it was a display of will under stress unequaled at the King Ranch table.

The next culture shock was only moments away. Richard, serving table that day, appeared at the chief's elbow with a large—very large—tray of sliced roast beef. Chief picked up the serving pieces, smiled at me, and worked his way from one end of the platter to the other, stacking on his plate every morsel, perhaps three pounds. A bit staggered, Richard returned to the kitchen. A rather strained wait while Leroy furiously carved, and the platter reappeared beside me. I took the conventional slice, the escort another, and the next Masai in line finished off the lot. Back to the kitchen, another wait, then a repeat, as Richard ever so slowly made his way around the table.

The escort leaned over to me, "Do you know what's going on?"

"You've brought us a bunch of very hungry people."

"No more than usual. When it comes to food, they have the custom of taking everything they're offered."

At the rest of their meals, the food arrived in small portions.

OUR DRIVE FELL into a routine. The chief relaxed in front beside me, chatting and asking questions the whole time. Behind, the others sat rigid and silent. When we aproached a gate, yards before I stopped, both rear doors nearly flew off their hinges as two of them made a run for the chain snap—apparently being the swiftest gate opener was a way of making points with the boss.

As we rode along, the chief occasionally interrupted his conversation with me to say to the others, "Good place for picnic." In unison, the reply from the back was "Ugh!" It being a bright, sunny afternoon, I imagined he was thinking about lounging in the shade of a nearby mesquite. Not at all. Again the escort furnished the explanation. The chief was spotting calves under trees in the distance and saw the makings of a picnic meal.

After we had been driving for several hours, Chief Mbarnoti expanded on this, when the escort bet him he could not find his way back to the headquarters. "Give me a piece of rope, a box of matches, and a knife and I would not need to find my way." When he got hungry, he said, he would rope a calf, snub it up to a tree, and prepare a meal. Then he would take a little snooze, awake refreshed, and go in search of the next calf.

I hope they left with some appreciation for modern beef production. They left me behind with the feeling that their exposure to our ways would have little effect on their aeons of tribal cattle tending.

CHAPTER ELEVEN

VERSAILLES VIA
FLUSHING MEADOWS

DURING THE 1960s, Bob added to his travel miles each year, without slackening the reins at home. Among others, two time-consuming chores demanded his attention: the cattle work on the two ranch divisions to the south, Norias and Encino, and overseeing the yearling Thoroughbred breeding and training. Added to these were the myriad administrative decisions concerning the things that poured into the office each day. In the decision-making process, as we have seen, he sometimes broke with the ingrained traditions that normally guided him—barging his steers across the eastern half of the United States was one example. On an early spring morning in 1964, he acceded to a friend's petition to do another pretty wild thing with his cattle.

Bob dropped his plan on me the morning after my barge ride up the Intracoastal Waterway with the first steer shipment. Having arrived home just before dawn, I planned to sleep in—the phone rang at 8:00 A.M.—the boss beckoned. I had laid my head on the pillow thinking the barge thing was about as far out as one could get in the cattle business—I was wrong!

Bob had received a phone call from a friend in Fort Worth, Angus G.

Wynne, Jr. Mr. Wynne and his family operated a Disney-type amusement park between Dallas and Fort Worth called Six Flags Over Texas, as well as other entertainment enterprises outside the state. Robert Moses was planning his 1964–1965 World's Fair in New York and was asking each state to subscribe a pavilion. The Wynnes had contracted to build a theater on the grounds to produce a musical, *To Broadway with Love,* and around the theater they planned several Texas attractions. One of these was a building—one large room, actually—where Angus wanted to exhibit a bull. Since the Santa Gertrudis was a Texas creation, would Bob consider sending one of his to New York? I was on my way east on the afternoon plane.

The boss's instructions were to check out the housing, make it into suitable quarters for a 2,500-pound bull, and see that the bull was delivered to the fairgrounds by the time the fair opened, two weeks hence. The next morning, my first stop was the fairgrounds, where I walked into the first of several hundred complications. The room, the bull's domicile, had been turned into a Louis XIV bedroom, lavish with pseudo-French furnishings: large porcelain vases on fluted columns, velvet curtains, needlepoint chairs, and gold-framed oil portraits of the bull's ancestors!

Only moments later, I was introduced to a small, delicate-featured man who was the interior decorator. Of course, I asked him the obvious question: Why the weird setting? He mumbled something about "King— King Ranch, bull king of herd" and disappeared. I never saw him again. Ridiculous as all of us were going to appear—bull included—it was too late and too expensive to rip the whole thing out and start over. I made do—sweating a bit at Bob's reaction when he saw one of his bulls turned into the biggest jackass in the bovine world. But he fooled me in his magnanimity on his first visit, a few days before the fair opened: "Nothing these goddam fools dream up surprises me."

Given an estimate of the crowds and the hours the fair was open, it was apparent that even the gentlest, most even-tempered bull would, in a few days, go off his rocker and wreck the place. Bob ordered up two bulls so that alternately one could rest in a nearby quiet and secluded location. So I had to find a vacant pasture on Long Island, not precisely ranch country. One can never foresee the outcome of a new adventure, particularly one as exotic as this. For me, the payoff for my Flushing Meadows experience was my making a friend and counselor of Max Hirsch. Bob's early instructions to me were, "Talk to Max first."

From the fairgrounds, I headed for Belmont Park close by, to Max's bungalow and office. Gnomelike, hunched behind his desk, little Max (he was an ex-jockey) turned the air blue with his view of the whole setup, then he gave me advice on where I could find the multitude of things I needed: mixed grain, bedding hay, hauling vans, halters, and headstalls, buckets, mops, the works. Best of all, with a phone call to a trainer friend he solved my most pressing problem—where to pasture the spare bull. Frank Horan boarded horses on his small farm near Syosett. I leased for the summer a paddock less than an hour's drive from the fairgrounds.

Even before the gates opened, it was obvious that the bull would need to be attended when there were people in the building. He was too big a target for small boys of any age, especially those millions of New Yorkers of nonagricultural background. ("Hey, kid, punch da moose wit ya whirligig!") Buck and Doe Run Valley Farms was just three hours away, and Helen Groves—who took a great and positive interest in helping her father—found young men with a livestock background who were willing to put up with the long hours for an opportunity to stay a few weeks in New York.

The first three weeks were a twenty-hour-a-day heart attack for everyone in that immense arena. It seemed no one was ready for opening day— but at the appointed hour Moses raised his staff and the gates parted. The unfinished bits had to be attended to in the few hours after midnight when the grounds were closed. Two days ahead of time, I installed the bull in his weird accommodations, hoping a bit of acclimatization would settle him before he faced the crowd.

The bull's name was Hoss, and he had been brought in from pasture in Texas—where he had been keeping company with forty cows—to put up with what we were told would be the world's largest number of people ever to assemble in one place. Bob had chosen the best candidate on the ranch to undergo the stress. Hoss was also a particular favorite of mine. Not only did he have an almost perfect masculine conformation, he was so gentle that when I drove into his pasture at home, he left the cows and came over to have his neck scratched. Yet he was a fine, virile breeder. Hoss faced the mobs and did not once snort, bow his neck, or roll his eyes.

The spare was a bull Bob had recently purchased at auction from his Houston friend Gus Wortham. He was a good-looking animal that had the advantage of already being halter-broken, a training that King Ranch bulls were not routinely put through. But this bull did not have the crowd empathy that Hoss displayed. In a day or two he learned to scatter the onlookers by snorting and battering his head into the welded pipe barrier—he could empty the building faster than the fire department. A tranquilizer appeared in order—we slipped it to him in his feed. But one cannot always predict the effect these drugs will have on large animals; a few of them experience a contrary reaction, becoming hyperactive. That is what happened in this case; in the middle of the night we had to wrestle the poor out-of-his-head behemoth into a van and head for the convalescent pasture.

Day by day, things settled in. Our crowd-shy bull learned to ignore the yammering out beyond his tail by lying down for hours at a time for prolonged snoozes. But this too worried me. Though I had their stall bedded with hay up to their knees, the building was on a concrete slab and they were beginning to get footsore. I ran to Max for advice; 90 percent of a trainer's physical problems are with the horses' feet. He had heard of a trotting track—over in New Jersey, he thought—that had recently covered the dirt course with a springy, synthetic matting so that they could race on rainy days. I located the track and got the name of the new product and its local agent. He was enthusiastic about trying it under cattle, got quick delivery from the factory, and supervised the installation. The covering worked perfectly; while springy, it was impervious to urine and manure. The pen could now be cleaned by hosing it down, sanitary conditions improved, and our bill for cases of air freshener appreciably diminished.

LIKE THE LONGSHOREMEN on the docks, the unions had a stranglehold on the fairgrounds, and they were having a field day. There were the Teamsters who drove the vans, the stevedore types who unloaded the hay and feed, crews to clean the floors, crews to clean the windows (one crew for outside windows, another for inside windows); specialization is a marvelous tool in the hands of union bosses. My stevedore encounter at the Port of Corpus Christi was my only previous brush with organized labor; I was a neophyte in dealing with them. By good fortune, we had assigned to our building a little fellow who taught me the labor relations ropes.

He was an Irishman hardly weighing ninety pounds, with a jug-ear-to-jug-ear grin and a ready wit. Though he was there all summer, I never learned his name. His job was to show up in the morning and sweep out the place. For some reason, he fell in love with the bulls, spending the whole day hanging around them. When his supervisor gave him a going-over for neglecting his other duties, he had himself appointed inside window washer. He helped the handler to clean up, feed, curry—anything that made him feel like a stockman. One afternoon I walked in to find him up on his window-washing ladder delivering a lecture to a group of mesmerized tourists on the virtues of the Santa Gertrudis breed of beef cattle.

The building had two sets of double doors, glass-paned. Another afternoon he was perched in the air on the outside, cleaning one of the open doors, when his union boss happened by. "Hey, there—off da ladder ya little pissant—don'cha know you're a inside washer!"

My union coach obediently climbed down, moved the ladder, closed the door, set up the ladder on the inside, climbed up again, and with his fetching smile stuck his head around the jamb and called out, "Go f—— yourself!"

For me, a lesson in successful arbitration.

Bob enjoyed his association with his friend Angus. He took a box at the Wynnes' theater for the season, and occasionally brought his friends from the track for dinner on the grounds and the evening performance. Our part of the Texas exhibit was a success, packing in the crowds. But the Wynnes learned, at quite a stress to their pocketbook, that crowds do not go to fairs to sit through musical performances. The theater folded in August, taking the rest of the exhibit with it. I faced an immediate, intricate problem. The theater operators had filed under the bankruptcy act, and the Texas exhibit assets on the fairgrounds were frozen—including one King Ranch bull. I went to Angus for advice—I had to see Hoss back to the ranch or not bother to make the trip myself.

"You can't haul him off, legally. Load him at 4:00 in the morning and get in line with the garbage trucks going out the gate."

"What if I'm stopped?"

"Then just unload him, turn him loose, and telephone the creditors to come and get him."

I didn't have a bit of trouble.

THIS THWARTED ATTEMPT to help his friends the Wynnes was of just marginal interest to Bob during the summer of 1964; he had a lot of business that brought him to the East Coast. Belmont Park was being rebuilt, and the New York Racing Association was undertaking to finance the construction. Bob, an association trustee, was attending frequent New York meetings.

William DuPont was Bob's friend and neighbor at Buck and Doe and the breeder of the best Santa Gertrudis herd in the East (his selection criterion: he liked his cows to have nice fat cheeks). He was visiting in Kingsville while Belmont was under construction. Ceaselessly outspoken, Mr. DuPont told Bob it was a mystery to him how the finest individual brains in the banking and investment worlds could form themselves into a committee and make such a hash of financing a reasonably simple investment.

Bob's Thoroughbreds were doing well at the races, but not well enough to suit him; he was expanding his breeding program. With his colleague

James C. Brady—the New York Racing Association president and the secretary of the Jockey Club—he made a trip to England to look over some
brood mare prospects.

Back in Texas, Bob took on other responsibilities. He entered King
Ranch into a partnership with Exxon to develop Friendswood, a community on the outskirts of Houston of high-quality homes and business centers. This was an outgrowth of the trust he put in a select group of his
friends—in their intelligence, judgment, and honesty—permitting him to
act with confidence and alacrity on the propositions they put to him. One
of these friends was Gus S. Wortham, the Houston philanthropist who had
founded the American General Insurance Company, headed it as president
and chairman for over forty years, and developed it into a national conglomerate. Bob had known Gus since the 1920s; their relationship was
further cemented when Gus, late in life, became a Santa Gertrudis breeder
and with his partner Sterling Evans developed a ranching and research
showplace just outside of Houston. Here is how Gus put Bob onto a lucrative real estate adventure.

AT A COCKTAIL party at the Bayou Club in Houston one evening, I spied
Gus standing alone on a second-floor balcony and went out to thank him
for steering the ranch into the promising land transaction just completed.
Gus laughed out loud, a thing he seldom did, and told me the story.

"That was about the goddamnest business deal I've ever been involved in!"

He had called Bob to tell him of a tract of land that was for sale just
north of Houston, 50,000 acres owned by the Foster Lumber Company that
was going on the market to settle an estate. For some reason, Gus was not
himself interested in it and was alerting his friend Bob to what he considered a timely investment. Bob told him that he would meet him at Hobby
Airport at 8:00 A.M. three days hence.

Gus and the real estate agent handling the transaction met Bob in
Gus's limo, chauffered by his longtime factotum and friend, a Negro gentleman of unsurpassed tact and courtesy. On the half-hour drive out to the
property, Gus explained to Bob, sitting in the front seat beside the driver,
why he thought the land would make a prime residential and business
subdivision in the burgeoning Houston market. Bob turned to the agent
and asked him if he could guarantee a clear title. The agent said, "Yes, Mr.
Kleberg, I can."

Bob: "OK, I'll take it. Let's go back to the airport."

Gus couldn't believe it; he pressed Bob to at least drive over the land before he made up his mind. Bob told him, "Gus, I know ranchland but I don't know anything about subdivisions. If you say it's a good deal, it's a good deal. Let's go back to the airport."

So the driver turned around and they headed back down U.S. 59. A little further on, Bob said to Gus, "I haven't had any breakfast. I saw a restaurant off the road a few miles up there; let's turn in."

Gus told him, "That's not a restaurant, Bob, it's a country club and I'm not a member. We can't eat there."

But Bob wanted to go in anyway; when they found the place he got out and headed for the entrance. Gus told his man to go in with him, and from this point on it is the chauffeur's story as later reported to Gus. In the main salon they found a man, a very large man, behind a bar polishing some glasses. Bob asked if they could get something to eat.

"Yo' a member?"

Bob confessed he was not.

"We don't serve nothin' but members. Can't serve you."

Bob asked politely if there was some way to make a temporary arrangement. No. The barkeep was formidable and adamant. Bob was turning to leave when the man called to him, "Yo' face is sure familiar—yo' have anything to do with horses?"

Bob allowed that he did.

"Racehorses?"

Bob nodded.

"Kleberg?"

Another nod.

"Mr. Kleberg, how do yo' like yo' eggs?"

The boss called for me as soon as he returned to Kingsville in the early afternoon. When I reached his home, he was on the telephone to the president of Exxon, Mike Wright. Exxon owned a real estate subsidiary that developed the subdivisions around the NASA Manned Spacecraft Center southeast of Houston; their work there was about done, leaving them with an organization without a mission. Bob was telling Mike that even though he had just bought some prime urban land, he knew nothing about how to go about getting it on the market. Exxon should take a half-interest in it and put their people to work developing it. Mike liked the idea; it came at an opportune time. But unlike Bob, he had to answer to a board of directors; he would let Bob know their decision.

Bob was jubilant—he knew he had them and for his part a $15 million deal had been wrapped up in just seven hours. Wagging his finger in my face, "Let that be a lesson to you. Always keep a lot of cash on hand. The man with the cash can act while the others are trying to put something together."

"Yes sir, Mr. Bob. Always keep a lot of cash on hand."

But he omitted telling me where and how this cash materializes.

BOB WAS ALSO TAKING more interest in government affairs. During the Roosevelt and Truman administrations, he had deferred to his brother Dick, who represented the ranch in Washington. With the Republicans returning to the scene under Dwight Eisenhower, Bob accepted an appointment to the quasi-governmental Committee for Economic Development and to the National Industrial Conference Board, taking an active part in formulating their agriculture recommendations. He was an enthusiastic Eisenhower supporter during the campaign, and Ike reciprocated by opening the White House door to him. In his own view, Bob thought himself too outspoken to enter the political arena, even as a friend and adviser. But the presidents whom he supported from the mid-1950s to the mid-1970s, Eisenhower and Richard Nixon, valued his company.

On one occasion, his plainspokenness surfaced before a distinguished audience. Eisenhower had invited a group of corporate and professional leaders to the White House for lunch, to hear Nelson Rockefeller report on his latest in a number of forays into Latin America to assess the proper level of American aid. Rockefeller, the Republican moderate (meaning leftist to this crowd), had challenged Eisenhower for the party nomination and lost, but Eisenhower had taken him under his tent.

Bob went back quite a way with the Rockefeller family. John D., Jr.'s older sons—including Nelson—were near his age. The Rockefeller-founded Standard Oil controlled Humble Oil and Refining and its successor, Exxon, the holder of the King Ranch mineral lease. So Bob had known Nelson most of his adult life.

Well into his recital, Nelson said, "And now I turn to agriculture." From one side of the dead quiet room came Bob's riposte: "Nelson, you don't know anything about agriculture."

Muffled gasps and snorts, Nelson's boyish, sidewise grin, and a president doing his level best to keep from exploding with mirth.

THOUGH BOB WAS A REGULAR on the Republican guest list, the lunch was but a warm-up for a much later White House spectacular, during Richard Nixon's first term. Invited to a formal dinner, Bob had checked in at his usual Washington lodging, the Ritz Carlton. Bob had at home an older retainer named Conrada. Conrada saw to his packing; on occasions such as this she meticulously put into his jewelry case the accessories for his white tie and tails. Just before 6:00, Bob began laying out everything and found his collar buttons missing. Jack Malone was dispatched to the restaurant to see if he could talk the maître d' out of his. No luck; he was wearing a tuxedo. Then Jack rounded up the bellhops, thrust bills into their extended palms, and hustled them off in taxis to the men's stores around the central city. The hotel manager was not a little put out at his help disappearing at the height of the checking-in hour. But one of them returned with the little brass buttons and a crisis was averted, for the moment.

The suiting-up went smoothly until Bob then discovered that his white vest was not there either—this time Conrada had really blown it. Now it was after 7:00; the shops were closed, even if one could be found that stocked such a special item. A moment's hard thinking. Desperation time—the boss went to the big boss. Picking up the phone, he told the operator, "Get me the White House."

To the White House operator he identified himself and asked for the president—a pause, and Rosemary Woods, the president's secretary, came on the line. The president was dressing, could she convey Mr. Kleberg's message? Bob explained his dilemma and told her, "As often as the president dresses for formal dinners, he must have more than one set of tails. I want to borrow his extra vest." Mrs. Woods said she would call right back; Bob countered, "I'll hold the line."

In less than five minutes, she had instructions for him: "Have your driver let you off at [a certain] entrance; a man will be waiting for you."

Bob did as he was told. A man opened his car door, saw him through the entrance and to a small door just to the right. It opened and Mr. Kleberg stepped in. There stood one of the White House butlers, holding a white vest in one hand and a chilled martini in the other. Mr. Kleberg donned the vest, downed the martini, and stepped out into the receiving line, to take the hand of the grinning, self-satisfied president.

WHEN I WALKED INTO his room the next morning, the boss was in great spirits, sitting in bed with a *leche colorado* in his hand, going over again with Jack the events of the evening. Then he turned to me, again the finger shake: "Let this be a lesson to you. When you're in trouble, go to the top, right to the top!"

THE CASE OF THE PIQUED PROFESSOR

Bob and the ranch teamed to create a magnet for agricultural scientists, drawing them to Kingsville by the score to compare notes with him and to assess his accomplishments on the ground. The largest gathering of a group of this sort was at the King Ranch centennial celebration in 1953, when he hosted nineteen of the top people in their fields. The most dynamic, the biggest character, and perhaps the most eminent of the group was Dr. Jan Bonsma of the Department of Agriculture, Union of South Africa.

Jan was especially keen to visit the ranch; like Bob Kleberg, he had created a breed of cattle to suit the conditions in his homeland. They are called the Bonsmara and Jan, a highly motivated and competitive man, saw the Santa Gertrudis as a rival and adversary. So he made a lot of comparative observations—not surprisingly, the Santa Gertrudis came up on the short end every time.

Discounting Jan's biases, he could easily have been the most astute observer of his time in any scientific field, in his ability not only to see but to interpret what he was seeing. His keen eye had given him the almost clairvoyant faculty of looking at a bovine and determining its level of fertility. For example, when shown a cow, Jan would ask her age. Then his evaluation might run like this. "Right, she had her first calf when she was two, her second when she was three, skipped calving when she was four, will have her next calf in five months, will drop two more, and then go barren." The owner, standing beside him with the record in his hand: "My God, the history's exactly right! How the hell do you know that?"

Jan: "I don't. The cow tells me."

By that he meant that over his career he had correlated every feature of the animal—from her nose to the hairs in her tail switch, including her ears, horns, rise of the shoulder, hair coat, skin condition, bone structure, udder—to her level of fertility. So he could spend hours having cows paraded before him and rarely miss their lifelong reproductive record by the count of one calf. It was a little spooky.

Jan was even more mesmerizing at cocktail parties. Standing in a circle of people, drink in his hand, he would make the round, assessing the guests' level for reproduction. Whether your assessment was high, low, or just average, it was an embarrassment that had no visible effect on the assessor.

Jan visited us a number of times and each time he was a little more dogmatic, a little more set in his outlook. I had given Bob one of Jan's papers outlining his criteria for fertility levels; Bob's reaction was that it was a brilliant combination of keen observation and common sense. But each of them kept the other at a distance; they never became real friends.

Bob was the more tolerant, accepting Jan's basic premises but rejecting his too highly refined conclusions. Jan had little patience with anyone who did not in one gulp swallow the corpus of his work.

His outspokenness once almost triggered an international incident in the main house dining room. It happened that Jan was visiting at the same time as the highest-ranking admiral in the Australian Navy. The admiral and his staff—four junior officers—were at the breakfast table when Jan came in. Following introductions, the admiral said that he hoped to go into the ranching business when he retired. Jan gave him a discourse on fundamentals, including his firm views on optimum nutrition levels for breeding animals. The admiral turned to Jan and told him, "I'll tell you why you have problems with fertility, doctor, you feed them too much protein, too much protein!"

Jan laid his fork beside his plate, bowed his neck, turned purple, and went off like a naval distress flare. "That is the most asinine statement I've heard in my whole life! Sir, you have no business running a navy—you're a blithering idiot!"

The admiral turned ghostly pale; doubtless it had been a long time since he had even been told no, much less received a dressing-down. His poor aides had a collective stroke—but what could they do, confronted with this overwrought civilian? The admiral rose ramrod straight from the table and headed for the door, his cortege by twos behind him. But it did no good—Jan brought up the rear. Left alone over my half-finished bacon and eggs, I heard the last, fading words as the group passed through the library and Jan said: "Stupid nonsense . . ." Within half an hour, the naval contingent had packed and was on its way. But Jan did not gracefully claim the field alone; he mumbled to himself during the rest of his visit.

Our last encounter was typical Bonsma. Jan had been brought back to the U.S.—by demand of our agricultural science community—to give another of his fertility demonstrations. It was held about 150 miles from my home, and I was late arriving. As I took my seat in the bleachers, a Santa Gertrudis bull was in the ring and Jan was in the midst of his evaluation.

"Let me demonstrate the problem we have here with a story. I have at home in Pretoria a dear Jewish friend who did not marry until he was over forty—he has had no children—he waited too late. These animals must be bred early or their libido is affected; they will not perform well in the herd."

The next time he gazed up into the audience, those remarkable eyes spotted me among several hundred spectators. "Why, John, we haven't met in years," and trailing his mike on a long cord behind him he came right up into the stand and sat down beside me. Forgetting the crowd for the time being, "Tell me, my boy, how have you been getting on?"

"Well, since we last met I've married. I was forty-eight at the time—have two children now and I'm expecting my third in a few weeks. What's the problem with that Jewish friend of yours?"

But it was impossible to catch Jan out. "Haven't I told you time and again, if you ever got around to it you would overpopulate that little village you live in?"

ANOTHER WORLD, DOWN UNDER

WE HAVE SEEN BOB'S interests expand in ever-widening circles. Now we reach his outer one; it extended over half of the globe, taking him to a continent that had called to him for over twenty years. In 1931, an eminent Australian, Dr. R. B. Kelley—head of the Division of Animal Health and Production, Commonwealth Science and Industrial Research Organization—visited the ranch and was mightily impressed with the Santa Gertrudis, even at that nascent stage in its development. He took back to Australia a bull that he bred into his experiment herd; the progeny indicated that these adaptable cattle were suited to the hot, dry Australian outback. Dr. Kelley spent time in the cow camp with Bob, and they corresponded when he returned home. Kelley was one of the major early influences on Bob's eventual decision to ranch in Australia.

The people suited Bob too. Most of their agriculturalists were stockmen, tall, rugged, open-handed and open-minded, outgoing, and by and large great swillers. It is often said that Australians and Americans are closer kin than Australians and the English.

But Bob's empathy for these fraternal people did not deter him from taking a thoughtful, step-by-step approach to making what eventually became his largest investment in a foreign country, the laurel wreath that crowned his later years. Above all, people were on his mind. He realized that while he could furnish the capital assets—the livestock—and the finance to start up, at the distance he would be from the operation, he could not be active in day-to-day management. His input would be confined to training and long-range guidance. He needed sound, intelligent, energetic partners to run the business on the ground. As described in Tom Lea's privately printed *In the Crucible of the Sun*, he went about finding them this way:

Through the National City Bank in New York and his friend Lew Douglas, former ambassador to the Court of St. James's, Bob was introduced to W. S. Robinson, Australia's premier businessman, entrepreneur, adviser to governments, intimate of Winston Churchill. W.S., a soft-spoken man whose intellect was as keen as that of any international figure in our century, had already assessed the potential for the Australian livestock industry that Bob Kleberg and his Santa Gertrudis might have. Acceding to Bob's request at their first meeting, he put into writing his thoughts on his country's agrarian future, the part King Ranch might play in it, and his recommendations for young, proven partners who might be directed by Bob in managing a complex breeding and beef-producing enterprise.

Robinson's choices were Sir Rupert Clarke, baronet, a pastoralist and investment banker whom Bob had already met; Peter Baillieu, W.S.'s grandson, a trained property manager; and Sam Hordern, one of Australia's leading businessmen-agriculturalists. Bob made minor partnership agreements with the three of them, with the caveat that W.S. hold the proxy to vote the King Ranch majority shares in the newly formed companies. Thus seventy-five-year-old Mr. Robinson had the clout to see that his recommendations were carried out in the way he had led his ally Bob to expect they would be carried out.

In choosing Peter and Sam, W.S. surrounded Rupert with his close and distant kin. W.S.'s grandson Peter was married to Edwina Hordern, a niece of Sam's. Though Rupert was not a branch of that family tree, by background, training, and temperament, he could more than hold his own in the company.

Regardless of bloodline, the partners were a good mix. Rupert had status in the financial world. His title was one of the few hereditary ones on the continent, a symbol of consequence among English-minded Australians. Peter was young, movie-idol-handsome, ranch-educated, and one of the most popular young men in the country.

Sam was "Mr. Outside." At forty-two the oldest of the three, he had an effervescent charm, a ready wit, a hollow leg, and was at the top of the agriculture and business worlds. Among other civic and professional responsibilities, he was the managing director of the Sydney Royal, Australia's premier livestock show—his connections extended right across his homeland.

The group stood apart from many of their compatriots in one sense: they were descended from the first settlers in Australia, and their ancestors—as they proudly pointed out at every opportunity—were convicted criminals exiled from England. During one of Sam's visits to Kingsville, Bob Wells's daughter married; Helen and Bob brought Sam to the wedding. During the reception in the Wellses' garden, Sam was summoned. Among the guests that evening was Mrs. Sarita K. East, the sole surviving direct descendent of Captain Mifflin Kenedy, the partner of Captain King. Mrs. East, along with her now deceased brother, had inherited Captain Kenedy's ranch, the second-largest in Texas, the 450,000-acre La Parra, located between the Laureles and Norias divisions of the King Ranch.

Mrs. East, an elderly widow, had been told that there was an Australian about, and she asked to meet him. During the course of their chat, she leaned toward Sam and gently asked, "Now, Mr. Hordern, I've been told that you Australians are descended from convicts. Is that true?"

Sam was ready, well equipped. "Yes ma'am, Mrs. East. All us Horderns are descended from convicts. Here, let me show you." And he opened his billfold, extracting an ancient tintype showing a line of seedy-looking emaciates shackled hand and foot to long chains.

"If you'll count three in from the left, Mrs. East, that fella standing there is great-great-grandfather Hordern. And you see there, he's wearing those shackles on his hand and foot—you know, after a time they rubbed those terrible dark, horny calluses.

"Will you believe it, Mrs. East, all us Horderns have inherited 'em, hereditary shackle marks!" And he pulled back his cuff in the subdued light to show the mesmerized lady what was probably his leather watchband.

A lifelong ranchhand, Mrs. East knew more about genetics than that, but she was far too genteel to call her new acquaintance to account.

BOB DID NOT LIMIT his business connections to this group. His International Packers friend, Tom Taylor, had already contacted him, indicating an interest in joining his company in some way with King Ranch in any future Australian venture. The partnership they formed, Associated Stations Proprietary, was separate from King Ranch, Ltd., (Australia) Proprietary, Ltd., the majority-owned King Ranch subsidiary. King Ranch, Australia, became the breeding enterprise and Associated Stations a commercial cattle-breeding and fattening operation. Between them, they showed Australian ranchers the way to improve their herd productivity—by using Santa Gertrudis bulls.

Through Associated Stations, Bob acquired another minor partner who was to have a lasting, judicious impact on the new company's business in the Australian north. Arthur Bassingwaighte was one of the top young men in the Swift packing operation in Queensland; he moved into management of the joint properties acquired by Associated Stations in the western part of the state and in the Northern Territory, eventually becoming the chief of the whole King Ranch investment down under. Though they sometimes had divergent interests and personality clashes, the partners were faithful in carrying out Kleberg mandates, and over a period of three decades they built the premier business in the King Ranch chain of foreign enterprises.

THROUGH A SERIES OF happenstances, I never traveled to Australia with Bob; though he was going out regularly and I was too, we never traveled together. When his friends accompanied him on his foreign property inspections, Bob generally did not say too much about the things they were seeing, letting their eyes be their primary receptors. Let me record my impressions from my first visit, in May 1960. They form a mosaic, a monument to a towering figure in Australia's agricultural advancement.

In 1960, King Ranch, Australia, operated seven ranches, or stations, located in Queensland, the leading commercial cattle state, in New South Wales on the temperate, more settled eastern seaboard, and in the largely undeveloped, unpopulated Northern Territory. My first stop was at Risdon, in southeastern Queensland, the home for the Santa Gertrudis imported from Texas. From the time they arrived in 1953, it had not rained on them; Australia was experiencing the worldwide drought of the 1950s that devastated the ranch in Texas. Bob was able to get only two shipments of purebred bulls and heifers—less than four hundred head in all—into the country before 1956, when a health-related ban was imposed on importing all livestock. To put this incomparably valuable breeding nucleus into the best pasture and climate on the continent, they were at this time being trucked to a new headquarters he had purchased just south of Sydney, where the seasons were gentle and predictable.

Despite the harsh conditions they had undergone, the first Santa Gertrudis (called "Santas" by the locals; "Gertrudis" is a tongue twister for

Australians) had been well received. Just months after they arrived, Bob directed his partners to hold an auction of ten of the imported young bulls. They brought an average of $2,595 a head, at that time believed to be an Australian record for any breed.

FOUR HUNDRED MILES TO the northwest of Brisbane lay the main commercial and fattening properties in eastern Queensland, a series of three stations—Elgin Downs, New Twin Hills, and Avon Downs—with an aggregate of 600,000 acres. The manager, Jack Cooper, gave me a short course in producing and selling Australian beef. Down under, ranches in the 1950s were not equipped with scales; unlike U.S. beef, which is sold by live weight, Australian beeves were sold by their weight skinned, dressed, and hanging in the packinghouse coolers. Generally the animals on the larger ranches were contracted on the property, meaning that both the buyer and the ranch manager had to be able to estimate, by looking at the animal in pasture, the weight of beef it would yield hanging in the locker.

On my first day with Jack, I went along with him to offer to a buyer 150 steers that had been gathered in a field near the house. He looked them over and wrote down his dressed weight estimate; the agent did the same. They agreed on a price, and the steers went off to slaughter in Rockhampton, on the coast about 150 miles away. Two days later we got the report. Jack had missed the average dressed weight of each steer by 1½ pounds! Mind you, he had to figure their total body weight in the pasture, how many pounds they would lose making the trip to the processor, then come up with a percentage of their live weight that was made up of muscle and bone. I could not believe anyone had an eye like that, but Jack just scoffed at me. "If I missed by three pounds, I'd hang up my hat and quit."

Jack was having his first encounter with Santa Gertrudis and I was curious as to how an older man, whose lifetime experience was with the traditional British breeds, would take to them. We were walking out to a water lot one morning to see some of the first purebreds he had received from Risdon, multiplications of the imports.

"How do you like them so far, Jack?"

"Bloody good, but I'm having trouble with ticks."

I could hardly believe it. Ticks transport a type of cattle fever from one animal to another by drawing blood from a sick cow and then biting a healthy one. All over the world, Santa Gertrudis had established a reputation for being resistant to ticks and other parasites, and right here on our own property we were having trouble. I told him so.

"No, no, you misunderstand me. This part of Queensland, it's ticky country and I've always felt cattle should carry a few ticks to ward off the fever." Jack's problem: "I can't keep any ticks on the bloody things!"

He had devised an ingenious arrangement to overcome his dilemma. Each evening he cut off the water in their trough, letting the cows drink it dry. The next morning, as we were doing, he went out and turned it on. The cows were standing around waiting, and as soon as they heard the splash they rushed the trough. Jack had put into the Santa Gertrudis herd four Shorthorn cows, long-haired old mothers that were covered with ticks under their matted coats. They nuzzled and pushed their way up to the water between the other cows, and in so doing rubbed up against them on both sides—transferring a few ticks in the process. Jack was making use of a sound medical practice, developing immunity by exposing healthy animals to a pathogen in small doses. He didn't know why it worked, but he knew that it did.

FROM ELGIN I FLEW SOUTH to see the national cattle show, the Sydney Royal. Our headquarters in this part of the country was the small property Milton Park, 2,997 acres in beautiful, rolling country quite like mother England, just seventy miles southwest of Sydney, the safe haven for the imported Santa Gertrudis herd being trucked down from Queensland. Peter Baillieu, his wife, Edwina, and their children lived in the English manor–style home, the kind in which Bob felt comfortable. Edwina's father, Anthony Hordern, had spent a lifetime developing the property, collecting trees and shrubs from over the world to create around the main house the most renowned garden in Australia.

While Milton was a secure sanctuary, the year-round green grass was a mixed blessing. It is bad for a breeding cow to get too fat; fat has a tendency to absorb the hormones that control her estrous cycle. Normally a mother cow's system will give preference to her developing fetus, or to producing a quantity of milk to nurse her calf, or both, over laying on fat. But when pasture conditions are extremely good and she is an efficient converter, she has the capacity to do all these things, and this is counterproductive; she becomes too fat to rebreed readily. This was the situation at Milton Park; fortunately it did not overly affect the herd.

ON MILTON I EXPERIENCED another first: an earthquake. Australia is probably the oldest continent in the world, and the most stable—earthquakes are almost, but not entirely, unknown. Just before 7:00 one morning, I was just putting one leg over the side of a four-poster bed up on the second floor when a rumble began, quite like a distant explosion, and the bed took off across the room. I managed to bail out and get to the window, to see the giant sequoia and eucalyptus trees swaying from side to side until their trunks were almost parallel with the ground. Time to get outta there—I headed for the door across the heaving floor, an oversized antique armoire chasing me and plaster raining down from the ceiling. As I reached the head of the stairs, it stopped; it had lasted forty-five seconds at most.

In the eerie quiet, I could hear Peter Baillieu calling to me from the front lawn. There I found him, all six feet six of him, dripping water and skimpily wrapped in an undersized face towel—he had been in the shower. Howard Douglas, the manager, was in his pajama bottoms with shaving cream over half his face. The only calm, collected one of the lot was Edwina, standing in the driveway fully dressed, svelte of figure and face, her two children beside her. We were exchanging experiences when Howard suddenly remembered he had a wife named Ruth, seen last in the bathtub. He flew up the front steps and flung open the screen door and there she was, soaking wet, struggling with a dress she had managed to get into backward. In the ensuing fracas, Howard lost several square feet of skin—Ruth took it off him over his abominable earthquake conduct.

When we made an inspection, we saw that the catastrophe was no joke. Fences and power lines were down everywhere, and several of the brick homes around the headquarters were partly or completely destroyed. Fortunately everyone was up and about, so there was no loss of life. The only injury was to one of the herdsmen, by a miracle only slight. He had been just opening a gate to turn out the heifers when the first tremor struck and three hundred females—half of last year's calf crop—stampeded over the top of him.

FROM SYDNEY I AGAIN turned north, headed for Brunette Downs in the Northern Territory. This station was 4,730 square miles in one block, 3,027,200 acres—one of the largest, but not the largest, single holding in the country.

In 1959, following Bob's inspection and assessment, his Australian partners negotiated the lease purchase of Brunette Downs from the previous owners, in the midst of the worst drought this part of the Territory had ever experienced. The normal annual rainfall was only twelve to fifteen inches; the year before, Brunette had gotten five. At that time there were just forty-six water wells on all the vast ranch. While there were good stands of dry grass remaining at a distance from the water, the pastures had been grazed out in a circle of four to five miles away from the wells. A cow had to walk nine miles or more in a round trip to grass, and then wait a day to a day and a half in a bovine traffic jam to get up to the water trough. The old ones and the calves couldn't survive that stress—half the herd, 30,000 head, perished. Bob took a gamble, at one of the longest odds in his long gambling career, that he could save the rest. He won—it rained.

Immediately, a water well contractor was hired to operate an innovative drilling rig, a rotary that used compressed air instead of water to flush out the cuttings. It drilled 110 wells in just over a year; drought was no longer a mortal threat. Anywhere on the ranch, an animal was no more than seven miles from water. During King Ranch tenure, Brunette went through equally bad dry spells, but not an animal was lost from lack of water or grass.

A CHARTER PLANE WAS waiting at Mount Isa, a frontier mining town in western Queensland—it would take me to Brunette. The pilot and I took off at midafternoon with a cargo of one Swedish cook, who had come into town to order supplies and was taking back to the station a full load of the local beer.

I had never seen a landscape like the one below us. Except for a very occasional fence, the hand of man was not visible on the level ground— there was not a house or a tree, a road or a moving vehicle, not even a stray animal. We may as well have been flying over the surface of a distant planet. The country was so flat that at the Queensland–Northern Territory border we flew over the world's longest straight-line fence, three hundred miles without an angle or bend.

I am a pilot and the gas gauges told me we had been too long in the air; the sun was setting ahead of us and there was no checkpoint on the ground to indicate we were approaching the Brunette airstrip. The young pilot beside me, almost a complete mute until now, told me he was looking for two small lakes just beside of the house, the only surface water in that part of the Territory. I glanced over my shoulder to see if the cook was conscious enough to spot a familiar landmark and I saw two dark, shiny blobs several miles behind us. We did a 180-degree turn and landed just at last light. Had we run out of gas—as we seemed determined to do—I think we could have safely set down even by moonlight, so flat and devoid of brush was the countryside. But what a long, dry walk to headquarters it would have been, guided by one hungover Swede.

Brunette Downs was more than a professional experience; I think it would have charmed, humbled, intimidated, beguiled, mesmerized, any thinking person who took the time to look at it. Its size alone was difficult to grasp by any terms, especially management—individual pastures enclosed over half a million acres each. Given a proper breed of cattle, three elements govern production on country like this: soil type, the perennial grasses, and rainfall. The soil was of fair strength like that of most semi-deserts; the native grasses—Flinters and Green Mitchell among them—were excellent. The Mitchell was especially good; the stands cured in the dry heat without rotting. Bob had staked his lease-purchase gamble largely on it—a strong grass plus adequate well water were the best drought insurance. The rainfall was a varied, chancy thing. Overall, the ranch could support about one animal on each 50 acres, though it was never stocked that heavily.

ADDED TO THE INSUFFICIENT number of water wells, the improvements were generally run-down when the King Ranch took over the lease. Land tenure in Australia is quite different from that in the U.S., and Bob was never entirely happy with it. In the northern areas particularly—Queensland, the Northern Territory, and Western Australia—nearly all of the land is owned by the state and territorial governments and put out to lease. At this time, the term of the Brunette lease was fifty years, the lease payments a very reasonable $1.12 a square mile. But when thinking about capital improvements, the lessees ever had on their minds that the money they were spending was not going into improving property they owned. The system had the long-term effect of holding back agricultural investment.

On Brunette, Bob did not let the leasing encumbrance restrain him from putting the place in first-class order. To get the fences, water wells, roads, and pastures into shape, he and his partners spent $2 million. The headquarters was particularly run-down. Bob felt that if he was going to ask people to live in this sort of remote outpost, he was committed to furnishing them with the most comfortable quarters he reasonably could. The manager's spacious home was in good shape; the other buildings were razed and replaced. With an exception. A tribe of aborigines lived in their own compound within walking distance of headquarters. Their houses were corrugated tin sheds that must have been like roasting ovens in the summer, but no amount of coercion could force them to give them up.

THE MANAGER, REGINALD GEDDES, greeted me at the airstrip, one end of which lay within fifty feet of his side porch. Though Reg had spent his working life in the territory, he had been employed by the ranch only a few months. Short for an Australian, stocky, taciturn, not given to throw away smiles, he was known to his young hands as the Napoleon of the Outback.

On my first evening, I sat down to dinner with Reg, his wife, his daughter, and the head stockman. As the World War II patriotic song had it, "There will always be an England"—or at least an English menu. My lifetime travels have convinced me that no matter where you drop an Englishman down, he will set an English table. Here we were, in a remote desert in the early autumn, the midday temperatures still climbing to 110 degrees and hanging near there into the evening, and we were sitting down to courses of roast beef, pudding with gravy, boiled vegetables, the lot.

Mrs. Geddes was determined to teach her aboriginal maids to serve at table—she sought the unobtainable. The girls were too shy to pass the dishes alone; they came in two at a time, even if carrying only a butter dish—constantly giggling, one hand over their mouths—to Reg's rising annoyance. By contrivance or otherwise, they managed to get themselves dismissed by tipping the hot grease in the roast platter into Reg's lap.

Morning came abruptly; a 6:00 siren got the day under way. Breakfast, then a fifteen-mile drive to the cow camp. The rain fell in the summer months; we were in the dry season and the roads were excellent, even though they were only a track as wide as an auto. There were thousands of miles of these trails; a heavy-duty maintainer, running from dawn to dark, could get over them only once a year. Throughout the Territory the Brunette road grader driver, Blader Jack, was famous for his lifestyle; his machine was his home. Two weeks of the year he brought his equipment into headquarters for an overhaul and went off on an extended bender.

Jack's rig suited his never-ending work. The maintainer towed a small house trailer of a high-wheeled, round-roofed design, like the ones in gypsy caravans. Following the living quarters was an open, four-wheeled flatbed carrying the fuel, tools, and supplies. Suspended between the wheels of the house trailer was a small, open platform. Jack always had three or more dogs in his troupe, and they spent their days trotting along in the shade of the caravan. When they tired, they jumped on the platform for a rest.

The most ingenious part of the two-car train was a wire chicken coop under the flatbed, home for a bantam cock and half a dozen hens that kept Jack supplied with fresh eggs. During overnight stops, he turned them out to scratch and exercise. At first light, Jack started the maintainer— squawks, fluttering wings, and the little birds ran for their box. While the engine warmed Jack climbed down, shut the door, and was on his way.

Jack told us that one morning about two weeks earlier he had pressed the starter, unthinkingly put the machine in gear, and driven off. He had bladed about two miles when he thought of his brood and rushed back to the coop. It was empty. But on the horizon down the road he just made out tiny dots, his flock waddling after him. No eggs for dinner that night, he said—exhausted hens.

ON BRUNETTE, I SAW my only Australian roundup in open pasture, Texas-style. This particular morning, the men were cutting out three-year-old steers to begin their journey to market. They didn't have the horses or the skills of our Latin cowboys. Often a steer would start his run on one side of the herd, dash straight through the middle with an aboriginal rider in howling pursuit, go out the other side and circle around—and do the whole chase over again. But they eventually managed to sort out the number they needed to make the long trek to market on the coast.

All of the cattle—bulls, cows, calves, steers, and spayed heifers—ran together. There were few small pastures available to segregate ages or sexes. When the market cattle had been sorted out in the roundup, the rest were trailed to the nearest corral. This set of pens was an ingenious thing, portable, made of sections of welded pipe. A ranch this size would have required dozens of pens to have one within walking distance of all the cattle. This portable contraption could be knocked down, stacked on a flatbed truck, and reassembled at the next cow camp.

The pens were the place where the branding, inoculating, castrating, and horn-tipping were done. Quite unlike our agile Quarter Horses, a twelve-year-old Percheron, a veritable tank of an animal, was used for roping. An aborigine prodded it over to the nearest yearling and draped, rather than threw, a stiff rawhide lariat around its neck. The patient horse, equipped with a horsecollar to which the rope was attached (Australian saddles, like British ones, have no horns), dragged its catch over to a set of panels that had, between them, two posts set close together. The rope slid along a panel, fell into the slot formed by the posts, and the yearling was pulled snug up against the boards; then the routine was carried out in the usual way. It went surprisingly fast; the crew of jackeroos was branding eighty to ninety head an hour. But somehow it seemed less colorful than the running, rope-swinging, dusty, noisy roundups in Texas. A bit of spontaneous excitement did occur when the half-trained Percheron wouldn't rein in and occasionally pulled a large animal over the top of the branding poles.

A DIGRESSION HERE, to examine the jackeroo system of training young men in agriculture, a custom quite uniquely Australian.

When a young man, raised on his family property, completes his education, he usually does not return home to work under his father. It is thought that with his mother close by, he won't get knocked about as he should to improve his retention level. So he is sent to another property and placed under a manager, usually a friend of the boy's father, who sees to it that he is treated like any other hand. Most surely, the manager himself has passed his own apprenticeship in the system. The trainee, or jackeroo, is paid peon wages for dawn-to-dusk work six or seven days a week, in rotation doing all the chores about the place. He stays at it two to four years, usually on the same property though sometimes, to get a varied experience, at two or three locations.

It's a great system for everyone. Aside from the training the young man ingests, it is a lifesaver for the ranch owner. With a population of some 15 million, two-thirds of whom live within 150 miles of the east coast, the bulk of this continent—the size of the mainland United States—is virtually uninhabited. Australia's most critical shortage is people, meaning the young person entering the labor market has the occupational spectrum to choose from. By far the majority decide to stay in the settled, civilized east. This would leave the agricultural sector inoperative were it not for the jackeroo system.

Brunette Downs was the first choice for a large number of these youngsters. Its remoteness and its size gave it a reputation somewhat akin to that of the King Ranch in Texas; it was renowned long before the King Ranch acquired it. So Brunette had a waiting list for jackeroo bunks, and at the time of my visit nineteen were employed. A new dormitory with a kitchen had been built for them, so they were pretty well provided for when working around the headquarters, quite different from sleeping on the ground in the camps. They were a fine crowd of brawny young extroverts with a lively curiosity about everything Texan.

ASIDE FROM A FEW permanent older men, often half-caste, the rest of the labor was drawn from the tribe of aborigines that lived on Brunette. The able-bodied men who were willing to work were on the payroll; the more shiftless lived on the dole. The federal government had an agency like our Bureau of Indian Affairs that cared for what the voters in the more civilized parts of the country considered a national treasure; one of the bureau's mandates was to preserve the aboriginal ways. These quaint tribal customs sometimes ran counter to the white work ethic.

For instance, one of the most sacred aboriginal ceremonies was the walkabout. Several times a year, usually when the cattle were gathered and a roundup was about to begin, the manager would sound the 6:00 siren and not an aborigine would appear. Checking the camp, he would find that the tribal elders had decreed a walkabout; clothes were piled in the doorways of the huts and there was not an able body around. They had gone native by going naked into the bush.

For days, the tribe wandered aimlessly, the men stopping at intervals to squat in the shade for a smoke and a natter while the women and children gathered supplies—chasing down lizards, gathering seed, grubs, plants, whatever. When they had had enough of their old ways, they returned to camp, put on their clothes, and went back to work.

While on Brunette, I was told a tale of the kind of bureaucratic nonsense that at one time or another infects every government. Since this part of the country was arid and tropical, it had the typical desert cycle of being fiercely hot during the day and freezing at night. The manager was notified that the agency wanted to study the metabolism of the aborigines on a walkabout: how was it possible that without clothes they could tolerate the daily cycle of extreme heat and cold? Would the manager kindly inform them the next time the Brunette tribe went off on one? He dutifully radioed when next he found the village deserted.

A day later, a civil service plane arrived loaded with the scientists and a ton or two of gear. Their equipment included an infrared scope, just recently developed by the military to provide night vision through specially equipped binoculars. Off the party set on the trail of the wandering aborigines. Their plan was to keep their distance in order not to upset the tribal routine, so during the day they stayed over the horizon. But after sundown on the first evening out, they crept in as close as they dared and set up their infrared apparatus. This is what they saw.

The women scooped out a shallow bowl in the ground and the children climbed in first, then the women, and the men on top. The pack of dogs, a dozen or more of them—mangy, flea-ridden creatures that followed the aborigines about—lay down around the rim. The team took turns operating the spotting scope. For a few hours, all was quiet; the temperature dropped, anticipation rose. Then they picked up the first sign of movement: a hand came out of the pit, grabbed a dog, and pulled it in. A few minutes later, another hand appeared; another dog disappeared. It kept up through the night until the tribe was covered with a layer of dogs. The chagrined scientists said to hell with it, packed their gear, boarded their plane, and disappeared. They were not heard from again.

Apparently this aborigine temperature control practice was no secret in the outback. There was even an Australian rock group performing in the States during the 1960s that called themselves Three Dog Night—a three-dog night is a very cold night.

ONE OF THE MANY things Bob was instrumental in improving in Australia's vast central region was the marketing process. The traditional way to deliver cattle to the packing plants was to walk them on cattle trails, just as we did here in the U.S. in the 1860s and 1870s. It was still the way thousands of head were moved out of the Northern Territory in the early 1960s. The government had formalized the system by designating trails across the vast expanses in northern Australia. These trails were marked by blading a strip about twenty yards wide; a trail boss was permitted to graze his cattle for half a mile on each side of its centerline. Government-maintained watering places were ten miles apart and the herds had to move at least ten miles each day, to keep the grazing on the lessee's land to a minimum. A prudent manager rode out and checked a herd before it passed off his property; sometimes a cow or two carrying his brand would join the exodus and the trail driver might overlook it.

Herds were sometimes on the trail for three years or longer, making a journey of over 1,500 miles. They would at intervals rest on rented pasture, or even pass from one owner to another a number of times. If the pastures were green along the way, they gained weight. But when a prolonged drought set in, the animals that should have been marketed first, the young and the old, became too weak to make the trip. They died on the range or on the trail. Before 1960, an estimated one-half the beef produced in the Northern Territory and in western Queensland never reached market.

By 1960, the railhead had reached Mount Isa in western Queensland, but the animals on Brunette still had to walk for more than a month before they boarded the cattle cars. This was changed by a machine called a land train, a fine piece of equipment that just suited this part of the world. It looked like a stubby freight train, with a large diesel cattle truck—a Leyman or Mercedes—pulling two cattle trailers the size of French boxcars. A unit could haul sixty to eighty head of grown animals over the graded roads, or even cross-country if necessary. Some of them were equipped with cowcatcher-like blades that pushed large boulders and the obstreperous, concrete-hard anthills out of their path. But there were very few of them around at this time, and the ones that were running were booked for a year or more in advance.

Trail driving in South Texas had ended before Bob came of age, but he had heard the stories of their risks and trials from his father and from Sam Ragland. Building the railroad that made it possible for King Ranch to ship its cattle to midwestern market centers was his father's greatest contribution to King Ranch's economic welfare. So Bob was convinced that the land train was a logical early investment. The ranch purchased its first unit shortly after the Brunette Downs lease was acquired; others followed. The machines ran almost continuously, day and night, moving stocker or fat cattle to market and returning with the myriad supplies required to maintain a station this size.

A REGULAR CHORE ON the ranch, the supreme chore, was inspecting the watering places. They were equipped either with windmills—enormous things by our standards, powered by thirty-foot fans—or with mechanical pumps run by diesel engines. Since in these temperatures a grown animal drinks about thirteen gallons a day, the wells and troughs had to stay in good operating condition. This meant inspecting them on the ground or by air every other day. When he wasn't needed to supervise other work, Reg Geddes drove the water well rounds; it also gave him an opportunity to check pasture conditions. I made these all-day trips with him. Since Reg was not one for idle chitchat, I eventually ran out of questions; the rides were monotonous, virtually silent, with only a break for lunch— camp bread and beef sandwiches, a tomato, and tea.

At noon one day we stopped on the trail, got out of the little Holden sedan, and hunkered down in the little shade it afforded. Sitting there on the ground with only the sound of the flies buzzing about our heads, chewing on the beef and looking out across a pasture that was dead flat with not a tree or bush to break the horizon line, I thought, "When we get in this car and drive off, it won't matter which direction we take, we'll be heading back. In all the world, this is about as far out as you can get."

The very sameness of the country was a mesmerizer—a tragic result of this had occurred only a few weeks before my visit. A young pilot had been hired to do the water well checking using a two-seater Cessna 150, a reliable little airplane, so stable it can almost fly itself. He did not return from a routine flight, on a bright sunny day in calm weather. He and his plane were found near one of the well sites, a long charred streak through the grass—he had flown into the ground at cruising speed. The investigators concluded that when he made a low pass and then lifted his eyes from the well, he had not been able to distinguish the ground from the horizon.

THE REMOTENESS, THE isolation, had its effect to some degree on all these people, upon their makeup, upon their relations with each other. The solitude was a tangible thing; I have never before or since experienced its depth. It was several days before its most pervasive element got through to me: the immutable silence. The wind spent itself getting this far inland, so it was usually calm. The birds congregated near roosts. While majestic sulfur-topped macaws and pink galahs sat by the thousands on the wind-mill towers and power lines, and the finches flitted in clouds through the small bushes around the water tanks, out on the treeless plains the sky was empty. So when one left the headquarters for the open country, noise and movement stayed behind. The silence was a cloak; it enveloped you. I began to understand how a person's ability to communicate could drain imperceptibly away.

The Geddes family was emblematic of exposure to these influences over time. Reg was a product of the outback, of the lonely life it mandated. If he had ever had the ability to nurture a relationship with those around him, he had lost it. He could give orders and receive them from higher up, but he was not able to exchange opinions, to perceive a divergent point of view.

Her years of exposure to this had taken its toll on Mrs. Geddes, a gentle, soft-spoken woman deprived of contact with the larger world. There was an outback practice that gave the wives an hour each morning on the two-way radio to chat with their distant neighbors. At 9:00, they took their cups of tea to the transmitter and settled down for a natter. Except for a two-week holiday with their family or a trip to the populated coast, this was their only social contact—a jumble of static-pocked, disembodied voices. The younger children attended school the same way, gathered around a radio, listening to a teacher some hundreds of miles away.

So a spouse faced almost certain war between the sexes, metaphorically handcuffed to his or her mate. Mrs. Geddes submitted and took direction from Reg. Among other couples, the wife resisted and overcame—and that usually meant quitting the outback, the husband taking up different work among townfolk.

There was an acute, sensible observer to this relationship: outback-raised daughter Fahey. Quiet, with a straight, regal bearing and a fluid stride, this beautiful young lady was reaching the end of her teens. Her only day-to-day relationships outside her family were with the jackeroos, whom she had over to dinner each Sunday evening, and with her father's overseer, who was smitten with her. Not a hint of resentment or rebellion rippled her tranquility, but escape was writ large in our offguard conversation. She became an airline stewardess and traveled the world, compensating for her lonely upbringing.

BRUNETTE DOWNS WAS Peter Baillieu's responsibility, and his most vexing, never-ending problem was keeping a good manager. He found some fine ones—mature men with a lifetime's experience in the outback who stayed on for years—but the others rotated in just a few months and he was forced to search again. The management reports from all of our foreign principals consistently began with an assessment of the staff; it was uppermost in their minds.

Of the duties Bob handed me, the business of finding qualified young people to settle on our properties around the world was the least rewarding. He or our foreign managers often asked me to locate trainees for our remote ranches, men with good educations and the initiative to think and act isolated from their superiors. I interviewed lots of them, young graduates who were fired up by the challenge of living and working in a foreign country. If they were married, their wives usually shared their enthusiasm; if a wife didn't, the man was not considered. The position generally entailed all the novice hoped for: an exotic setting, lots of challenges, an independence he could not hope to attain in the U.S. until middle age, higher-than-average wages.

Almost inevitably, the wife did not adjust. The husband was out in the pasture all day, putting into practice the exciting things he had been educated to do. She was in the house, often isolated by the language, the difference in class of the hired hands' wives around her, her ties to her family and friends severed. I could not help but be sympathetic; it was more than a young woman could normally be asked to bear. The good and able man, just learning the ropes, was left with a choice between his job and his mate. Inevitably, they returned home.

With the unmarried men, the situation was different but just as acute. They had left their hearts and minds behind with some young woman they had been courting. Their imagination ran riot at the turns their long-distance love affair was taking; their thoughts were on the next excuse to run home on leave. They lasted even less time than the married ones. My batting average was near zero. Over time, it proved better to hire a native of the country; they were not as well educated or trained, but they were acclimated.

BACK ON THE QUEENSLAND east coast, Mr. Kleberg made in 1959 another spectacular gamble, an innovation in a rain forest not previously undertaken on such a scale anywhere in the tropics. It got the attention of the Australian agricultural community. Again, the development was a result of a decision based, at least in part, on his incredible eyes and on his perception of what his eyes told him.

The windward side of the Cape York Peninsula in northeastern Australia, jutting into the Coral Sea, is one of the few high-rainfall zones on the continent. The low mountain slopes along the peninsula's spine force the moisture-laden clouds drifting in from the sea to a higher, cooler altitude, where they precipitate into drenching rains. Here on these hillsides and partly on the coastal plain, Rupert Clarke showed Bob an undeveloped jungle and swamp. The continentwide drought of the 1950s still vivid in everyone's mind, the rainfall here was a fascination, an average of 168 inches. One year, the area received over 300 inches. Australian planters had cleared some limited acres in this region to grow sugarcane and bananas, some bananas over a foot long. But at the price that slaughter cattle commanded, no one had thought of ranching the verdant, remote forest.

Bob, too, was dubious about keeping cattle under these exotic conditions. The conventional thinking in the agricultural research community was that grasses grown in excessive rainfall had such a high moisture content—as high as 92 percent by weight in some species—that the animals grazing on them filled up and starved, taking in mostly water. But at Rupert's urging, he agreed to go north to take a look. One look was sufficient.

On their inspection, they were bumping through some open forest when Bob spied a bull, a wild one that had probably escaped from one of the properties down on the coast. He got only a glimpse of it before it disappeared into the undergrowth, but that glimpse told him the animal was in fine condition, his ribs well covered, his hide sleek. It meant that the types of grasses growing here were sustaining fodder after all, taking their necessary allotment of minerals from the soil, generating proper amounts of protein; it indicated to him that cattle could indeed do well under these conditions. But he was prudent enough not to risk a bankroll on one sighting.

On the King Ranch, Bob had cleared over three-quarters of the 825,000 acres of mesquite and kindred noxious growth. His manager, who designed the heavy machinery for this specific task, was Lowell Wilkinson, a mechanical wizard with an innovative mind. Bob dispatched Wilkie to Tully River, the valley he had driven over, with instructions to collect as much data as he could and come home with a recommendation on whether King Ranch should put its foot into that impenetrable growth. Wilkie reported that using the heaviest equipment obtainable, working on a 50,000-acre tract, the land could be cleared for $20 an acre. The other improvements—fencing, roads, homes and outbuildings—would bring the total cost to within $30 to $40 an acre. Not a bad shot—the final bill was $31.13, exclusive of the well-appointed main house.

Bob sent Wilkie back, with a load of Texas heavy machinery, to clear the eucalyptus and mangrove trees and the undergrowth, and to haul out the logs. After a few tries, Wilkie learned that even his giant Caterpillar D-9s could not shove over 100-foot-high trees that were eight to ten feet across at the base. So he did what he had done at home—he improvised. With his mechanics and welders, he constructed a heavy steel ball, eight feet in diameter, with lugs circling it in bands. Through it ran a shaft with swivels on each end, and to the swivels he attached 150 feet of ship's anchor chain. With a D-9 pulling each end of the chain, he renewed the attack. The rolling ball struck a towering tree trunk, the lugs dug in, the ball climbed, and the chain gained the purchase to pull the tree over, bringing its roots out of the ground. With this gadget, Wilkie's drivers were able to roll through the forest with the speed necessary to get the trees down, load the logs, clear the debris, and plant an appreciable acreage in grass between rainy seasons.

The boss selected the guinea and parra grasses that were proving themselves on other King Ranch tropical pastures. Within five years, the new ranch, Tully, was transformed from unproductive jungle into one of the most efficient beef factories in the world, with a carrying capacity of 30,000 head of cattle. For Rupert Clarke, Bob even had an experienced man available, one of the few in the world who had managed tropical, high-rainfall pastures. Neil Alderman had run the Braga Brothers livestock operation in Cuba; he had become a refugee at the same time as Tash, just when Tully needed a man to get the stocking operation under way.

Bob envisioned Tully as a fattening range for steers produced on the western properties when rainfall in the outback was normal. But he harbored a more basic, urgent reason for making this unusual outlay. There was an ever-present danger that a prolonged dry cycle in the northwest would bring on losses in his Santa Gertrudis cow herds, the prized breeding stock that had taken generations to reach purebred status. Tully would prove of inestimable value when these other properties went into one of their periodic droughts—it was a safe place to truck them. The haven, in Bob's mind, was worth the outlay.

EACH YEAR, KING RANCH, Australia, held an auction of some of its top-quality bulls, and each year several hundred were sold at private treaty. Imaginative Australian cattle breeders used those bulls to grade up a large number of quality herds. The best of them were monuments to Bob, herds ideally suited to their adopted country. In two decades, the Santa Gertrudis grew from a few hundred young imports to the top-ranking breed in the country. At the end of Bob's life, the Australian properties seemed King

Ranch's most promising asset. It turned out they were, but not in the way he envisioned. In 1989 they were sold at auction for a handsome profit.

TWO ACROSS THE HIGHLANDS

Nearly every visitor to the ranch added to our view of the world. But there were so many—thousands—that most did not stand out in a special way. On a few occasions, two unrelated visits combined to create a lasting memory; such was the case when Ian Grabowski and Michael Leahy came to see us.

Their trips to Kingsville were separated by almost a decade, yet their lives were bound in a unique and indivisible way. Both were Australians, both were explorers and pioneers, both possessed unremitting courage and foresight. Grabowski's Slavic name came from his Finnish father, but his stature, bearing, speech, and outlook were pure down under. He had devoted his life to aviation, and his trip to the ranch had the frontier-exploring overtones of a man who dreamed of new routes to fly, wild lands to tame.

Grabowski visited us in November 1952 to talk over with Bob the possibility of King Ranch's joining him in setting up an air beef operation across northern Australia. During World War II, a line of military airfields had been built along the north coast, in anticipation of a Japanese invasion. They were abandoned after the war, but the runways were still there. Grabowski planned to build small slaughter facilities on some of these fields, bring in cattle from the remote stations in Queensland, the Northern Territory, and Western Australia, kill and skin them, hang the sides in large transports, and immediately fly them to a high altitude where they would chill during the trip to the east coast processing plants. It was novel—it held promise—but Grabowski was never able to get all of its diverse elements off the ground.

Although at this time Grabowski was working on an Australian enterprise, his experience and reputation were based on his exploratory flying adventures in New Guinea, hence his longtime ties with Michael Leahy. Mick Leahy was an Australia–New Guinea legend. He landed in the Mandated Territory in 1926, one of the earlier prospectors for gold in the upland riverbeds. With his partner, he was the first explorer to penetrate the valleys and plateaus in the central highlands, coming upon indigenous tribes totaling nearly a million natives who had inhabited the region from aeons past. Until this time, the rest of the world had no knowledge of the existence of this mass of people. This race of Papua New Guineans was the last of the large anthropological groups to be discovered on this earth.

During Leahy's second trek into the interior, arrangements were made to supply his party by air; Ian Grabowski was the pathfinder pilot who flew the material in, thereby proving that it was possible to develop the uplands solely by air service, using the planes and communications of the 1920s. It took a lot of ingenuity—and guts.

As Mick Leahy advanced into unexplored country, his party staked out and smoothed runways so that Grabowski could land. This they did by locating a reasonably level, open piece of ground in a valley and then marshaling the natives to run up and down it, flattening the tall grass by pounding it into the turf.

When the strange bird appeared overhead, the locals thought they were about to be paid a visit by one of their gods; they went down on their hands and knees. According to Grabowski, when he landed and climbed out of his little biplane—all six feet one and a half inches of him, dressed in white coveralls, a flying helmet, and green goggles—the small, frightened natives fell flat on their faces, a lot of them fainting dead away. Mick Leahy walked over and removed Ian's goggles, showing them there was a man inside— they were still not convinced. Only when they were allowed to feel Ian up and down, eventually discovering his genitals, were they satisfied he was indeed a man. But the airplane mystified them—they were not able to find the genitals under it.

MICHAEL LEAHY AND his wife arrived at the ranch in March 1959, on a trip to New York where he accepted an award from the Explorers Club. I was looking forward to hearing more tales like those told by the personable, outgoing Grabowski, but I was disappointed. While Leahy had gone into ranching in New Guinea after World War II and had a professional interest in seeing the King Ranch operation, he was withdrawn, reluctant to talk about his unique adventures. Like so many men of unparalleled accomplishment, in his own mind complete fulfillment seemed to have eluded him. For one thing, he never found the gold that had lured him into prospecting, though his contemporaries of considerably less intelligence and vision had found a limited number of paying deposits.

Later, I asked some of his Australian acquaintances why Leahy was so reticent to speak of his experiences. They told me that he had come under criticism from the authorities, and gotten into quite a donnybrook with them, over the independence of Papua New Guinea. In 1931, nomadic tribesmen attacked his prospecting camp—Leahy, his brother Dan, and several of his men were wounded. Michael received a severe ax blow to the head that affected him for the rest of his life. They killed six of the attackers—they felt they had no other recourse to avoid being massacred as they fought their retreat to the coast. But from their offices in the city, the administrators viewed this and other skirmishes as acts of unwarranted aggression.

BOTH ARE GONE NOW, two pioneering individualists of pronouncedly different character, yet each a link connecting the roving reed boatmen of the Indus with the astronauts. In Kingsville, on our own small frontier, it was a privilege to have them pass by.

CHAPTER THIRTEEN

FROM THE NEW CATTLE
WORLD TO THE OLD

THE LAST OF BOB KLEBERG'S great efforts lay across the Atlantic, on the shores of the Mediterranean. Until the middle 1960s, he evidenced little interest in agricultural opportunities in this part of the world; it could not compete with the immense potential that slumbered on the plains and in the forests of the Western Hemisphere and Australia. But he was accumulating more and more European and Middle Eastern friends who urged him to at least take a look at their homelands.

One of these had had an early, telling experience with another of Bob's friends and associates. Bob Wells, his tax adviser, had previously had a career with Standard Oil in Latin America, stationed in Buenos Aires. At one point, Wells was the personnel director, in charge of giving aptitude tests to potential employees.

One morning two Greeks, just off the boat, presented themselves, applying for jobs as laborers. They took the required tests, and when the results were reported to Wells he called them in. To one: "You show you have the requisite skills; we're prepared to offer you a job in the oilfields in Salta."

Turning to the other: "Your test shows you have no aptitude for the oil business. I'm sorry, we can't hire you. What do you want to do—stay together or take the offer?"

They decided to split up. They were penniless and one needed to work to carry the other until he could find a job.

The one who showed no aptitude for the oil business was named Aristotle Onassis. So much for those mind-twisting tests.

In the late 1960s, Mr. Onassis arranged a meeting with Bob in New York; he made an offer to join Bob in a clever, innovative venture. Onassis owned a whaling fleet operating in the Pacific. He foresaw the industry's demise and was feeling his way into transforming his large investment: a factory ship that processed the whales and a fleet of small hunter craft. At their get-together in Bob's Pierre apartment, Onassis proposed that, utilizing Bob's knowledge of livestock production and distribution, they set up a slaughter and packing business on the west coast of South America. He planned to convert the factory ship into a packing plant and use the fleet of fast, shallow draft hunters to go into the ports in Colombia, Ecuador, Peru, and Chile, buy fat cattle, and transport them to the offshore plant for processing. The system would open a market to the region's underpriced steers while avoiding the risk of making substantial investments in packing plants in politically shaky countries.

Bob and Onassis got on well—Bob liked him. But before the plan could be developed, Onassis had an offer from a Japanese firm to buy the fleet. He sold; nothing came of the idea.

Onassis did influence Bob in a quick, one-sentence way. One of the crew on Bob's plane told me this story. Bob had been visiting with Onassis in London and offered him a lift to New York. They arrived at the airdrome together. Onassis, stepping out of the limo and inspecting the Grumman Gulfstream I turboprop the King Ranch owned at that time, turned to Bob: "Ah! The poor man's jet." That did it; Bob had been thinking jet. Commitment immediately took hold.

Onassis and others planted a seed in Bob's mind to look into the profitable business opportunities their part of the world offered. To prepare himself, Bob traveled in Italy, Sardinia, and France, and met property owners in Greece and some of the other Mediterranean countries, gaining from them the impression that there was a market for Santa Gertrudis breeding cattle in southern Europe, the Middle East, and North Africa. Nearly every contact made a proposition to King Ranch to come into their country. Bob declined; his ways of doing business and his goals were not compatible with theirs.

In the middle 1960s, tourists were overrunning Europe and most of them were Americans, beef eaters every one. Cattle ranchers in the region had a market incentive to increase herd size and herd quality, on a foundation of animals adapted to their climate. Spain seemed a logical place to make an inroad into this trade. Most of its land was arid and rocky, suitable only for livestock, and its beef prices were the highest on the continent. The timing was right; Spain was just upon entering the European Economic Community.

Since the Cuban debacle, Bob's former partners, the Braga brothers, had from time to time tried to interest him in their homeland. In 1967, Riondo Braga persuaded Bob to accompany him on a trip to the locale around Seville, where the country is similar to our arid Southwest. They landed in Portugal, drove to the Spanish border, and Ronny almost lost Bob along the way. There was good river-bottom land for sale near Lisbon at some of the lowest prices in Europe. A few months after Bob's trip, I walked over farmland there that I thought could support a cow to three acres, for sale at $150 an acre. But Portugal was held back by its infrastructure and its markets. Roads were poor, packing facilities few and antiquated.

In Spain, Ronny showed Bob the southwestern borderland. Though suitable properties were on the market in the region, an almost insurmountable difficulty for the buyer was putting together enough acreage to create a ranch of a viable size. Unlike the British, the Spanish landowner does not follow the tradition of primogeniture; each of the children inherits. Over the centuries, this has resulted in an ownership map that looks like an ad for a carpet sale; the individual fields are about that size. Spanish agriculture is stifled by this practice—generation after generation subdividing plots until they reach minuscule proportions, down to three-quarters of an acre in many instances. It was almost impossible to piece together enough contiguous land to operate a profitable ranch, by Kleberg definition. Bob's credo was, the further from home a property, the more cows it had to carry. The administrative overhead required to look after it—travel, dealing with governments, communications—was fixed. The revenues had to cover these long-distance expenses, added to the normal overhead, before a reasonable profit could be realized.

But as it happened, the tenure system played into Bob's hands. A property named Los Millares—forty miles north of the port city of Huelva and a stone's throw from the Portuguese border—had been divided into four sections in the will of the deceased owner, each of his children inheriting a tract. But none of them were satisfied with their share, so they eventually decided to sell and divide the money. It was no picnic, coming to terms with four wary siblings who were at each other's throats, but over time individual deals were finally struck. When the ranch was put together, the Braga brothers took a minor interest, continuing their partnership with King Ranch that had begun fifteen years before.

Almost all of Los Millares's 18,687 acres was marginal land, the topsoil thin, with an underlay of blue slate. King Ranch, España, eventually farmed and ranched 24,700 acres, nearly all of it the scrubby, hardpan soil that characterized Los Millares. Most of Spain is arid and this corner of the country was no exception; rainfall averaged around fifteen inches. The land rolled and the shallow valleys were infested with scrubby brush; but the trees were a noble stand, oak and cork. There were no native perennial grasses that could sustain a reasonable year-round stocking rate—lots of improvement work was indicated.

Bob found his Spanish manager before he even had a property in mind. His nephew, Bobby Shelton, whom he and Helen had raised, had just married and was spending some time working on the Argentine properties under Juan Reynal. Bobby had made friends with a young Englishman, Michael Hughes, who was employed by one of the international British ranching and packing firms. Michael had a solid multinational background; educated in England and the U.S., he was fluent in Spanish and French and had been on several foreign assignments. A big, good-looking fellow of reserved manner, he had fine livestock credentials. Bobby invited Michael to the ranch, where Bob met and liked him; they found an early rapport. So after a thorough checkout with his business friends on trips to Argentina, Bob was ready to make Michael an offer when the Spanish enterprise began to develop. A lot of Michael's time, over the next three years, was taken up settling with those dissident Los Millares owners.

Michael was able first to purchase the portion of the ranch where the headquarters was located. The buildings were impressive but neglected. The home and attached chapel, about 150 years old (new by Spanish standards), was large and comfortable. Designed in the traditional Iberian style, the large, high-ceilinged rooms suited the climate. The carriage house, shops, and storage sheds were grouped in a square around the home, forming an immense enclosed patio. Like most Spanish country homes, on the outside it was a bit foreboding—a white-walled, red-tiled fort.

We again ran the steeplechase—over one regulatory hurdle and then another—of exporting a consignment of 40 Santa Gertrudis bulls and 280 heifers, along with a Quarter Horse stallion and a few mares. Southern

Spain is home to an indigenous breed of cattle that was the best suited for crossing with Santa Gertrudis of any the boss had found over the world. The Retintos were large animals of a solid red color that almost exactly matched their imported mates and of good clean bone. The cows were fertile, delivering strong, active calves. And they were available locally, at a hefty price.

Along with the cattle and horse shipment to the port of Huelva went a lot of equipment: fencing, tractors, discs, building hardware, a sort of a ranching Noah's ark. It was cheaper to ship from a Gulf of Mexico port than to obtain comparable material in Europe.

Of the improvements the land needed, the most pressing was developing the water supply; the pastures could not be stocked without it. Though the rainfall was low, catchment dams large enough to hold a two-year supply were constructed. There was a shallow underground water stratum underlying the ranch that in places seeped out from the base of the low hills. On one of his stateside visits, Michael and I went out to a King Ranch property in West Texas to see a clever horizontal drilling rig (vs. the conventional vertical one) that was increasing the flow in some seeps. The simple, relatively inexpensive machine bored into the sides of the hills to tap these small springs. It appeared that it might work on Los Millares, so a rig was shipped over. It did, in fact, help increase the water supply.

There was also an irrigation canal running through the ranch, owned by the government. Los Millares had the right to draw water from it, but Michael did not want to open the gate by becoming beholden to the local authorities for his water supply. The Spanish bureaucrat is basically honest, but is the most infuriating record keeper in the Western world. Every comma had to be in place on twenty-four notarized copies of every document before the paperwork went forward, to the next bureaucrat. It took a little more time than forever, so Michael kept our contacts with them to the minimum—not an easy thing to do in a country with a centuries-old bureaucratic heritage.

BOB'S LIFELONG INTEREST in wildlife made him especially enthusiastic about its potential on this ranch. Los Millares was home to one of the largest populations of rough-legged partridge in Western Europe. In Spain, as in most Western countries, the wild game is the property of the landowner. The partridge was in demand, a sought-after gourmet dish; it provided a subsidiary income for the ranch. Harvest time was the best time of year to be in Spain. At autumn shoots the owner invited in friends, furnished the shotgun shells and the food and drink, and at the end of the day presented each guest with a brace of birds. The remainder of the bag went to market. It was considered a good day when, at sundown, a thousand braces were laid out in the patio. Anything less was a reflection on the shooters.

These morning outings began while the patchy fog hung in the swales between the low hills, condensing on the grass. In the chill, everyone gathered at the first line, each shooter—there were usually eight—assigned two ranch-hand assistants: a loader and a retriever. They cut brush and built crude blinds down a valley floor facing the adjacent rise, and laid out the guns and ammunition.

When everything was ready, the loaders on the shooters' right and the retrievers behind and on the left, Michael signaled the gamekeeper and the first drive began. The gamekeeper had rounded up the ranch hands and a cadre of moonlighting workers from around the neighborhood, about twenty in all. Swinging long sticks, these drivers advanced toward the blinds from about a mile away, whistling and beating the bushes. Like pheasants, though slightly smaller, the partridges are good runners; the beaters had to spook them to make them fly. They usually went airborne on the far side of the hill, just crested the peak, and glided down toward the blinds.

The beaters, not far behind, were getting within firing range. The hoots and yells began: "I'm here! Don't shoot! Behind this tree!"

At first I wondered at the commotion; soon I learned. The tip-off came on my first morning out, from the behavior of the man in the adjoining butt. He was a retired bullfighter named El Litri and he had his own suite serving him: loader, retriever (two-footed), and retriever (four-footed—a German dog). El Litri opened a case, took out an English cap, one with earflaps that he tied under his chin, and a heavy tweed coat with a collar that buttoned around his neck. Then he fitted on a pair of shooting goggles. Overdressed it seemed to me; it was a cool fall day, but I was comfortable in a light sweater.

Spanish guns are competitive in the extreme—get the bird and damn anything in the sights. The first wave was on us—the firing began— smoke obscured the targets—confusion prevailed. My retriever pointed and grunted in one ear; the loader, mumbling in the other, grabbed the gun the instant the second shot went off, regardless of my position. I followed overhead only the birds that were directly above me; my companions on each side weren't so inhibited. When a bird came in low, between the blinds, they swung and fired right down the line. The heavy clothing came clear to me—pellet protection; all day I was peppered and stung by spent shot.

When the whistle blew to signal cease-fire, my retriever went into a frenzy, running, grabbing every bird in sight. Apparently his standing for the day depended on my score; he did his part by piling as many birds as he could behind my blind. The bullfighter's cleverly trained dog ignored the birds in his territory, leaving them to his two-legged counterpart while he skipped off to bring in everything he could pick up behind the blinds of the other shooters. When he flagrantly snatched a bird away right under my feet, the bullfighter grabbed him, cursed him good, and boxed his ears, but he didn't return the bird. That was part of the training; the dog probably thought it was being rewarded.

When the birds were gathered, mules were led up with large baskets roped to their flanks. The bag was counted and loaded and the line was moved to another location selected by the gamekeeper. Blind building again, beaters out, and the drama was repeated. While this was a bird shoot, a hare occasionally broke cover. Light brown, medium-eared, they were amazingly agile for their size, twice that of our jackrabbit. When one of these terrified animals saw the line, it invariably turned and ran straight down it, giving everyone a shot. One raced past me—I ignored it. But my loader wasn't having any of that; yelling "Conejo! Conejo! Mire el conejo!" he grabbed my gun barrel, pulling it down to help me aim. Spanish peasants prize one rabbit over a sackful of partridge.

By late morning, three flights had been shot. Refreshment time— pulled by two more mules, an open wagon arrived loaded with trays of cold shrimp, mussels, sliced ham and sausage, vegetable salads, red and white wine, and sherry. Eating, drinking, rehashing the shooting, comparing scores (waging a battle with your facial muscles when you found you had bested the other fellow) took up the middle of the day. Then a short siesta under an oak, and everyone moved out for the three afternoon drives.

Mr. Kleberg was a safari man; from Texas to Latin America to Africa, he had had some of the finest game shooting the sport had to offer. These Millares days ranked in his mind with the best in his experience. One of his most valued possessions was a pair of Purdey 12s. To be out on his ranch with them on a brisk autumn day, his loader at his side, along with his friends harvesting his birds, seemed to me a fitting if modest bonus for a lifetime devoted to propagating wildlife.

I have been told that the partridge shooting on Los Millares was the finest in Europe. I cannot vouch for that and it didn't matter; it certainly was a substantial source of supplemental income—and a joy. When the property was eventually sold to a Swiss, he bought it with no intention of ranching. He wanted it only for the shooting.

THE SPANISH RANCH WAS never a fit with the other King Ranch foreign operations, mainly because it was too small. In developing his markets, Bob was at a disadvantage because he had no experience dealing on this scale. On a trip in May 1974, he saw the first of the first-cross heifers bred on the ranch, by the imported Santa Gertrudis bulls and out of the Retinto cows, and was convinced that the Millares country was strong enough to raise fine animals. He instructed Michael to buy more land; there was some available at the twice-the-value-of-the-animals formula, but not much. The most opportune road to a sustained profit was to make the ranch into a high-quality breeding center, then undertake an aggressive marketing campaign in the Mediterranean countries that had need for warm-climate-adapted bulls. This was never done because the small numbers of animals raised each year did not justify the cost and time to make the marketing effort.

THERE WAS ANOTHER facet of King Ranch, España, that was unique to Bob's experience. The previous owners had kept a herd of three hundred Spanish fighting cattle, the Toros Bravos. Known to the aficionados by their brand name, Concha y Sierra, this herd had one of the finest reputations in Spain for strength and bravery. But the previous owners had not given the breeding program the attention it merited and the herd had degenerated. Bob now had title to as unpredictable and cantankerous a herd of bovines as existed in the animal kingdom.

His inclination at the outset was to sell them, but Michael convinced him that this would not be good public relations for a foreign company attempting to establish a good rapport with local stockmen, especially our close neighbors, nearly all of whom had a few of these animals. The Spanish treated the Bravos with reverence; downgrading them would be a slur on the national pride. So the cow herd was reduced by half; about 150 were retained for breeding, with the agreement that they would be quietly disposed of at a later time. But this was not to be. The boss and everyone else got hooked on them. Michael cultivated some of the better breeders and learned the intricacies of making the proper matings, of selecting and testing them.

The theory among students of the race is this: the fighting bull inherits his strength and stamina from his father and his intelligence and bravery from his mother. Consequently, all of the heifers were screened for their courage before they were placed in the breeding herd. They were tested when they were about 2½ years old, in an event called a *tienta*—it was a high point in the year on the ranch. Neighboring Toro Bravo breeders and their families were invited, along with the stars of the performance, two or three retired matadors living in the province. Adjacent to the main home was a small bullring with the fixtures necessary to handle these strong, active animals. The ring had a corral built into it, so that the heifers could be sorted and released into the arena one at a time. Around its circular eight-foot-high wall, there were two openings, overlapped on the inside by a stout wooden barrier, so that a man entering the ring could edge in sideways but the animal could not force its way out. Overlooking the ring, a small covered stand accommodated the spectators. Chilled sherry and refreshments were spread on a board.

On one particular morning, two matadors had accepted Michael's invitation, an older fellow named Emilio Olivios and a younger one, Julio Vega. Olivios was especially a character, still full of life's juices, though over the years any number of quarts of them must have gushed out of him—he told me he had thirty-four horn-wound scars, one from his thigh to his chest. Following one heave-ho, he married his intended in the bullring infirmary, on the operating table, convinced he would never leave the room alive.

The *tienta* began when a rider, the picador, entered the ring; he was a necessary performer in this drama: the villain. His horse was heavily padded and one eye was blindfolded, so that the horse could see the wall but not the center of the ring. The rider was dressed in the traditional uniform of his calling: a round, flat-brimmed hat with an oval crown and a strap under his chin, a short, close-fitting jacket, plain trousers, his right leg encased in a stout metal shield that looked like a piece of carried-over medieval armor, which it easily could have been. Under his right arm was a wooden shaft about eighteen feet long, tipped with a sharp steel point. Just behind the point was a metal ring that acted like a stopcock, to keep the point from penetrating any more than just the skin.

When the picador was in place, to one side and facing the corral gate, the first heifer was released into the ring. She usually charged most of the way across, came to a four-footed, spraddle-legged halt, and looked around. If she immediately saw the horse and rider, turned, and charged, she showed promise. As her horns hit the padding, the picador set his lance into the depression between her shoulder blades, breaking the skin but not damaging the muscle. If despite the pain she kept at her charge, twisting her horns into the padding, another plus.

Then the matador stepped out from behind the barrier, unfurling his large cape, yellow on one side, magenta on the other, and the picador withdrew his lance. The matador attracted the enraged animal away from the horse, enticing her with his moving cloth toward the center of the ring, where he took her through two or three passes. In a final flourish, he turned her so that the picador again came into her view.

Here the animal passed or failed. If, with the punishment she had just taken fresh in her memory, she without hesitation charged again, she had the bravery and single purpose the judges were seeking. If she hesitated, pawing the sand a few times with a front leg before boring in, that was acceptable but not high scoring. To raise her head, look the horse over, and turn away—worse still, to run to the gate where she had entered—eliminated from her further consideration. Some of these feisty little females—you might recognize the type—charged their tormentor three or four times in a furious frenzy before the foreman signaled to turn them out of the ring; they were the best of the lot, expectant mothers of noble bulls.

As they left the ring, they were marked with the sign of their destiny; their horns were tipped. The left tip only was cut if they had failed their exam, both left and right if they were to become future breeding cows. At this point, the weakness in the economics of breeding fighting bulls was exposed. Thirty to 40 percent of the females failed the test; they were not fit to breed bullring-class bulls and traditionally they were not considered fit for much of anything else. An immediate sale in the beef market was the only option for the owner. Since they are a slow-maturing breed and thin—weighing only a little more than half as much as their sisters in other breeds at this age—they brought very little money. Toro Bravo breeding was not a profitable business.

An interesting facet of these animals, little known, is that of all the world's breeds of cattle, they have the highest ratio of muscle (red meat) to total body weight. Michael knew this and he reasoned that since the heifers had so little value as beef animals anyway, he should keep them and breed them to Santa Gertrudis bulls, getting higher return from the calf than he could from the mother. This would take advantage of their ability to produce red meat while the Santa Gertrudis would infuse their offspring with the ability to reach earlier maturity and a larger size. Such proved the case; the calves quickly grew into acceptable beef animals. The experiment opened to Los Millares a new market: the sale of Santa Gertrudis bulls to breeders of fighting cattle for use on their reject heifers.

AT A *TIENTA* THERE WERE usually twelve to twenty heifers to test. After the matadors had practiced their skills and shown off for the small audience, the amateurs had their opportunity. All the young men on the ranch wanted a go; the adulation a matador receives in Spain far outranks that of a movie star, and nearly every lad dreams of a shot at these nearly insuperable heights. Following the young aficionados came the rank amateurs, those of us who had been sipping the sherry during the morning and had had our courage bolstered to the level that made this bullfighting business appear an overrated lark.

Bob was invited to take a try, but a few months before he had made his debut in a ring in Mexico and he wanted no more of it. A ranch belonging to the Sorda-Madaleno family bred bulls of the Presidente Prudente bloodline, some of the best in the New World. Bob had been invited to one of their *tientas* and reckoned he would go the young people one better. He spurned the proffered cape and unfolded his pocket handkerchief. Flicking his minuscule *capa* before the heifer's eye, he confidently awaited the charge. *Whommph!* The heifer zeroed in on his midriff, a far larger and more tempting target. Down he went and the animal went over him, and his hosts thought for sure they had killed their distinguished guest. But she didn't get her horns into him—no harm was done, aside from a few days of midsection tenderness. It was far from the first time a Kleberg had been tossed and run over by an irate female. So Bob declined the offer, leaving the U.S. flag to be flown by a more expendable member of the party.

All my life I have been a bullfight nut, so I was a patsy for this setup. I couldn't wait to get the cape in my hand and face off with this diminutive, low-risk, six-hundred-pound heifer, by my estimation. But in the time it took me to climb down from the stand and get on a level with her behind the barrier, she miraculously gained a formidable four hundred pounds. The snickering Spaniards around me handed me the little red cape, just slightly larger than the boss's handkerchief, and shoved me into the ring. Then they commenced pounding on the barrier to attract the heifer's attention.

The four-legged proof of my folly turned, facing me. Another transformation—here came a veritable locomotive engine, coal black, snorting and throwing up plumes of dust, pointing a set of yard-long, lancet-tipped horns straight at me—at least a ton of lacerated, bleeding, very angry, female malice.

Essentially, the cowboy working in the corral, whose aim it is to get close to an animal to bind and throw it, rather than find himself draped over its horns, is using the same tactics a matador uses in the bullring. The ability to get in close is based on the obvious difference between man and beast: the man is two-legged while the animal is four-legged. Therefore a man can maneuver in a smaller radius than a bull, which must stop on his front legs and then two-step in a circle with his hind feet to reverse direction. The matador's survival secret: as the bull thunders past him, he dances toward the tail instead of moving to the side or in the direction of the bull's charge. It's physically impossible for the bull to change direction before the matador is set for another pass.

I had been taught this by the cowboys and I prepared to stake every inch from my thighs to my armpits on it. The heifer lowered her head and came at me, whooshed through the little red rag I thrust out as far as I could, rubbed off some hair and gore on me, and kept going. I extended that one step toward her tail, skipping about ten yards to give myself a little better margin. What an exhilarating sensation! I was in a bullring, I had completed a pass, I was alive and well! The system worked! She came at me again, again the pass, and again and again and again—I had the caping part down by now but I had neglected to ask how to break it off—how to quarter across the ring to reach the barrier and get the hell out of harm's way. My solution was not the one Manolete would have chosen—I wore the poor young thing down and tiptoed out behind her. But not before I heard the boss's voice from up above. "Don't press your luck. Get outta there before I have to take you home on a board."

Michael went on to improve the herd; though we never got top prices, he had bulls fighting in the major rings in Seville and Madrid. But it wasn't worth the time and attention the program demanded. Eventually Bob agreed it was best to dispose of the lot of them.

WHILE BOB KNEW THAT it was not likely that he would ever be able to make Los Millares the size he felt he was justified in running at a distance, I think he had a further goal in mind. He saw it as an entrance for him and his family into another segment of the international world of commerce, a vehicle to make contacts with some of the top people in the European agribusiness community, people who would be useful to him and to those coming after him. The connections were made—in Spain, France, Italy, Greece—but they did not mature into meaningful associations.

A SPANISH CONNECTION

The effort Bob extended to visitors directed to him by our State Department was mainly for the visitors' diversion: to show them a little of the American ranching scene, however atypical. There were exceptions, people genuinely interested in ranching economics and techniques. One of

these was Rafael Cavestany, minister of agriculture for Spain. Sr. Cavestany and his party visited Bob in mid-1955, long before Bob became interested in setting up shop in the minister's country.

Cavestany was a gentleman in every sense: tall and erect, erudite, with
a dignified, reserved Spanish air occasionally fractured by a refined sense
of humor. The State Department let us know that while the minister did
not always agree with his boss, Francisco Franco, the dictator had a high
regard for Cavestany's ability and integrity. One of the members of the
party was the director of the Spanish Agriculture Research Institute. He
told us of the minister's accomplishments during his term in office. One
particular innovation has stayed with me over the years.

Sr. Cavestany's *estancia* was near Avila, northwest of Madrid. Com-
muting from the capital, he spent his weekends managing his property.
After World War II, Spain was troubled with two related agricultural problems: the lack of storage space to protect the cereals grown there, and the
lack of capital to build proper silos. However, the economy was being
boosted by an increasing tourist trade; foreigners were attracted to Spain
in part by its rich, turbulent history and the artifacts that history had
spawned. Driving back and forth to Avila, Cavestany passed any number
of castles and fortresses, now fallen into ruins, built by the Christians to
defend against the Moors.

Putting all this together in his mind, Cavestany formed a brilliant plan
to enhance at once several areas important to Spain's future: they could
restore the facades of the old buildings—much cheaper than attempting to
refurbish the whole structures—then seal the walls and roof and use them
as grain silos. This would give the villages where these monuments were
located the appearance they had had in their medieval heyday, increasing
tourist traffic across the countryside, while providing an ancillary benefit to the agricultural economy. It worked out that way. Quite a number
of the more important ruins were restored, even to building insets behind their windows and openings to give an illusion of depth to their
forms.

IN THE LATIN TRADITION, the minister was unquestionably the god-
father to his close-knit extended family. He had along with him his wife
and a daughter and his sister and brother-in-law. On a Sunday afternoon,
we were sitting around the pool at the main house watching a crowd of
children splashing around in front of us. Beaming, Bob turned to the minister, "Those are my great-nieces and -nephews."

Sr. Cavestany asked, "How many do you have?" To which Bob was pleased to reply, "Eight." The minister rose from his chair and came over to shake Bob's hand, telling him what a blessing it was to have a large family. Feeling expansive, Bob courteously inquired how many the minister had.

Cavestany: "Fifty-four."

CHAPTER FOURTEEN

DECISION MAKING, THE CONTORTED PROCESS

POSSIBLY I HAVE GIVEN the impression that Bob's marathon travels were primarily inspection jaunts, to plan and upgrade future work. They were, of course, but in tandem with the business problems came the problems raised by the almost constant push and shove between his partners, managers, stockholders, and officers in the subsidiary businesses. As arbitrator, he was responsible for adjudicating their differences, his decisions final, no appeal. An example: the interplay that went on during the course of just one visit—from July 7 to July 25, 1971—to England, Spain, and Morocco.

The boss and I left Kingsville on the G-2, along with his niece Ila Clement, the daughter of his older sister, Henrietta Larkin Armstrong, and Ila's husband, Jim Clement, the manager of the main office and the ranch's subsidiary domestic businesses. The first overnight stop was New York, where Bob wrapped up the complicated three-country deal to purchase the Thoroughbred stallion Canoñero, described earlier.

The following morning, we continued on to London to join the chairman of King Ranch, Australia, Sir Rupert Clarke, his wife, Lady Katherine, and their daughter, Vanessa. Rupert had put together a three-way partner-

ship involving the creation of a new Thoroughbred breeding farm in Australia, the principals to be King Ranch, Lord Derby (previously mentioned
in connection with the Buckpasser/Buffel episode), and Rupert. During the
stopover, Bob and Rupert went out to the earl's family home, Knowsley
Hall, and overnight firmed up the ownership and administrative participation of the three partners in the new venture.

Back at Claridge's Hotel in London the next day, Rupert had another
proposition for the boss. In Australia the Angliss family—among the largest ranchers in the country—had decided to sell out their extensive holdings, and Rupert had arranged for King Ranch, Australia, to make first offer. Rupert went over the Arthur Angliss proposal, which Bob felt was out
of line; he thought the company could be bought for $10 million. To Bob,
Rupert didn't contest the figure; instead he took me aside to tell me that
an insurance company was also interested. While Rupert felt we must offer
$10.5 to $11 million, he could spin off some of the ranches, leaving King
Ranch, Australia, with an investment of $5 million. You have probably
gathered that all of this was not for my edification—my mission was to
convey it to Bob where, in the event of an adverse reaction, I would be
standing under the fallout. While I did not relish the role, I saw it as a part
of my duties—to act, when circumstances indicated, as intermediary between the CEO and the principals.

While the Angliss proposal was under consideration, Tom Taylor arrived in London with a tender from Deltec. Things had not been going well
for Mr. Dauphinot in the ranching and packing businesses in Argentina
and Brazil; he had decided to restructure his businesses and needed cash to
do it. Rupert had gotten wind of a possible sale of all of Deltec's interests
in Australia, and as usual had thoroughly done his homework. Deltec
owned the leases on two large adjoining properties on the eastern Northern
Territory border, just across the fence from one of the Associated Stations
properties in Queensland. Lake Nash and Georgina Downs together were
2,969,600 acres carrying 35,000 head of cattle. Deltec also owned 20 percent of F. J. Walker, one of the country's leading meat-packing firms. All
three of the properties were sound ones; Walker was generating a 10 percent
annual profit. The package, net of cash and debt, might be had for $3 mil-
lion. But the buyer would need to forgo a return for two years in order to
rebuild the herd.

Rupert and everyone else in the King Ranch camp, foremost Bob,
wanted to make a clean break with Deltec. But Tom pushed an alternate
Deltec proposal. They needed $3 million within three months to recover
Swift from receivership in Argentina. In addition, they wanted to sell their
other food-processing businesses and go into brokering meat in Latin

America. So Tom offered their Australian interest for $3.5 million, with the provision that Deltec could buy back 25 percent in two years, their option. Here Tom had a vested interest: with the prospect that Deltec might in the future again be doing business in Australia, his experience had value for the company.

Meantime, everyone had moved with the boss from London to Madrid, where he had several decisions to make concerning new property acquisitions in Spain. Settling in at the Ritz Hotel, the parties began the dickering over the two Australian propositions before lunch, went through the afternoon, evening, and far into the night. It was complicated by the fact that two of the King Ranch's top people who had journeyed to Madrid for the discussions—Francis Herbert from Brazil and Arthur Bassingwaighte from Australia—also managed properties for Deltec. Even though Tom Taylor was nominally over them, there was no question that their loyalties were to Bob, cattleman to cattleman. No one was interested in the Deltec option; a clean break was the only suitable solution. But Tom balked at this. His position and principal interest lay with Deltec; though he had never been comfortable in his diminished role, selling now would mean his long association with the Australian and South American companies would be over.

So here we were, locked in a smoke-filled room without the smoke. (Oddly, for men of our age, no one in the group smoked.) Tensions mounted—they were bound to under the circumstances. Each man had his agenda, each agenda was different from the others. Even the two Australians, Rupert and Arthur, were poles apart. Arthur was the cattleman, the Queenslander; Rupert, the financier, Melbourne-born. Arthur thought in terms of huge holdings of semiarid land carrying hundreds of thousands of commercial cattle. Rupert was attuned to small, developed properties running fine purebreds. Rupert fixed on land tenure, favorable leases, low-interest rates in the Australian or Eurodollar market. Arthur's interest was in the pasture: beef turnoff at the most efficient rate.

Tom Taylor and Francis Herbert were linked, like two prisoners handcuffed together who wanted to take off in opposite directions. Though Francis was employed by Deltec, he shared Bob's reservations over that company's commitment to the cattle business. He was also aware that King Ranch would stand behind him in any settlement that was made between the two companies. Tom, normally unflappable, was in an emotional state because of the schizophrenic position Clarence Dauphinot had put him in over these negotiations. At one point, Francis took Tom into another room for a little lecture. In cutting a deal, he said, Tom must stand by Bob. Francis pointed out to him that over the years Bob had always stood by him, even to the point of buying into Deltec to bolster Tom's position.

Tom had other problems; Rupert was circling for the kill. Rupert could not see a position for Tom in the new alignments: "What does he have to offer?" When I reported this friction to Bob, he gave me the background. At the acquisition of the Tully River rain forest property in Australia in 1959, Tom wanted Arthur, his man, put in charge. For his part, Arthur did not have much confidence in running cattle in the wet tropics. Rupert, the top King Ranch official in Australia following the death of W. S. Robinson and the loss of Sam Hordern in an auto accident, wanted to run it himself. As always, the call was left to Bob, and Bob chose Rupert. Rupert had not forgiven Tom for trying to lock the gate on him.

Bob listened, went off to take naps, drove in the countryside to look at properties Michael Hughes had located, and waited. He would not let the group forget that the Angliss buyout was a viable alternate to dealing with Deltec and instructed Arthur to offer them $10 million, walk in, walk out. Arthur did not think they would accept it, as it would come to only $60 a head for their 167,000 cattle alone, but he would try.

At 2:00 one morning, after the first-night marathon had been extended two more days, Bob still seemed relaxed, willing to wait: "Let everything happen in its own time." More avenues were open to him than to Deltec in this situation; time was on the side of the man with the cash. A deal was eventually struck with Deltec, on Bob's terms, and King Ranch took over their interest in Australia.

This abbreviated summary, involving property acquisitions in three different countries (and not including a third Australian offer that got considerable attention) was not an exception to the Kleberg routine; it was more the rule, almost a way of life. When there was nothing more to add to the discussion that almost constantly buzzed around him, it was left to him to render his judgment. He unfailingly made it, stuck with it, and moved on.

The next move he stuck with too—the most exotic, in many ways the most frustrating, of a full lifetime of creating ranches.

HIS MAJESTY KING MOHAMMED V

The visit that most taxed our resources, and our ability to adapt, was the descent upon the ranch by His Majesty King Mohammed V of Morocco.

A request to Bob for King Ranch to be included in the royal procession across the United States came weeks in advance. As soon as he agreed—perhaps "capitulated" is a better word—phalanxes of security people poured through the front gate: the FBI, the Secret Service, the State Department Secret Service, the Texas Rangers, the State Highway Patrol, each with no knowledge of and not much interest in the others' plans to provide the royal protection. Their modes of operation were poles apart also: the FBI smooth and adaptable; the Secret Service inflexible, feet solidly on the ground; the Texas Rangers good ole boys who were on their home turf.

When a chief of state tours the country on an official visit, our State Department renders full ceremonial honors—leading to further interservice complications. For instance, on arrival the dignitary's national anthem shall be played. Since the king and his party were landing at our local Kingsville Naval Air Station, the Navy was saddled with the musical rendition and with providing the military honor guard. But they could not come up with a copy of the Moroccan anthem. They did locate an officer who had been stationed in the country and thought he remembered how it went. He spent several days humming while the band tried to pick up the tune.

The day arrived, the planes touched down on the air station tarmac— two of them, one carrying the king and his party of forty-five, the other bringing in the baggage, both eight hours late. The king had brought along his younger son, a forward-thinking young man who had dispatched an agent ahead of him to line up girls at the stops—the agent had oversupplied him in Dallas and the son disappeared overnight. On the morning of their departure to Kingsville, the king had gone into His Highness's bedroom to wake him and discovered him missing. His coat had been thrown on the bed and out of it had tumbled a fat roll of large bills. The king pocketed the money and walked away. The son appeared about noon, found the money missing, and began screaming to the security people, mainly to divert the heat he was getting from his father. Pandemonium—and the king said not a word. Finally he relented, produced the bankroll, took his son aside to point out his indiscretions in language absolute monarchs reserve for their children, and they headed for the airport.

So by the time he arrived, His Majesty was not in the best temper. The ladder was wheeled up to the plane door and he stepped onto the platform, followed by the United States chief of protocol, Wiley Buchanan. The honor guard cracked to attention, the band sailed into the anthem. The king descended the stairs, spotted a line of limousines at a distance—and with his djellaba flying in the wind, he stalked over and climbed into the backseat of the first one.

Buchanan was in panic pursuit. "Your Majesty, they're playing your anthem!" A disbelieving head appeared around the door, a nonplussed look. Then Mohammed dutifully took up the burden of his office, stepped out and came to attention, the strange sounds squeaked to an end, and he inspected the honor guard. Meanwhile, the rest of the party lined up, some in military uniform and the rest in striped cutaways, patent leather shoes, and red fezzes.

As large as the main house is, it could not sleep forty-five. We had asked the State Department to sort them out by rank so that we could accommodate the lower end at a motel. Somehow, word of this arrangement got through to the entourage at the airport, so when the line of cars pulled up to the house, all the doors flung open and a thundering herd swept into the hallways. Bedroom doors crashed against walls; when vacant beds were hunted down the fez-headed, cutaway-suited functionaries leaped into them, staking their claim. There they lay, ramrod stiff and unyielding. They were determined not to be separated from their lord, the center of the action.

Bob Wells, who spoke a smattering of French, made the rounds, explaining to the prone functionaries that this was a matter beyond the ranch's control; they had been assigned their places by their own people. To a man, this made not a bit of difference. Finally, a general with enough clout to speak for the king ordered everyone out of bed, lined them up, made the assignments, and made them stick.

Meanwhile, there was the matter of the king's accommodations. A few months before his visit, Mr. and Mrs. Kleberg had made a trip to England, where Helen had purchased antique furniture for one of the large corner suites. It had just been redecorated and made ready to receive its royal visitor. His Majesty was escorted in; he inspected the bathroom, made a circuit around the four-poster bed, remarked to his aide that he thought he felt a draft, and headed for the hallway.

Opening doors, sniffing and rejecting, he circled the upper balcony until he came on a cubicle at the back of the house furnished only with an iron cot—it was used by baby-sitters as a napping room. This became the royal enclosure, the king on the cot and his valet curled up at the foot, on the floor. The abandoned suite has since become known as the King's Suite, though a king thus far has spent only about a minute and a half in it.

Remarkably, following these opening confusions, things went fairly well. The reason was that everything revolved around Mohammed; when he moved, everybody moved. An example: He was in the country to have a digestive malady treated, a serious one that we were told eventually killed him. So he barely touched the food that was prepared for him by his personal chef. At table, he picked at it a few minutes, gave up, and rose. Forty-five sets of knives and forks hit the plates in unison, chairs screeched, and the assembly came to attention: meal over, move out. Also, the fact that they would not think of touching alcohol in the king's presence made it far easier to settle them in at night.

While the king had brought along his top military staff, the officer with the clout was a little colonel, his personal aide-de-camp. Mohammed was an enthusiastic and expert horseman; he had expressed a desire to ride one of the ranch's Quarter Horses. The night of their arrival, the colonel came to me, towing an interpreter by the sleeve. The following morning the king wished to take his ride in western clothes; would I please provide an outfit?

Normally guest attire was not a problem—the ranch owned a downtown shop that stocked everything that was needed. But we had been through this before: in new clothes the wearer always looked like an outlander who had just detached the labels. Since Bob was away in Argentina and he and Mohammed appeared to be about the same size, I brought out some of his clothes—a hat, a worn tweed coat, khaki shirt and trousers, scuffed but sparkling boots—and sent them to the king's room. In only a few moments, a highly agitated colonel reappeared. Through the interpreter: "You have sent the wrong clothes! It's a military uniform!" I explained that most of the people on the ranch wore khakis, not jeans. That was only part of his hang-up. He demonstrated, with gestures, that he wanted one of those Buffalo Bill leather jackets with the strings hanging from the sleeves.

Back and forth we went. In exasperation, I finally told him, "Look, we have a saying in Texas: You pay $150 for your hat [remember, this was 1957], $150 for your boots, and $1.98 for everything in between."

His facial expression brightened. "I'll tell the king."

The next morning His Majesty, mounted on the top stallion of the breed, Hired Hand, and, accompanied by his host, Chairman of the Board Dick Kleberg, Jr., took a ride through the pastures. It appeared to us, and to the press corps, as if it was a daily routine they had followed for years.

The end of the visit emulated the beginning. On the morning of his departure, the king ordered his secretary to telephone his oldest daughter, with whom we understood he was particularly close, in Rabat. Of course, the request was handed over to his hosts, and a six-hour marathon with any number of overseas operators ensued. By midafternoon, His Majesty's patience was at its end, and he decided he would wait no longer; the party headed for the Naval Air Station. I left behind frantic instructions to transfer the call to the Navy operations office and joined the caravan.

When the cars drew up, we could hear the commanding officer through an open window. "No! no! operator, don't break the connection! The king is here, hang on!" Gently we tried to rush Mohammed inside—it was futile—monarchs move at their own unhurried pace. His Majesty seated himself at a desk, put the receiver to his ear, listened a moment, and dropped it back into the cradle. "I hear a static."

The captain looked as if a bomb had gone off in his belly—yeomen rushed off to try to reestablish the connection—Mohammed sat back, folded his hands in the sleeves of his djellaba, and waited. To divert him, the captain called in his weather officer with satellite photos taken a few hours before over Morocco. Mohammed was fascinated; it was probably the most interesting thing he had seen in this strange land. So the time passed quickly, the operators came through, and father and child had a half hour's chat. The lot of them then went directly to the plane, and our collective sigh of relief, whisking down the tarmac, helped get them airborne.

Over the years, King Ranch attracted a number of reigning and unemployed monarchs; Mohammed was the most regal, and possibly the most intelligent, of them all.

CHAPTER FIFTEEN

THE TRIALS OF
THE TWO KINGS

AT ONE TIME OR ANOTHER, all of us are asked for advice, give it, and then regret we did. Bob's last foreign foray proved to be that way—a request for advice that roller-coastered into his most modest but at the same time least rewarding offshore enterprise.

Through the Braga brothers, in February, 1967 Bob attended a reception in New York for His Majesty King Hassan II, son of Mohammed V. The king was accompanied by his sister, Her Royal Highness Princess Lala Niza, the wife of Ahmed Osman, one of the king's ministers. During the course of the evening, Bob was told that the king was interested in enlarging the beef output in Morocco; the country needed higher quantity and quality to satisfy its growing American tourist appetite. But Morocco had no qualified people in animal science; their agriculture, especially their herd tending, was of the primitive, nomadic type.

At that time, Bob's interest had recently been piqued at the opportunities in this part of the world, and it centered on the Mediterranean basin. He replied that on his next trip to Europe he would find time to spend in Morocco, to assess their potential and make any recommendations he might see that would be useful. The princess and her husband made arrangements for His Majesty to extend the invitation. So later in 1967, Bob first set foot in North Africa, spending a month traveling the country.

He found the Moroccan coasts on the Mediterranean and the Atlantic hot and desertlike. The uplands—in the foothills and the higher elevations of the Atlas Mountains, notched by shallow valleys—were cooler, more fertile, and received a higher rainfall. Some of the land was held by the crown, the rest was in private hands. All of the decent valley land was overgrazed by the nomadic Bedouins, who herded their few cattle, sheep, goats, donkeys, and camels from one grassy patch to the next, mowing it to the rocks and bare earth, then striking their black wool tents and moving on. They had the habit of watching the horizon. When they spotted an occasional black cloud that might herald rain, they noted the direction. In about two weeks they headed for it, putting their animals on the fresh emerging plants before they had time to mature, a pasture-depleting practice of incomparable efficiency.

When Bob returned to Kingsville, he wrote a report detailing his observations and made recommendations on where and how the king might direct his people to initiate a government-sponsored ranching enterprise. He thought that was the end of it. It wasn't. The king replied by offering to enter into an equal partnership with King Ranch, the government supplying the land, the ranch providing the improvements, livestock, and management. Bob saw Morocco as an economical way to enlarge his opening into the European market; by producing beef outside the continent, he would have far cheaper land with lower labor costs, yet be close enough to have ready, competitive access. He accepted the challenge, entering for the first time into a fifty-fifty ownership, with a bureaucracy holding the other half. The decision sowed the seeds of lots of acrimonious wrangling.

The Santa Gertrudis breed was a natural for the country, so the first priority was to get a herd settled on the land that the government put into the company. By agreement, a valley called Adarouch (Arabic for "footprint of the jackal"), aligned north-south about thirty miles south of Meknes and bisected by the Meknes-Marrakech highway, was chosen as the site for the new operation. The initial acquisition was 25,000 acres, equipped with a comfortable home but with no other improvements. The government obligated itself to add 25,000 acres a year until the ranch totaled 125,000 acres. Michael Hughes was appointed to manage this investment in tandem with the one in Spain; he began work immediately on the minimum improvements needed to handle the livestock: the fences, corrals, lanes, watering places, and quarters for the workers' families. The grazed-out land required a lot of attention. Bulldozers were brought in to uproot the scrub, tractors deep-plowed, and fertilizer, annual and perennial grasses, and legumes were laid down.

From the beginning, it wasn't easy. To get things moving, Michael had to offer his resignation to our Moroccan directors and demand theirs before they would divvy up their half of the input. But within a few months, Ranch Adarouch began to bloom and its new headquarters was a model for the country.

In Kingsville, arrangements were under way to make the usual cattle and equipment shipment. Since competition between breeds was not a factor and high-quality breeding stock was not in demand in Morocco, Bob did not feel that the grading-up program merited selections from his top animals. In Texas he put together a consignment of Santa Gertrudis bulls from his best commercial herds—the ones he had given his attention to over the years on Norias—and added to them a smaller group of young bulls from the Buck and Doe Run Valley Farms in Pennsylvania. To gather the females he needed, he innovated. The grading-up program was far enough along in Argentina to produce young females, two- and three-year-olds, that were of excellent Santa Gertrudis type, though not purebreds. A shipment of these young Argentine crossbreds was the foundation of the Adarouch breeding program. Joined with the Norias bulls, they made an admirable base upon which to build a commercial herd. All together, 269 Santa Gertrudis bulls and 249 heifers landed on the ranch.

Thus Bob made a two-step movement through his foreign operations. Recall that the best Santa Gertrudis to leave King Ranch went to Argentina; their progeny did them proud. Therefore he had an alternate source to his Texas herd when it came time to stock the Morocco ranch. From Texas to North Africa by way of South America.

Meanwhile, Michael Hughes and his foreman were buying native cows to begin their grading-up program, generally animals of mixed French–North African breeding. With the exception of a small herd of Yugoslav cattle I had seen years before in Israel, this lot was by far the worst herd of cattle I had ever laid eyes upon. Hardly a cow would have weighed 600 pounds; they were small-boned, mineral-deficient, disease-ridden little things that did not seem to stand a chance of producing a marketable baby. Nearly all of the cattle of the country were like that; there was no better quality available. Inexplicably, Bob seemed little concerned over the poor base upon which he had to build, putting his faith in his big, long-bodied Norias bulls. They justified his confidence; the calves out of these runty cows outweighed their mothers by the time they were old enough to breed.

A number of times Bob had visual, vocal proof that the Adarouch improvement program was being accepted by the Arabs. The highway passing through Adarouch was a thoroughfare for produce buyers, who bartered for vegetables, grains, and slaughter livestock from the small farmers along its route. Occasionally Michael had herds pushed up to the fence next to the road so the boss could look them over. Within minutes the shoulder was littered with battered pickups and flatbeds, their drivers bunched up in the bar pit making shouting, hand-waving bids for the fat calves.

KEEPING TO BOB'S preference for having meals outdoors, each midday the Moroccan hands set up beside a running stream an Arab tent, round with a conical roof, multicolored, tall and cool. Here they cooked for Bob's party. He asked Michael to roast a native calf so that he could compare the meat's flavor and texture with that of the crossbreds when they came on. Michael gave the order to the cook, who had experience only with spitted sheep—so he roasted the 450-pound calf the same length of time he allotted for 100 pounds of mutton. Six men staggered into the tent to set before the boss a low table with the brown and sizzling calf spread-eagled on it. Bob was ceremoniously handed a native dagger—in it went to carve a slab of loin. Boiling hot blood squirted over everyone—if the poor thing had still had its head, it probably would have jumped off the table and headed for the river, just as the cook and his helpers did—they made themselves scarce.

MORE THAN ONCE, I have mentioned the adaptations King Ranch made to the customs of the countries where it operated. Morocco was not an exception. Take the practice of tending a herd in the Arab world. The aeons-old tradition was to keep a man on foot day and night living with his animals. Good fencing made this obsolete, but that had no effect whatever on the ancient profession of the herdsmen. They were going to find employment living with any herd roaming Arab ranges, or place before the king's men their grievances over these strangers defiling their ancient customs. Adarouch acquiesced; out on the range a man or boy—draped in a filthy djellaba and carrying a stout shepherd's pole—tended each herd, even though the herd was quite capable of tending itself.

The nomads created another problem. They were squatting all over the countryside, their disease-ridden animals mingling with the ranch herds. Their goats, sheep, camels, and donkeys—with their more efficient sets of upper and lower grazing teeth—were taking the sparse grass, denuding the land. These people tended to return, year after year, to the same campgrounds where they had left behind crude lean-tos and mud-plastered

ovens. When Michael complained to his men about the problems the Bedouins were creating, King Hassan sent back word: "As soon as they move
on, bulldoze their campsites and put up the fences."

Nor were the locals done with seeing that Michael adapted to their
version of doing business, burnoose-style. The Adarouch Valley was a long
trough with the highway running the length of its floor, the ranchland
extending up toward the ridge on one side. Up on the inaccessible, cool,
pinnacle-strewn skyline, farmers cultivated one of North Africa's oldest
and most profitable crops: kef. Kef is a mild form of marijuana favored by
Moslems, who are denied the jollies of alcohol. The reclusive farmers were
not a problem, except at harvest time. On moonless nights, they loaded
their donkeys with their kef bales and set off down the hillsides to the
highway where they had scheduled rendezvous with their buyers. If they
encountered a fence along the way, they cut it and moved on, leaving behind mixed herds of wandering cattle and playing hell with the breeding
program.

Having had this experience during the first kef harvest season, the following year Michael sent word up to the farmers that he was fencing off
several lanes from the high end of the ranch down to the highway. They
were advised to use these lanes and told that the ranch hands would be
patrolling to see that they did. The arrangement worked; the farmers were
not interested in calling attention to their secretive, illicit trade through a
confrontation. Apparently the business, like its kind around the world,
already entailed enough risk. Two days before we arrived at the ranch on a
visit, the hands found a man murdered beside a water hole in one of those
lanes.

OUR FIFTY-FIFTY ARRANGEMENT with the government created for Bob
another sticky problem, aside from jurisdiction over day-to-day management. Around the world, he had maintained sole ownership over the purebred Santa Gertrudis females, selling only bulls to his partners and to other
breeders. This practice kept in his hands control over the foundation herd,
those animals which, on both sides of their pedigree, descended from the
King Ranch's bull Monkey. Therefore he was able to individually select
every Santa Gertrudis that went into the purebred or grading-up programs.
Others might have had the ability to do this, but by having one expert—
one set of eyes—make the judgment, high quality plus year-after-year uni-
formity were assured.

So the King Ranch created a separate corporation under Moroccan law,
controlled by two kinds of capital stock that put the control of the com-

pany owning the purebreds in King Ranch hands. A small property called M'Sellet, just a few kilometers from the outskirts of Rabat, was leased to accommodate this herd and the best of the native Tarentaise heifers that had been purchased for the grading-up program. M'Sellet was leased from a French colonialist, Raul Estrad, who had been clever and enterprising enough to hang on to his property when the newly independent monarchy had confiscated most French lands. Raul became the ranch manager under Michael and was invaluable to the company for his agriculture background and for his lifetime experience in the country.

The French-Moroccan relationship was ambivalent at best. Nearly all upper-class Moroccans were French-educated, including King Hassan II; French was their second language, perhaps even their first, since they spoke it to each other. They shopped in Paris, played on the Riviera; they loved everything French; they loathed Frenchmen. This created a dilemma for us. The colonialists who had not fled the country were the only trained agriculturalists in Morocco. Our nationalistic, excessively touchy, bureaucratic partners insisted in every dialogue with them that the ranch replace Raul with a native and hire more Moroccan assistant managers. They looked upon the setup as a free training ground for young people who would eventually replace all the resident foreigners. Understandably, Bob saw turning over management to a bunch of untrained amateurs as a certain formula for disaster. The matter was a festering sore during our entire experience in the country and never was fully resolved.

AT ONE POINT, KING RANCH Moroccanization degenerated from a three-act misadventure to a slapstick comedy of errors. Bob came to realize that Michael would need high-placed assistance to represent his views to his government partners. He had made friends with—and appointed as president of the company—one of Morocco's leading industrialists and advisers to the king, Othman Benjelloun. Othman was as cosmopolitan and erudite as one would expect of a man who represented Swedish Volvo in his country and in other parts of North Africa, exporting to neighboring countries and to China automobile accessories and heavy machinery. Quietly, effectively, in England and the United States, he was also the leading arms procurer for his government during its sporadic conflicts with the Polisario guerrillas. Small, impeccably tailored, with remarkable energy and an exceptionally level head, Othman managed to balance on a tightrope stretched over a wide chasm between the two equal partners.

ON THE COAST NEAR KENITRA, about fifty kilometers north of Rabat, three of Morocco's few permanent rivers converge to form a swampy delta. The rivers had been dammed in the uplands to provide irrigation, and Michael wanted Bob to see the fertile plains that had been formed by access to this water. He needed a safe farm to produce hay for his cows during the dry season and hoped that the government could be persuaded to add some of this irrigated land to the partnership.

On a December visit in 1972, when the ducks had migrated down from northern Europe, Othman arranged a shoot for Bob in the coastal marshes. We stayed overnight in a nearby hunting lodge, and in the predawn, donning our wading gear, we sloshed behind our guides into the reeds. The ducks squawked and groused all around us and took to the air—in the dark the confused guides had led us right into the middle of several thousand of them. Apparently it was the only raft of birds on the North African coast—we did not see another duck the rest of the morning.

By 8:00, without firing a shot, we gave up, reassembled at the cars, and drove through citrus orchards to one of the irrigated meadows where we hoped to find jacksnipe. We did—we also found several hundred Arabs. They materialized from beneath the trees, chasing our caravan down the road shouting for employment as jacksnipe beaters, or for just a handout. Abdelbaki Doukkali, our cohost, a leading naturalist and a member of one of Morocco's most venerable families, rounded up the mob, sorted out about thirty to hire as beaters, and paid the rest one dirham apiece if they would agree to leave. They did, the beaters spread out and went to work, and we got in some decent shooting, for a while.

When we returned to the cars, we found a group of the constabulary waiting. Their young senior officer was the local game warden, new to his post, full of himself to the point of seeming to swell in indignation as he lectured us. Two weeks before, a man had been found murdered nearby. While not too pointedly fingering us as suspects, he demanded to see the permits for our guns. The hunting lodge proprietor was responsible for providing them, but this minor expense he had forgone. Othman, Abdelbaki, and the military went at it. For over two hours they listed for the stony-faced warden the people in and out of government who would vouch for us. He was unmoved by the litany—in the end he began gathering up Bob's treasured Purdeys, along with our lesser weapons.

As I have pointed out, Bob did not have an undue attachment to possessions, but those Purdeys were an exception—the stuff hit the fan and flew all the way back to the royal palace. Instructing Othman to translate word for word, he told the warden that he expected to have his guns back within twenty-four hours and he expected to receive them in Rabat. The young man went from pale in the face to purple to pale again, climbed into his jeep, and left us to watch our shotguns disappear down the dusty road.

Back in Rabat that evening, we were invited for drinks with Ahmed Osman, the former minister to the king and U.S. ambassador who was now the prime minister, and his wife, Princess Lala Niza, at the new Dar es Salaam Country Club. By this time Bob had unwound and enjoyed needling the smiling but slightly stiff-mouthed and embarrassed Osman over the events of the morning. A few minutes later, Osman excused himself and made for the telephone. He had something on his mind that involved his friend Bob, and he had no intention of having it sidetracked by a country game warden and a box of twelve-gauges.

Later in the evening, Osman drew Bob aside to tell him that recently Moroccan relations with Washington had been deteriorating. Could Bob arrange for him as soon as possible to meet with President Nixon? Bob had been one of Nixon's early presidential backers; faithful to his creed, he stayed with Nixon long after Nixon's more intimate associates had run for cover. He assured Osman that it could be arranged, and it was.

When we reached Bob's suite in the Rabat Hilton, the phone was ringing and there was an accumulation of messages at the desk. Would Mr. Kleberg honor the newly appointed minister of agriculture by paying him a call at 9:00 the following morning, at which time the minister wished to make Mr. Kleberg a presentation? At the appointed hour, a brief, rather frigid ceremony came off wherein the minister, in the presence of the game warden's superior officer and other department dignitaries, returned Bob's Purdeys to him. The minister's remarks were a bureaucratic mind-boggler—he managed to slide down a verbal razor's edge without even nicking his pin-striped pants. While he profusely apologized to his guest for the inconvenience he had been caused—for the lack of hospitality and consideration, for nonrecognition of the value to His Majesty's government of so distinguished a friend of Morocco—his national pride would not permit him to say that the game warden was in the wrong or even that he had overreacted.

Following this somewhat strained introduction to the minister, Bob settled in for a discussion on the future of Ranch Adarouch. Michael had several points to raise: the length of the leases on the land, the need to keep the purebred herd separate from the commercial cattle, the urgency of providing irrigated land so that a hay supply would be assured, the problems caused by the government's not honoring its commitment to put more acreage into the partnership. Bob explained to the minister that past experience had taught King Ranch a lesson: the further a foreign holding was from Texas, the larger it must be to become viable. At Morocco's distance, it was mandatory for the ranch to support 40,000 cows to be profitable. The minister was hesitant to commit himself to even 50,000 acres from the present 25,000. He proposed an association of small neighboring farmers, each of whom would put their land into a cooperative alongside Adarouch. We conjured up in our minds a vision of a directors' meeting under this kind of setup! Even if all this came off and Adarouch eventually grew to the minister's 50,000 acres, it would carry only 16,000 animals at best. The two principals were poles—and cultures—apart.

Bob asked if there were any questions. The minister's first: Will you consider hiring a Moroccan manager? Bob pointed out that Morocco was not a cattle country; therefore there were no trained ranchers available. Not in the best humor over several less-than-satisfactory turns the interview had taken, he turned to Othman and again asked him to translate his exact words. He told the minister that he would never have undertaken a development in Morocco without complete control. King Ranch had been offered opportunities all over the world—in countries where it had its biggest landholdings, the governments had offered him even more land. He said he came to Morocco only because Michael was available to manage; otherwise he would not have done it.

The message got across. The minister assured the boss that he did not want to replace Michael, he just wanted Moroccans in responsibility under Michael, rather than Raul, a Frenchman, to facilitate solving Morocco's problems (meaning the heat the minister was taking over the locals' being shut out). Bob replied that he had no objection to this. All but one of the King Ranch's foreign operations were managed by nationals of the countries where they were located. So far, we had not been able to find that caliber of man in Morocco.

Despite the differing views of our mission that had been aired, the meeting ended upbeat. Bob assured his counterpart that when a country had good cattle standing over good grassland, the two became a permanent asset, like forestland—an asset that could be taken to any of the world's banks to secure a loan. The minister replied that for years Morocco had concentrated on fruit and grain production: "Now it is time to feed the grain to cattle."

THE INCIDENT INVOLVING the ducks, snipe, and shotguns was but one of our wildlife misadventures. His Majesty is an avid golfer and his royally sponsored courses must be among the most beautiful and best-maintained in the world. Othman told him of the flocks of wild turkey he had seen roaming over the ranch in Texas, and the king indicated he would like to see a few of these exotic birds released on one of his golf courses. Bob handed over delivery to me.

Trapping the birds was not difficult. Our wildlife manager, Bill Kiel, had a great deal of experience moving them around the United States to restock areas where they had been hunted to extinction. So in due time we had twenty mature gobblers and hens boxed and ready for air shipment. I kept a monitor on them from the time they went aboard the plane in Corpus Christi; the next day I learned they were sitting in an overheated metal warehouse at Kennedy Airport. The Pan Am dispatcher reported that they had not arrived in the four-hour time frame required to get them on the Rabat flight.

I pointed out to him the susceptibility of all birds, especially turkeys, to heat stress. Since these were wild creatures, the state did not allow us to put a value on them. But it had cost us five thousand dollars to capture and transport them—if Pan Am lost them, we planned to file a claim for that amount, naming him as the responsible party. If they arrived dead, King Hassan would take up the matter with Pan American in a manner he deemed appropriate. "Yes sir, Mr. Cypher, I see the forklift headed for the plane right now!"

By coincidence, the shipment arrived while the king was hosting a meeting for the heads of the North African states at one of his homes in the countryside. The officials at the airport, seeing His Majesty's name on the manifest, loaded them on a truck and sent them on their way. When they arrived at the compound, a guard peeked between the slots, saw birds, and waved the driver toward the kitchen. The poor, exhausted travelers were trussed up and laid out on the floor awaiting the cook's inspection. Since they were not on the menu, the cook thought they were one of His Majesty's last-minute whims—he stroked his knife and leaned over the first bird. Just then, a minister in the know sauntered through, took in the scene, and spared the cook, the guard, the airport officials, and sundry other participants their sovereign's displeasure. As far as I know, the descendants of those overpampered American fowl are still living out their idyllic lives along the royal fairways.

As the 1970s got under way, meat production became a goal Morocco could not afford to pursue. With little to generate foreign exchange except their supply of rock phosphorus—a commodity in surplus in international trade—the government was strapped to pay its escalating costs for arms to pursue the guerrilla wars. The tensions caused by the restrictions this overriding burden placed on the economy, plus the pressure to which the armed services were being subjected, led to a nascent revolutionary movement against Hassan and his authoritarian form of government.

During the July 1971 trip to England, Spain, and Morocco, we were in

London when we received word from Michael that there had been an attempt on the king's life at his birthday celebration. The troops assigned to guard him and his guests at his seaside palace at Skhirat, south of Rabat, were ordered by their officers to open fire. Ninety-nine guests and staff personnel were killed, 133 wounded, but the king was spared.

The airports were closed and we were on the point of canceling our visit when we learned that the officers responsible had been rounded up, tried, and executed, and that relative calm had returned to the country. Bob decided that even though we would likely not accomplish much in view of the political unrest and uncertainty, he needed to see what progress had been made at the ranches. His government partners were expecting him—he also thought he should show his solidarity with them and with the king by putting in an appearance. We found the countryside calm and orderly, but we spent a lot of time waiting in line at the innumerable roadblocks thrown up along the highways.

There was a sidelight to the incident—amusing, as it turned out, though it might not have been. On our arrival at the Ritz Hotel in Madrid, we were waiting for the elevator when the door opened and out stepped a pale, shaken George Moore, the retired chairman of the First National City Bank in New York. "Look what I just found in my mail!" and he handed a telegram to his friend Bob. It was an invitation to the king's birthday party. For some years, George had been Hassan's financial adviser and frequent golf partner. He was at his vacation home in Soto Grande when the message arrived at the hotel—it had missed him by two days. Otherwise he would have caught the first plane over to Rabat and would have found himself standing in the midst of the carnage, or a part of it.

A FEW MONTHS LATER, we learned that there had been another try at His Majesty. He was returning with his personal staff and members of his family from France in an Air Moroc plane when it was attacked by a Moroccan Air Force fighter. The plane fired an air-to-air missile that must have been improperly armed—it passed through the body of the Boeing 727 without exploding. The plane was able to land at the Rabat airport, and the king and his party took shelter in a grove of trees alongside the runway as the fighter strafed the sitting duck on the ground. Again Hassan escaped unharmed, and it must have appeared to his followers that truly he was a direct descendent of Mohammed and under his protection.

These incidents were but the high drama in a continuing state of unrest and preoccupation over the border disputes that embroiled the country in the late 1960s and early 1970s. Agriculture—indeed, all of Morocco's plans to shift its economy out of the third world orbit and to catch up to its peers in Europe—took a backseat to settling these conflicts.

A ranch, like a herd, must ever continue to grow or it dies. Failing to improve, Ranch Adarouch, like an unkempt jalopy on half-inflated tires, coasted to a stop—then began an inexorable backward slide. But in 1974, this was in a future misted by our inability to conjure up a King Ranch destitute of Bob Kleberg.

CHAPTER SIXTEEN

WE SAY GOOD-BYE

AS I DESCRIBED IN THE beginning, Bob Kleberg's last visit to Morocco in 1974 had a different character, a darker hue. His plans were to stop over in Spain to look at a property that could be added to Los Millares, then take on several problems in Morocco, where Michael had located a ranch on the north coast that the government might have been able to acquire. Bob had brought along his three oldest grandchildren, Helen, John, and Emory Alexander, along with a young French friend of Helen's, Corine Hendricks. From Morocco he planned to take the group of young people on safari in eastern and southern Africa.

For Bob, it was a long, grueling trip that almost immediately began to take its toll. Even though we made the fastest Atlantic crossing in our experience—four and a half hours from St. John's, Newfoundland, to Madrid—he had drunk too much and was in a sour, complaining mood by the time we reached the hotel. Every day, his only good times were his first two or three hours out of bed in the late morning. From the prelunch cocktails until we got him to bed at night, the climate around him deteriorated. I credited it to the fact that all of us were getting older and the boss was the oldest among us, seventy-eight on his last birthday. More and more, he did not accept with good grace the advancing years.

Bob loved his grandchildren and often took them with him on his travels. But they were just turning from adolescence to adulthood; their agendas were no longer necessarily his. So each day there was lots of discussion, leading to bickering over our schedule: who would go where when.

Another grind on our tempers, and this was generally true during all of our travels, was a lack of sleep. The children, our hosts, and their wives were able to get away for a nap at times during the day, but for me and the others on business call, this was a seldom-afforded luxury. Each morning we needed to organize our plans—arrange transportation, meals, plane schedules—before the boss was up and ready to go. At night, even if he decided to turn in at a sensible hour, I felt responsible as his surrogate to his guests, some of whom invariably lingered after dinner. This meant seeing the last one to bed. I seldom reached my room before 1:00, sometimes around 3:00, to go over the notes for the next day before the light went out. Great fun occasionally, deadly every night.

The property in Morocco that might have been added to the joint venture—near Tétouan on the Mediterranean side of the Straits of Gibraltar—turned out to be a disappointment to Bob, further stretching his temper. The soil was a barren clay studded with dwarf palms; about a third of the grazing land turned to swamp during the rainy season. The young people got bored and testy during the long day, nipping at their grandfather's heels, for which they were returned a few snarls. By the time we reached the last day of the trip, I planned to leave for Paris when they departed for Kenya. I was of a mind to return to Kingsville and begin looking for a job. I could not see how I could be of further use to King Ranch or to Bob Kleberg, given our deteriorating relations over the past three weeks.

His last stop in Morocco, on the morning of July 3, was at the royal palace, where he had an appointment with the king. From the palace he went directly to the plane for the first leg of his safari, a stop in Nairobi. I had scheduled a noon flight from Casablanca, so under the hotel portico I put him in Prime Minister Osman's sedan, said good-bye, and was never in my life more relieved to make an exit.

I HAVE SINCE LOOKED back on that June–July episode as one of the more thickheaded in my career. While I put the root of the boss's dark spirit on his age and his drinking, I did not suspect that he was ill, really ill. Anyone exposed to the length and fraternity of our relationship should have spotted the cause behind something new and unfamiliar developing in the other—I did not.

But by late August 1974, Bob was back at the ranch, refreshed, relaxed, his usual self. His shooting had been successful, especially he had been able to bring home a trophy lion, a prize that had eluded him on his previous safari. In southern Africa he had visited Botswana and had been taken out on the Kalahari Desert. The Kalahari Desert took him—he fell in love with it. A partly unexplored open plain, as level as his King Ranch and just as devoid of surface water, it is one of the world's largest and most under-utilized grasslands. Like King Ranch, it is underlaid with a water table that can be pumped by windmills. On his return, the first thing he told me was that his next foreign venture would be in the Kalahari. By happy coincidence, the Botswana ambassador to the United States had visited in Kingsville during the time Bob was in his country, so I had a contact in Washington to make the initial inquiries.

Also, the Amon Carter Museum of Western Art in Fort Worth wanted to mount a major show of the photographs made on the ranch by Toni Frissell, Helen's friend, during the early 1940s. Toni was one of the stars in what must have been the finest group of photographers ever assembled during their era, the heyday of the Time/Life organization. During the early months of World War II, when Toni's travels were restricted, she spent a lot of time with Helen on the ranch, a Leica constantly in her hand. Toni had given her negatives to the Library of Congress, so the director of the museum, Mitch Wilder, and I spent a week in the library basement choosing several hundred candidates for the show. We also discovered, in the cabinet next to the one we were culling, Toni's voluminous file of her photo sessions with the fresh, young, voluminous Elizabeth Taylor. Part of that week was lost in extraneous visual activity.

Bob and I had several pleasant evenings together at Norias, going over the prints to select the ones he felt best depicted the ranch of 1939–1943. Then September was upon us, the dove-shooting season was about to begin. Bob was spending all of his time on the southern ranch; I did not go down every day. There was a lull in activity; he passed on to me the things he wanted me to do over the telephone. So I had not seen him for several days when, one midmorning, I was out on the street in Kingsville and found him in his parked car across from our office.

I crawled into the backseat, next to Adán, and got a shock. Bob's face, including the whites of his eyes, had turned a rather fluorescent yellow. My instant gut reaction was, the ole liver has finally succumbed to a life-long alcohol bath. He told me that he had just come from our local doctor, that he had jaundice, but that there were so many causes for the condition that it could not be diagnosed here. The doctor urged him to immediately put himself in the hands of a group of diagnostic physicians in Houston.

But Bob had a horse running at Belmont on Saturday and he very much wanted to see the race; he decided to put off entering the clinic until he could fly from New York to Houston on the following Sunday, five days later.

Neither I nor any of his family could change his mind, though even to laypersons like us, his condition was obviously acute. Helen went from her farm in Maryland to New York to join her father; she had a rough four days. He began feeling bad, worse each day, and took to the liquor cabinet to offset it. Even the horse ran badly; the week was misspent.

Meanwhile, Patricia was within a few days of baby time, our second child. I was strung out between not wanting to leave her for a moment and my duty to the boss, who needed to have someone with him, especially now. He flew alone from New York to Houston and checked into a lavishly appointed suite on the top floor of St. Luke's Hospital in the Baylor Medical Center; I was told it had been furnished for Lyndon Johnson. I met him there at 10:00 on a Sunday evening; he looked like hell warmed over and felt the same way.

Early the next morning, a team headed by the chief of diagnostic medicine of the Kelsey-Seybold Clinic, Dr. Kelsey, went to work. The series of examinations, lasting three days, was inconclusive; more and more Dr. Kelsey became convinced that this was not a simple case of liver failure, either from an infection or from excessive alcohol processing. There was no question that, in some way, the liver was affected; Dr. Kelsey told Bob that for the time being any further drinking was out.

Even in a situation as serious as this, there were funny moments. A series of doctors spent several hours taking Bob's medical history. When they got to the part concerning the frequency and amount of his liquor intake, he was a study in smooth, evasive equivocation. "Sometimes one before lunch; one, even two sometimes before dinner." Oh boy! "Sometimes" was the key they never focused on, thinking it meant one or two or none when he was actually telling them one or two or infinity. But to credit his willpower, when he was told that it was harmful to his health and would interfere with his treatment, he did not ask for another glass. Friends soon learned he was in town; he had lots of them in Houston. So they began dropping by in a widening stream. He had me stock the bar in the suite and offered drinks all around—but he never took one himself.

At this late hour, I got another lesson in his capacity for work. Most of his tests were completed on his first full day in the hospital, leaving us a few days together while they were being evaluated. He accomplished more in each of those days than I had seen him turn out in several normal ones at home. For fourteen hours without letup, except for brief meals, he either dictated to me, had me placing overseas calls, or was on the phone himself. Shorthand is not among my talents; so I wrote as fast as I was able, signaling frequent stops or slowdowns, which he tolerated even though he sometimes lost his train of thought. Then, while he was on the telephone beside his bed, I ran to a pay booth to read everything to Lee Gillett in Kingsville. She had it in the mail by that evening.

HIS CLOSE ASSOCIATION with Richard Nixon had brought Bob under the eye of the attorney general's investigation into the Watergate affair. Specifically, they were interested in his campaign contributions. Did they exceed the limit? Before he entered the hospital, he had set up an appointment to make a deposition in the matter. This he did, from his hospital bed, before the government people, with Leroy Denman the only representative in his behalf. The question-and-answer session went on for several hours. I have read the document; it is over an inch thick. The people who later reviewed it said they had never seen a performance like his. Without a note to guide him, he answered their questions as completely and as factually as if he had been surrounded by a score of prompters and stacks of briefing books. The only reservation he made concerned citing dates— he had no memory for them. The day of the week—or month—weekdays or weekends—had little meaning for him.

WHILE BOB HAD SAID nothing to his family or to his other associates about his plans to retire, he had asked me to look into the possibility of purchasing another home for him. To the end, his mind was on his horses. Adjacent to King Ranch, Kentucky, was a piece of property called the Steel Farm, the property of a widow who had for years leased her pastureland to the ranch. On it was a nice home; Bob wanted to buy it and make it his headquarters for looking after the racing operation. But he added, "Don't think I'm pulling out entirely; I'll keep my hand in at the ranch!"

He asked me to do this on his first day in the hospital; I was not able to even open the negotiation in his name.

The test results were inconclusive; Dr. Kelsey advised exploratory surgery. Two days before his operation, Bob's oldest granddaughter, Helen Alexander, joined her mother at her grandfather's bedside. Of daughter Helen's six children, Helen was the most interested in the Thoroughbreds and had become a devoted student of pedigrees and performance. Bob dictated a letter to me turning over the management of the horse operation to her during his convalescence. He never took back the reins. Helen took up this legacy, built by her grandfather for King Ranch, by mastering a complicated business, easing out of racing and concentrating on the more lucrative side of breeding and selling yearlings, putting the stable on the black side of the ledger, and then closing down the operation at a tidy profit. He would have been a proud grandfather had he lived to see Helen elected a member of the Jockey Club, the affiliation he most prized during his lifetime.

Helen has been true to her grandfather's legacy in the Thoroughbred world. Making her home in Lexington, she has formed her own stable and is currently breeding and racing horses, successfully, in her name.

MY LAST TRIP TO ST. LUKE'S Hospital, holding my breath as I left Patricia looking like a very large grape, was the night before his operation; I arrived at dinnertime to find him surrounded by his family and friends. He was in good spirits, enjoying himself, telling tales and listening to our banter, until the nurse arrived with a sedative that was preliminary to the operative procedure. The next morning at 6:00, Helen and I were there to accompany him to the operating room door. As they rolled him through, he looked at me, trouble written on his face, and turned away.

ONE OF BOB'S GREAT-NEPHEWS, Dr. Richard Sugden, was doing his residency at St. Luke's and was in the operating room during the first part of the surgery. The diagnosis that this was not a simple case of jaundice brought on by liver failure was a correct one. Richard told Helen that when the surgeons examined Bob's liver, unbelievably it appeared to be that of a twenty-four-year-old man.

At midafternoon, Dr. Seybold came out to report that he had excised a doughnut-shaped tumor that had grown around the duct leading from the liver to the intestine, shutting it off and accounting for the symptoms of liver failure. The pancreas was also involved; his condition was serious. When the doctor told Helen that her father would be in intensive care for several days under around-the-clock observation, Helen asked him to make every effort to see that all the nurses were pretty ones.

Great-thinking daughter—nothing could have done more toward his recovery.

Bob lived for three weeks after the operation; daily the prognosis became more negative. He had to endure a second operation and a tracheotomy to relieve his breathing, which left him unable to speak; a pad and pen were provided so he could communicate. On one of his visits, the doctor asked Bob if there was anything he could get him that would make him more comfortable. Bob wrote, "Vodka tonic." To the end it demonstrated that he not only knew what he wanted, he used some clear reasoning to attain it. A vodka tonic was a drink he rarely took. But of all the highballs on his list, it was probably the mildest—he must have figured that if he stood a chance of getting one at all, this would probably be it.

The doctor was sympathetic, but in the interest of protecting his patient's perforated digestive tract, Bob didn't get it.

FROM HIS FRIEND TOM LEA, he received a last gift, dedicated to one of the crowning accomplishments in his long career. Bob had taken Tom with him on his last trip to Australia, so that Tom could write a history of King Ranch developments out there and illustrate it with his paintings and sketches of the different ranches. Tom was able to bring to the hospital copy number one of *In the Crucible of the Sun* and place it in his hands. Bob could respond only with a nod and a smile.

A copy of this privately printed work has since been given to the libraries of each of the land grant colleges and universities in the United States.

ROBERT JUSTUS DIED during the evening of October 13, 1974. His funeral, four days later, was a grand thing. It was held inside and on the lawn of the main house on a bright autumn morning, where he was bid good-bye by a gathering of a thousand or more from all over the country, a sizable delegation from Mexico, and friends and associates from the countries where he had gone to ranch. There was mourning, of course, but the mood seemed mainly one of poignancy—saying good-bye to the *patrón* who had to leave us, and to his El Dorado world, his unique creation, that instinctively all felt we would never see again.

Bob had left instructions that at his funeral his liquor and wine cellar was to be emptied and put out for his friends. Helen complied—along with a camp lunch, bottle after bottle of century-old cognacs, rare vintage wines, and private-label bourbons and scotches went down a considerable number of uneducated and, I fear, unappreciative gullets.

Then the funeral cortege, mile upon mile, pulled away from the main house and from his cottage nearby, headed south to Norias. In the remote sand dunes, in a pasture called San Ignacio, there is a little island surrounded by a lake, fed by a trickle of water from a flowing well. During the day deer, javelina, turkey, coyotes and raccoons and other small creatures, and birds, singly and in flocks, come to drink. Ducks stop in during the season; the water teems with largemouth bass. On the island, under a sheltering grove of oaks, Helen lies; it was her favorite fishing cove. There Bob joined her.

Level on the ground, unobtrusive in the natural beauty that surrounds them, rest two simple marble slabs, gifts of their Mexican friends. On Bob's is written the message that he carried with him through his life, words that were the sum of his being, the canon that formed and guided him: "Your life is an expression of what you are."

VIEWED FROM TWENTY years' hindsight, it seems that Bob's accomplishments have largely been erased: His efforts to build outside of Texas have been leveled; the ranches into which he put so much of his later life have been sold—they no longer have the form or function he gave them. At home his beloved Thoroughbreds are dispersed, his Santa Gertrudis herds and Quarter Horse bands reduced.

Though the corporation has diminished, the fault cannot be laid entirely at the feet of the present shareholders; they no longer have access to the mineral income that Bob used as his brick and mortar. Perhaps most important, because of his intelligence, drive, relentless tenacity, and fortitude, the ranch in South Texas, whose suzerainty he grasped just as he rose from boyhood, is still intact, still serving his country and the world, providing us a bountiful supply of high-quality protein.

In a hundred years, the structure of all of our present-day industrial giants will have changed. If General Motors and General Electric still exist, their roles in our economy will be far different than today. But in the pastures on the coastal plain in Texas, good cattle will still be standing over good grass. Absent a future Bob-like Kleberg rising during the era, it is possible that they will not be King Ranch cattle or King Ranch grass, but the function, the relationship that has over five centuries bonded one to the other, will be as strong as ever it was.

AS I HAVE FOR MOST of my life, in the evenings I drive in the pastures near my home, occasionally stopping to watch a herd of deer graze, to count the points on a well-antlered buck, to sit quiet as a flock of gobblers or a covey of quail amble toward their roosts. I hear it then—I hear the land breathe—the soft respiration of a living thing. That's foolishness, of course—dirt doesn't breathe, at least not audibly. Reason tells me it's just the gentle sundown breeze moving through the feathery mesquite leaves, swaying the smaller branches. Still, the land seems to emit an immutable life—apart—transcending ownership—beholden to no higher order than the Order that brings the rain and the frost, the heat and the cold. Its self-sufficiency, its independence, overreaches humankind's relatively brief few million years here on earth, making us mere custodians during our minimal time.

If there is anything approaching the eternal, it's the sea—and the land. While on the land the trees are majestic, stately, the grass is inevitable—it has claimed its place since the earth cooled; it will endure until the final conflagration. Bob's goals and faith were bound to these seas of grass—the rippling pastures he saw around him he believed were the land's most beneficent yield—and around them he formed his life, his creed: No excuses.

In Kingsville

1994

Aberdeen Angus breed, 13, 142
Abolengo ranch, 143–144
Aborigines, 173–174, 176–177
Adarouch ranch, 210–212, 216, 220
Africa, 2–3, 149–152, 221, 223. *See also* South Africa
Africander breed, 15–16
Aguay ranch, 144
Airplanes, 77, 84–85, 135–136, 188
Alcohol use, 2, 44–49, 224
Alderman, Neil, 183
Alexander, Deaver, 49, 64
Alexander, Emory, 2, 221
Alexander, Helen (daughter). *See* Kleberg, Helen King
Alexander, Helen (granddaughter), 1–2, 221, 225–226
Alexander, John, 2, 221
Alligators, 98, 101
Allred, James, 66
American Quarter Horse: in Brazil, 124, 133; breeding of, 12, 14–15, 54; and Mohammed V, 207; in Spain, 190–191. *See also* Horses; Thoroughbred horses
American tourists, and beef demand, 76, 189, 209

Amon Carter Museum of Western Art, 223
Angliss, Arthur, 202, 204
Antunes, Augusto T. A., 1, 129–130, 134–135
Aramburu, Pedro Eugenio, 148
Argentina: and Deltec Panamerica, 127–128, 202; hunting in, 144; King Ranch in, 129, 141–149, 211; political climate of, 141–142, 148–149; Santa Gertrudis breed in, 142–145, 211; and water, 146–147
Armstrong, Henrietta Larkin, 64–65, 201
Armstrong, John B., 64
Armstrong, Thomas R.: and alcohol use, 45; and foreign investments, 88; gift for, 103; and hunting, 21; and Thoroughbred racing, 64–65
Associated Stations Proprietary, 167–168
Australia: aborigines in, 173–174, 176–177; and Associated Stations Proprietary, 167–168; and Brunette Downs, 171–175, 179–180; cattle transport in, 178–179; clearing land in, 91, 182–183; drought in, 168, 171–172,

178, 183; earthquake in, 170–171; grasses in, 94, 170, 173, 182–183; and International Packers, 129; isolation of, 179–180; King Ranch in, 91, 165–184, 204, 227; land of, 172–173; personnel in, 165–167; roundup in, 175; Santa Gertrudis breed in, 165–166, 168–169, 183–184; Thoroughbred horses in, 56, 202; training system in, 175–176; Tully River ranch, 91, 181–183, 204; water in, 168, 171–173, 178–183
Azy, Benoit, 118

Baillieu, Edwina, 166, 170–171
Baillieu, Peter, 166, 170–171, 180
Barbosa da Silva, Ambassador, 1
Barker, E. J., 74
Baruch, Bernard, 64
Bassingwaighte, Arthur, 168, 203–204
Batista, Pedro, 60
Batista y Zaldívar, Fulgencio, 78, 89
Beinecke, Walter, Jr., 86
Belmont Park, 58, 61, 154, 157, 224
Bemelmans, Ludwig, 32–34
Benjelloun, Othman, 214–215, 217
Berry, Red, 70
Big B Ranch, 40, 86–87
Blader Jack, 174–175
Bonsma, Jan, 162–163
Bonsmara breed, 162
Boyce–Rotchford, Cecil, 56
Braciaria grass, 92
Brady, James C., 158
Braga, George: and Cuba, 40, 75–76, 79, 89; and Morocco, 209; and Spain, 189–190
Braga, Riondo, 40, 75, 79, 189–190, 209
Brahma breed, 13, 96, 126
Branding, 31
Brazil: American Quarter Horse in, 124, 133; and Antunes, 129–130; cattle breeding in, 123, 125–126; clearing land in, 122, 132–135; and Deltec Panamerica, 127–129, 134, 202; grasses in, 124–127; and Herbert, 1, 123–124, 130–135, 137, 203; Indians of, 122, 131–133, 136; Jari

Company, 135–138; King Ranch in, 121–138; land of, 122–123, 130–131; and Mosquito, 122–124; Pará Ranch, 133–134; Santa Gertrudis breed in, 122, 124–126; SUDAM project in, 130–135, 138; and Taylor, 121–122; water in, 123
Breeds and breeding. *See* American Quarter Horse; Cattle breeding; Thoroughbred horses; and names of specific breeds
Brooks, Chet, 70
Brooks, Oakley, 134
Brown, Edgar, 68
Brown, George, 68–69
Brunette Downs, 171–177, 179–180
Buchanan, Wiley, 205
Buck and Doe Run Valley Farms, 112–118, 155, 211
Buckpasser (Thoroughbred horse), 7–8
Buffle (Thoroughbred horse), 7, 56

CAEMI, 129, 135
Campbell, Phillip Pitt, 9
Carmen ranch, 143–144
Castro, Fidel, 40, 78–80, 89–90, 111, 138
Cattle: diet of, 12, 15–16, 78; herd instinct of, 27, 100; quality of, 78; and roundup, 25–32, 99–101, 175; transport of, 112–118, 178–179. *See also* names of specific breeds
Cattle breeding: in Argentina, 142–145; in Australia, 165–166, 168–169, 183–184; in Brazil, 123, 125–126; conference on, 4; in Cuba, 74–75; and drought, 15, 39; in Great Britain, 12–13, 71, 142, 144; at King Ranch, 12–14; in Morocco, 211; and roundup, 25–32; in South Africa, 15–16, 162; in Spain, 190–191, 196; in Venezuela, 99–100. *See also* names of specific breeds
Cavazos, Lauro, 146
Cavestany, Rafael, 199–200
Cedral ranch, 96–104
Celestino, 93

Charolais breed, 118, 137
Chessire, Sam, 19–20
Chigüiri, 101–102
Churchill, Winston, 166
Clarke, Katherine, 201
Clarke, Rupert, 56, 166, 182–183, 201–204
Clarke, Vanessa, 201
Clearing land: in Australia, 91, 182–183; in Brazil, 122, 132–135; in Cuba, 75–76; in Texas, 75–76; in Venezuela, 91–93. *See also* Land
Clegg, George, 14
Clement, Ila, 201
Clement, Jim, 201
Colombia, 96
Committee for Economic Development, 160
Companhia Auxiliar de Empresas de Mineracão Internacional (CAEMI), 129, 135
Compañía Ganadera Becerra, 75–80
Compañía Venezolana de Ganadería, 96
Concha y Sierra, 194–198
Connally, John, 66–67
Cooper, Jack, 169–170
Corpus Christi, Port of, 114
Corrida, 26, 31, 100–101
Creed, Rufus F. S., 49–52
Cuba: and Castro, 40, 78–80, 89–90, 111, 138; cattle breeding in, 74–75; clearing land in, 75–76; grasses in, 77; and King Ranch, 40, 74–80; land in, 75–76, 78–80; Santa Gertrudis breed in, 74–75; and Tash, 123; and Venezuela, 88–90
Cullen, Hugh Roy, 68
Culling, 29
Curry, Leroy, 150
Cypher, John: in Australia, 168–184; in Cuba, 76–79; relationship with Kleberg, 1–4, 40–41, 44; in Venezuela, 94–95
Cypher, Patricia, 3, 103, 224, 226

Dauphinot, Clarence, Jr., 127–129, 202–203
Dauphinot, Penny, 128

De Cröy family, 118–120
De los Reyes, Gustavo, 89–91, 93–97, 100, 103–104, 107
Deltec Panamerica, 127–129, 134, 202–204
Denman, Diana, 133
Denman, Leroy G., Jr., 39–41, 128, 133, 225
Denman, Leroy G., Sr., 39–40
Derby, Lord, 55–56, 202
De Sevoia, Maria Gabriella, 118–120
Diet of cattle, 12, 15–16, 78
Dillon, Douglas, 46
Dogs, 20
Douglas, Howard, 171
Douglas, Lew, 166
Doukkali, Abdelbaki, 215
Drought: in Australia, 168, 171–172, 178, 183; and cattle breeding, 15, 39. *See also* Water
Dulles, Allen, 89
DuPont, William, 157
Durham, Ed, 9, 20, 28–29

Earthquake, in Australia, 170–171
East, Sarita K., 167
Eisenhower, Dwight, 160
El Abolengo. *See* Abolengo ranch
El Cedral. *See* Cedral ranch
Emert, Mary Lee, 125
Emert, Pete, 125
Encino, as division of King Ranch, 26, 153
English pointers, 20
Estrad, Raul, 214
European Economic Community, 189
Evans, Sterling, 158
Exxon, 17–18, 105, 158–160

Fanjul, Christina, 90
Farish, Will, 17
Fences, in Venezuela, 93
Fitzsimmons, Hugh, 66
Flinters grass, 173
Florida, 40, 85–87
Ford, Whitey, 63

Foreign investments. *See* names of specific countries
France, 188, 198, 214
Franco, Francisco, 199
Fraser, Simon Christopher Joseph, 71–73
Friendswood, 158
Frissell, Toni, 223
Frondizi, Arturo, 142

Geddes, Fahey, 180
Geddes, Reginald, 173, 179–180
General Motors Corporation, 113
Gillett, Lee, 41–42, 225
Gimson, J. F., 109
Golden retrievers, 20
Goulart, João, 130, 138–140
Government affairs, 30, 66–71, 160–161
Grabowski, Ian, 184–186
Grant, Arthur, 114–115
Grasses: in Australia, 94, 170, 173, 182–183; in Brazil, 124–127; in Cuba, 77; management of, 94; in Morocco, 211; and scale, 126–127; of South Africa, 126; in Spain, 190; in Texas, 16, 125–127; in Venezuela, 92, 97, 107. *See also* names of specific grasses
Great Britain: cattle breeds of, 12–13, 71, 142, 144; cattle companies of, 26, 107; and Royal Worcester Company, 107–110; and Thoroughbred horses, 55–56, 158
Greece, 88, 188, 198
Green Mitchell grass, 173
Groves, Helen. *See* Kleberg, Helen King
Guggenheim, Harry, 64
Guinea grass, 77, 92, 94, 107, 183

Handcock, Bull, 56
Harrison, Gerard, 113, 117
Hassan II, King of Morocco, 2, 42, 209, 213–214, 217–219
Hawaii, wasps of, 127
Hendricks, Corine, 221
Herbert, Francis: and Brazil, 1, 123–

124, 130–135, 137, 203; and Irwin, 125
Herbert, Martha, 124
Hereford breed, 12–13, 142
Hirsch, Buddy, 59, 61
Hirsch, Max: and Santa Gertrudis bull, 154–155; and Thoroughbred racing, 41, 54, 59–61, 64
Holmes, Mona, 83
Horan, Frank, 155
Hordern, Anthony, 170
Hordern, Sam, 166–167, 204
Horse racing, 7, 59–66, 157–158
Horses, 14–15, 28, 96–97, 175. *See also* American Quarter Horse; Thoroughbred horses
Hughes, Michael: and Morocco, 2, 204, 210–214, 216–218; and Spain, 190, 194, 198
Humberto II, King of Italy, 118
Humble Oil and Refining Company, 17–18, 21, 84–85, 160
Hunting: in Argentina, 144; and dogs, 20; and Humble Oil and Refining Company, 21; on King Ranch, 18–22; and land value, 96; in Morocco, 215–216; in Spain, 191–194; in Venezuela, 102–103. *See also* Wildlife management

India, 13, 126
Indians. *See* Native people
International Packers, 121–122, 125, 127, 129, 167
Iran, 2
Irwin, Monte, 124–125, 146
Italy, 88, 118, 188, 198

Jari Company, 135–138
Jockey Club, 62, 69, 158, 226
Johnson, Belton D., 9, 49, 66

Kalahari Desert, 223
Kazickas, Joseph, 105–106
Kef, 213
Kelley, R. B., 165
Kelsey, Dr., 224–225

Kenedy, Mifflin, 167
Kennedy, John F., 138
Kentucky, King Ranch in, 45, 53, 56, 225
Kenya, 2
Kern County Cattle Company, 26
Kiel, Bill, 217
King, Henrietta M.: and Denman, 39; homes of, 22; marriage of, 45; and railroad, 14; and ranch management, 5–7, 11; and trust period, 17
King, Captain Richard: alcohol use of, 44, 48; as founder of King Ranch, 5; homes of, 22; and Kenedy, 167; philosophy of, 38; and roundup, 26; and sheep, 144
King, Richard (cousin), 8–9
King Ranch: in Argentina, 129, 141–149, 211; artists visiting, 23–24, 107–110; in Australia, 91, 165–184, 204, 227; Australians visiting, 184–186; authors visiting, 32–34, 71–73; in Brazil, 121–138; and cattle breeding, 12–14; as corporation, 11, 23; in Cuba, 40, 74–80; divisions of, 26; in Florida, 40, 85–87; homes of, 22–23, 94, 122–123, 143; hunting on, 19–22; in Kentucky, 45, 53, 56, 225; management of, 5–7, 11–12, 23; mineral resources of, 11, 17–18, 87, 105, 160; in Morocco, 2, 209–220; in Pennsylvania, 112–118, 155, 211; photographs of, 223; ranchers visiting, 71–73; road system of, 12, 27; and roundup, 25–32; royalty visiting, 118–120, 204–208; scientists visiting, 49–52, 105–106, 161–164; size of, 26; in Spain, 2, 189–198; State Department visitors, 138–140, 149–152, 198–200, 204–208; in Venezuela, 40, 88–107; and wildlife management, 18–19, 217–218. See also American Quarter Horse; Cattle breeding; Thoroughbred horses; and specific people and ranches
Kleberg, Alice King, 5, 45
Kleberg, Caesar: alcohol use of, 45; and

horse breeding, 14; relationship with Bob Kleberg, 7–8; and Thoroughbred horses, 53, 55–56; and wildlife management, 18–19
Kleberg, Helen Campbell: and Argentina, 141; death of, 40, 48–49, 80, 228; and Frissell, 223; and hunting, 19–22; marriage of, 9–10; and Thoroughbred horses, 14–15, 53–54
Kleberg, Helen King: birth of, 9; and Brazil, 122–123; and Buck and Doe Run Valley Farms, 113–114; and New York World's Fair, 155; relationship with father, 49, 224, 227; and Thoroughbred racing, 63
Kleberg, Richard M.: childhood of, 5–6; and government affairs, 160; and ranch management, 11, 23; and Santa Gertrudis breed, 6, 13–14; as speaker, 4
Kleberg, Richard M., Jr., 38–39, 207
Kleberg, Mrs. Richard M., Jr. See Scott, Mary Lewis
Kleberg, Robert J., Sr.: alcohol use of, 45; and cattle breeds, 13; and grasses, 126; and Port of Corpus Christi, 114; and railroad, 14; and ranch management, 5–6, 11
Kleberg, Robert Justus, Jr.: alcohol use of, 2, 44–49, 224; childhood of, 5–6; and daughter, 49, 224, 227; death of, 227–228; early adulthood of, 6–8; family attitudes of, 8–9; fear of old age, 3, 82–83; forms of address for, 8; and grandchildren, 2–3, 63, 221–222; and hunting, 18–22, 96, 102–103, 191–194, 215–216; illness of, 222–227; lifestyle of, 1–2, 37; management style of, 11–12, 23, 35–42, 45, 76, 111, 201–204; marriage of, 9–10; personality of, 6, 42–44, 106–107, 224–225; philosophy of, 4–6, 12, 37–38, 41–42, 137, 228; physical appearance of, 35–36, 54; relationship with Caesar Kleberg, 7–8; relationship with Cypher, 1–4, 40–41, 44; and wildlife management, 18–19,

96, 191–194, 217–218; and women, 9, 80–83. *See also* American Quarter Horse; Cattle breeding; King Ranch; Santa Gertrudis breed; Thoroughbred horses
Kleberg, Sarah, 9

Lagere, Tad, 63
Lala Niza, Princess of Morocco, 42, 209, 216
Lambadora grass, 97, 100
Land: in Australia, 172–173; in Brazil, 122–123, 130–131; in Cuba, 75–76, 78–80; in Florida, 86; in Morocco, 2–3, 210; ownership of, 88, 138; philosophy concerning, 38, 92; rain forests, 91–92, 131–132, 181–183; in Spain, 190, 194; and SUDAM project, 135; in Texas, 15, 22, 84; value of, 95–96; in Venezuela, 90–91. *See also* Clearing land
Land train, 178–179
Latin America. *See* names of specific countries
Laureles, as division of King Ranch, 26
Lea, Tom, 54, 166, 227
Leahy, Dan, 185
Leahy, Michael, 184–186
Lee, Robert E., 38
Legumes, 94, 211
Lehmann, Valgene, 18
Lincolnshire Investment Company, 107
Lindner, Doris, 107–110
Lombardi, Vince, 63
Longhorn breed, 12
Longoria, Shelby, 65
Los Millares, 189–198
Ludwig, Daniel K., 107, 135–138

Malone, Michael J. P. (Jack), 40, 76–79, 94, 161
Manatí Sugar Company, 75
Marabou, 75–76
Marcus, Stanley, 108
Marshall, Douglas, 68–69
Marx, Roberto Burle, 123
Masai tribe, 149–152

Mbarnoti, Edward Carlow, 149–152
McCombs, Holland, 5
McCready, Robert, 118–120
Media, and cattle transport, 115–116
Médici, Emílio Garrastazú, 130–131
Mediterranean region, 187–188. *See also* names of specific countries
Mendoza, Eduardo, 106
Meturet, Diana, 21
Milton Park ranch, 170
Mineral resources, 11, 17–18, 87, 105, 160
Mohammed V, King of Morocco, 204–209
Monkey (bull), 13, 213
Moore, George, 2, 129, 219
Morocco: cattle breeding in, 211; and France, 214; grasses in, 211; and Hughes, 2, 204, 210–214, 216–218; hunting in, 215–216; King Ranch in, 2, 209–220; Kleberg visit to, 221–222; land in, 2–3, 210; nomads in, 212–213; problems in, 218–220; royalty of, 2, 42, 204–209, 214, 216–219; and Santa Gertrudis breed, 210–211
Moses, Robert, 154
Mosquito (Brazil), 122–124
Mosquitoes, 100–101
Mostrenco ranch, 91–96, 107
Muñoz, Adán, 9, 20, 41–42, 82, 223
Murphy, Charles, 27, 71, 73

National Industrial Conference Board, 160
Native people: of Africa, 149–152; of Australia, 173–174, 176–177; of Brazil, 122, 131–133, 136; of Morocco, 212–213; of Venezuela, 99–101
Natural gas, 105–107
Neiman Marcus stores, 108
Nellore breed, 126
News media, and cattle transport, 115–116
New York Racing Association, 62–63, 157–158
New York World's Fair, 153–157

Nomads, in Morocco, 212–213
Norias, 22, 26–27, 153, 227
Northway, J. K., 13, 57–58

Ocean Transport, 105–107
O'Keeffe, Georgia, 23–24
Olivios, Emilio, 195
Onassis, Aristotle, 188
Oscuro ranch, 146–147
Osman, Ahmed, 209, 216, 222

Pará Ranch, 133–134
Pari-mutuel betting, 66–71
Parra grass, 183
Pennsylvania, 112–118, 155, 211
Percheron, 175
Perón, Evita, 141
Perón, Juan, 141–142, 145, 148
Phosphorus deficiency, 16
Piranha fish, 98–99
Port of Corpus Christi, 114
Portugal, 189
Posey, Clayton, 136
Pratt, Wallace E., 17
Prince, Billy, 128

Quality, of cattle, 78
Quarter horses. See American Quarter
  Horse

Racing, 7, 59–66, 157–158
Ragland, Sam, 6, 178
Railroad, building of, 14, 178
Rain forests, 91–92, 131–132, 181–183
Ranch Adarouch, 210–212, 216, 220
Ranch horses. See American Quarter
  Horse; Horses
Ranches. See specific ranches
Real estate, and Friendswood, 158–160
Red Poll breed, 74
Retinta breed, 191, 194
Reynal, Abbott, 129, 146–149
Reynal, Jeannie, 145
Reynal, Juan, 143, 145–146, 190
Rhodes, Cecil, 126
Rhodes grass, 126
Riverole, Sandra, 1

Roads, 12, 27, 130–133, 174
Robinson, W. S., 166, 204
Rockefeller, John D., Jr., 107, 160
Rockefeller, Nelson, 107, 160
Rogers, William, 90
Roosevelt, Franklin D., 6, 160
Roundup: in Australia, 175; and brand-
  ing, 31; and cattle breeding, 25–32;
  and corrida, 26, 31, 100–101; and cull-
  ing, 29; history of, 32; and horses, 28;
  and King Ranch layout, 26; setting of,
  26–27; in Venezuela, 99–100; and
  weaning, 29–30
Rouse, Howard, 45
Rousuck, Jay, 65
Royal Worcester Company, 107–110
Russians, and Santa Gertrudis breed, 80

Saint Augustine grass, 86
Sanchez, Alvaro, 86
Sandifer, Joe, 20
Santa Gertrudis, 22–23, 26
Santa Gertrudis breed: in Argentina,
  142–145, 211; in Australia, 165–166,
  168–169, 183–184; and Bonsma,
  162; in Brazil, 122, 124–126; and
  Connally, 67; in Cuba, 74–75; de-
  mand for, 87; development of, 12–
  14; in Mediterranean, 187–188; in
  Morocco, 210–211; and New York
  World's Fair, 153–157; ownership of,
  213; porcelain model of, 107–110;
  recognition of, 6, 13–14; and Rus-
  sians, 80; in Spain, 190–191; and
  Toros Bravos, 196
Scale, 126–127
Schwartz, Morton, 54
Scientific research, 15–17, 49–52,
  105–106, 127, 161–164
Scott, Mary Lewis, 39
Seeligson, Arthur, 66
Sheep, 144
Shelton, Bobby, 9, 82, 190
Shelton, Joseph H., 9, 46
Shorthorn breed, 12–13, 118, 142
South Africa, 15–16, 126, 162. See also
  Africa

Spain: American Quarter Horse in, 190–191; cattle breeding in, 190–191, 196; grasses in, 190; and Hughes, 190, 194, 198; hunting in, 191–194; and King Ranch, 2, 189–198; land of, 190, 194; Santa Gertrudis breed in, 190–191; and Toros Bravos, 194–198; water in, 191
Staddlehofer, Emil, 79
Standard Oil, 21, 64–65, 160, 187
State Department visitors, 138–140, 149–152, 198–200, 204–208
Stewart, Plunket, 112
Stieglitz, Alfred, 24
Strauss, Bob, 66–67, 69
SUDAM, 130–135, 138
Sugden, Richard, 226
Superintendency for the Development of Amazonia (SUDAM), 130–135, 138
Swift, Geraldine, 121
Swift and Company, 78, 121, 202

Tarentaise breed, 214
Tash, Lowell, 16, 75, 79, 123
Taylor, A. Thomas: in Argentina, 142; in Australia, 167; in Brazil, 121–122; and Deltec Panamerica, 127–128, 202–204
Taylor, Elizabeth, 223
Texas: and Aguay, 144; clearing land in, 75–76; drought in, 39; grasses in, 16, 125–127; land of, 15, 22, 84; and Longhorn cattle, 12; and natural gas, 105; and pari-mutuel betting, 66–71; ranch life in, 10; roundup in, 25–32; and state politics, 30; trail driving in, 178; water control in, 97, 146; wildlife management in, 18, 96. See also King Ranch; and specific people
Texas Racing Association, 66
Thoroughbred Club of America, 69
Thoroughbred horses: and American Quarter Horse, 14; in Australia, 56, 202; breeding of, 54–57, 157–158, 201–202, 225–226; in Great Britain, 55–56, 168; and Helen Campbell

Kleberg, 14–15, 53–54; and Hirsch, 41, 54, 59–61, 64; and pari-mutuel betting, 66–71; racing of, 7, 59–66, 157–158; stallions, 54–56, 60–61, 201; yearlings, 57–59, 153. See also American Quarter Horse; Horses
Ticks, 169–170
Toros Bravos, 194–198
Tractors for Prisoners trade, 80, 86
Transportation: airplane, 77, 84–85, 135–136, 188; of cattle, 112–118, 178–179; railroads, 14, 178; roads, 12, 27, 130–133, 174
Truman, Harry, 160
Tully River ranch, 91, 181–183, 204

Vega, Julio, 195
Venezuela: cattle breeding in, 99–100; clearing land in, 91–93; and Cuba, 88–90; El Cedral ranch, 96–104; as fattening ranch, 95–96; grasses in, 92, 97, 107; Indians of, 99–101; and King Ranch, 40, 88–107; land of, 90–91; Mostrenco ranch, 91–96, 107; and Ocean Transport, 105–107; roundup in, 99–100; water in, 97–98
Visitors to King Ranch: artists, 23–24, 107–110; Australians, 184–186; authors, 32–34, 71–73; ranchers, 71–73; royalty, 118–120, 204–208; scientists, 49–52, 105–106, 161–164; State Department visitors, 138–140, 149–152, 198–200, 204–208

Wages, 36
Walker, F. J., 202
Wasps, and scale, 127
Water: in Argentina, 146–147; in Australia, 168, 171–173, 178–183; in Brazil, 123; control of, 97–98, 146–147; and drought, 15, 39, 168, 171–172, 178, 183; in Spain, 191; in Texas, 97, 146; in Venezuela, 97–98
Weaning, 29–30
Wells, Bob, 76–79, 167, 187–188, 206
Widener, P. A. B., 64
Wilder, Mitch, 223

Wildlife management, 18–19, 96, 191–
   194, 217–218. *See also* Hunting
Wilkinson, Lowell, 182–183
Wilson, Sam, 113
Women: and Kleberg, 9, 80–83; as
   wives of ranchers, 10, 125, 180–181
Woodlands Stud, 56

Woods, Rosemary, 161
Wortham, Gus E., 155, 158–160
Wright, Mike, 159
Wynne, Angus G., Jr., 153–154, 157

Zebu breed, 126